Symbol Emergence Systems

Tadahiro Taniguchi

Editor

Symbol Emergence Systems

An Interdisciplinary Discussion about
Cognition, Language and Society

 Springer

Editor
Tadahiro Taniguchi
Graduate School of Informatics
Kyoto University
Kyoto, Kyoto, Japan

ISBN 978-981-95-1326-0   ISBN 978-981-95-1327-7   (eBook)
https://doi.org/10.1007/978-981-95-1327-7

This book is an open access publication.

Translation from the Japanese language edition: "記号創発システム論" by Tadahiro Taniguchi,
© Tadahiro Taniguchi, Editor 2024. Published by Shin-yo-sha. All Rights Reserved.

This work was supported by Japan Society for the Promotion of Science KAKENHI (JP21H04904 and
JP23H04835)

This Springer imprint is published by the registered company Springer Nature Singapore Pte Ltd.
The registered company address is: 152 Beach Road, #21-01/04 Gateway East, Singapore 189721,
Singapore

If disposing of this product, please recycle the paper.

Preface

Since ancient times, humankind has created and relied upon symbol systems. Language is the most well-known example, but it is by no means the only one. From cave paintings and rituals to tools, numbers, laws, and currency systems, our civilization has been built upon a rich variety of symbolic structures. While certain forms of communication using signs are observed in the animal kingdom, no other species has developed symbolic systems as complex and flexible as humans have. The capacity to generate, manipulate, and share symbols is a fundamental force that has shaped humanity and enabled the construction of civilization itself.

Yet despite their centrality, we still do not fully understand the dynamic nature of symbol systems: the principles by which they are formed or the powers they possess. In the humanities and social sciences, semiotics has long grappled with such questions. However, the field has remained largely disconnected from engineering and informatics, limiting opportunities to explore symbol emergence in the context of AI and robotics.

Human society is undoubtedly upheld by these dynamically emergent symbol systems. And now, into this society, we are witnessing the arrival of generative AI: systems built on large language models that have ingested massive amounts of linguistic and multimodal data, acquiring a remarkable degree of complexity and flexibility. These systems are beginning to participate in our symbolic environments. The age of generative AI marks the dawn of a new era in which humans and AI must learn to coexist.

My academic background lies in engineering and information sciences, where I began my research career in fields such as human-computer interaction, artificial intelligence, and robotics. Along the way, I encountered constructive approaches that intersected with my long-standing desire to understand the human mind. This convergence led me to create a new research domain.

In AI research, the so-called "symbol grounding problem" presents a fundamental challenge: How can artificially created symbols be meaningfully connected to real-world experience? However, I have come to believe that the very premise of this question may be misguided. Symbols are not merely external representations, such as words or signs, but are also deeply intertwined with internal representations, such as concepts, which evolve dynamically through self-organizing processes grounded in sensorimotor interaction with the environment. Unless we clearly distinguish between these internal and external symbol systems and understand their respective dynamics, it will remain impossible to build AI that can meaningfully engage with the real world.

During the early 2000s, as a graduate student at Kyoto University, I encountered many ideas that deepened my inquiry into this problem. Through the emerging field of cognitive developmental robotics, I was introduced to developmental psychology and neuroscience as they relate to AI and robotics, and in turn to Piaget's theory of cognitive development. Through studies on autopoiesis and foundational informatics (or neo-cybernetics), I also came across Jakob von Uexküll's Umwelt theory and other constructivist traditions that emphasize subjectivity and autonomy.

In retrospect, the common thread running through these influences was a focus on the subjective experience and meaning-making of individual agents, including Peircean semiotics. Yet I gradually realized that our existing theories around cognitive developmental systems were insufficient. It was not enough to model individual development alone, nor was it sufficient to simulate social dynamics through artificial societies or multi-agent systems. What was needed was a framework capable of integrating both cognition and society: a model of their co-evolving dynamics.

This realization led me to formulate the idea of *Symbol Emergence Systems Theory*. Around the same time, my work in artificial life and complex systems exposed me to the concept of *emergent systems*, which are frameworks characterized by micro–macro loops, layered interactions, and the spontaneous formation of order. I became convinced that such a perspective was essential for developing a theory about the dynamics of symbols and meaning.

Symbol Emergence Systems Theory challenges the view of symbols as static, absolute entities. Instead, it frames them as dynamic constructs that continuously emerge through social interaction and contextual adaptation. Many approaches in AI take a "ground truth" paradigm, wherein symbols are treated as correct answers to be taught to the machine. Such views risk excluding cultural diversity and rejecting uncertainty, leading to narrow conceptions of intelligence. This challenge persists today in debates surrounding AI alignment in the age of large language models.

If we are to envision a future of true human–AI coexistence, AI and robots must become systems capable of continually co-constructing symbolic environments together with humans.

The first articulation of Symbol Emergence Systems Theory took shape around 2010. Since then, over a decade of research has developed under the umbrella of *Symbol Emergence Robotics*, yet the theory's full scope has remained underexplored. This book represents the first comprehensive attempt to articulate that broader vision. It brings together leading scholars from a range of disciplines—philosophy, linguistics, sociology, and the humanities more broadly—to present this theory as a truly *transdisciplinary* intellectual movement.

The theory is not confined to individual agents. It reconsiders how intelligence, culture, and meaning emerge within social symbolic systems. In that sense, it aspires to serve as a meta-theory within AI and cognitive science: a more inclusive systems theory for the symbolic dimension of human–AI interaction.

More than fifteen years have passed since the initial conception of this theory, but its relevance has only grown. As the generative AI era unfolds, and the power and structure of language are reexamined with renewed urgency, there is a growing need for a unified framework that can integrate symbols, meaning, intelligence, and society.

It is a profound joy for me that this new intellectual movement, which took root in Kyoto, Japan, a city with over twelve centuries of cultural and scholarly heritage, can now be shared with the global community in English. I hope this book will inspire new perspectives and contribute to the growing discourse in this emerging field.

Let us begin.

Kyoto, Japan   Tadahiro Taniguchi
April 2025

Introduction

The Era of Generative AI: Language and Symbols

Advances in artificial intelligence technology entered a new phase in the 2020s, with enormous societal implications.

Generative AI, such as large language models like ChatGPT, has begun to change the way we engage in linguistic communication in our lives. Large language models, trained on massive corpora to predict the next token, which can be called a subword, were able to achieve a significant level of natural interaction that was previously unseen in AI even in the 2010s. The ChatGPT, released by OpenAI in the late 2022, sparked a global boom in generative AI throughout 2023 and continues into 2024.

The technological phase transition that gave rise to generative AI is not solely attributable to advances in machine learning techniques or increased computational power. It is deeply related to the inherent power of "language" itself—and even to the foundational reasons for its very existence. Language, a creation of humankind, implicitly encodes the cumulative layers of our culture and civilization. This latent power of language now appears to have been unleashed by large language models. As a result, no one can yet say for certain what the full capabilities of these models are. Much of the AI research conducted around 2023 focused on revealing their nature—through approaches such as prompt engineering and beyond.

From the perspective of semiotics, language is one form of symbol. Humans are the only species capable of using symbols not only for communication but also to generate written texts, create social norms, develop systems of ethics and law, accumulate scientific knowledge, and ultimately build entire civilizations.

What is particularly remarkable about symbols is that, although they may initially have no intrinsic meaning, they acquire meaning when created by humans and shared within a community. The forms that symbols can take are virtually limitless, ranging from gestures and pictograms to facial expressions and beyond.

While discussions about symbols often tend to center around language due to its practical prominence, the term "symbol emergence systems" in the title of this book refers to a broader notion of symbols—those that emerge through shared meaning-making processes across various forms. Please understand that this concept includes the full breadth of symbolic phenomena.

The era of generative AI can also be regarded as a time when language-producing entities have emerged beyond human beings. While these entities are not identical to humans, it has become remarkably easy today to create AI systems that can engage in human-like conversation to the extent of deceiving people on social media as bots, or to serve as conversational partners for language learners. In a certain sense, they seem to handle the meaning of words in ways that rival human capabilities.

Without a doubt, we have entered a new era in the environment surrounding language. The qualitative transformation triggered by generative AI based on large language models is likely to rival the cultural revolution brought about by the invention of the printing press. In such an era, we must strive for a more panoramic and systemic understanding of symbols and language not only to design AI and robots that can engage with language more appropriately but also to shape a society that can coexist meaningfully with these emerging entities.

Toward an Transdisciplinary Integration of Symbol Emergence Systems Theory

The academic concept of "symbol emergence systems theory," which serves as the central theme of this book, began as a line of philosophical inquiry initiated by the editor, Tadahiro Taniguchi, nearly two decades ago. Since then, it has been gradually developed in collaboration with numerous researchers. The theory was first introduced to the general public in Can We Create Communicative Robots? A Constructivist Approach to Symbol Emergence Systems,[1] where the meaning of symbols was discussed from a systems-theoretic perspective. From its inception, the theory was conceived to include not only AI and robotics but also the generation of meaning in human symbolic activity, extending to discussions in the humanities.

As the theory evolved, emphasis was placed on applying the constructivist approach not only through simulation but also through physically embodied robots. This development led to the emergence of the research field known as "symbol emergence in robotics."[2] While this trajectory fostered significant progress in the 2010s, it also led to a common misconception that the theory was solely a robotics-centered, engineering framework around related academic communities. This impression was further reinforced by the author's own academic grounding in AI

[1] Tadahiro Taniguchi, Can We Create Communicative Robots? A Constructivist Approach to Symbol Emergence Systems, NTT Publishing, 2010, (in Japanese)

[2] Taniguchi, T., Nagai, T., Nakamura, T., Iwahashi, N., Ogata, T., & Asoh, H. 2016 Symbol Emergence in Robotics: A Survey. Advanced Robotics, 30(11–12), 706–728.

and robotics. Although scholars in the humanities offered rich discussions and sympathetic engagement, expanding the theoretical scope beyond engineering remained a persistent challenge.

At the same time, a different kind of difficulty emerged for students and researchers in engineering: the absence of structured resources that explained the philosophical and humanistic foundations underpinning symbol emergence in robotics. As this book attempts to show, the theory intersects with a wide array of disciplines not only in science and technology but also in the human and social sciences. These connections go beyond what can be covered by a single educational curriculum, and many of the contributing disciplines have not explicitly connected themselves to fields like AI, robotics, linguistics, or cognitive science. In this sense, symbol emergence systems theory is inherently interdisciplinary and integrative by nature.

This book was written in response to that context. Rather than presenting a conventional linear exposition, it aims to offer a web-like mapping of keywords and concepts that form the intellectual landscape of symbol emergence systems. The related fields are vast and diverse. Consequently, this book is not designed to be read in a self-contained, chapter-by-chapter fashion. Instead, it invites readers to reflect on the interconnections among ideas and to use these as stepping stones toward further exploration—through additional literature, dialog, and inquiry.

Structure of the Book

Part I: Foundations of Symbol Emergence Systems

This section introduces the core concept of symbol emergence systems by grounding it in semiotics and the philosophical foundation of pragmatism. It emphasizes the importance of taking the internal perspective of the agent—drawing on Jakob von Uexküll's Umwelt theory and Jean Piaget's genetic epistemology. It also incorporates insights from neo-cybernetics and foundational informatics, which offer dynamic and systems-based views of information and meaning. These perspectives converge through the lens of constructivism. The approach here is fundamentally transdisciplinary, laying the groundwork for bridging fields from engineering to the humanities.

Part II: Symbol Emergence in Robotics

This part introduces symbol emergence robotics as a constructive approach (in the sense of "building to understand") toward modeling symbol systems. After outlining the essence of this approach, it explores developmental examples such as infant language acquisition and concept formation. It also introduces basic ideas from probabilistic generative modeling, serving as a foundation for understanding more advanced topics like the free-energy principle and the notion of world models.

Part III: Cognitive Development in the Environment

Here, the focus shifts to humans as adaptive agents embedded in dynamic environments. The section explores constructive approaches to cognitive developmental systems and brains. It discusses how recent advances in deep learning intersect with these ideas, and introduces developmental and neuro-robotics as embodied experimental frameworks. On the theoretical side, attention is given to the free-energy principle and predictive coding, which are gaining prominence as candidate unifying principles of brain function. These models are also linked to affective phenomena such as curiosity and emotion. The discussion of world models is expanded through the lens of representational learning.

Part IV: Embodiment, Mind, and Consciousness

This section addresses two key concepts often underrepresented in AI studies implicitly influenced by functionalism: embodiment and consciousness. It connects philosophical and engineering perspectives by introducing embodied cognitive science, enactivism, and phenomenology, leading into deeper explorations of consciousness. The notion of consciousness is also discussed in relation to the societal recognition of AI as "others." This part concludes by linking these ideas to AI and society—serving as a conceptual bridge to Part V.

Part V: Dynamics of Culture, Norms, and Language

Focusing on the emergent nature of culture and language, this section extends symbol emergence theory into the domain of society. A key theme is the formation of emergent symbol systems through micro–macro loops of individual adaptation and collective structure. Topics include the concept of the "semiosphere" from cultural psychology, the evolution and emergence of language, and the rise of large language models (LLMs) in the 2020s. LLMs are portrayed as emergent artifacts of symbol emergence systems trained on vast human-produced corpora and instantiated in massive neural networks. Beyond language, the section considers the emergence of norms, ethics, and legal systems as higher-order symbol systems, emphasizing that these too are outcomes of collective adaptation in symbol emergence systems.

Part VI: Symbol Emergence Systems and beyond

Returning to the general theory, this final section reexamines symbol emergence systems in light of AI advances and social developments in the 2020s. It introduces a constructive model of decentralized representation learning, interpreting symbol emergence as decentralized concept formation across agents. This idea is elaborated as collective predictive coding, extending the micro–macro loop framework. A three-layered model of intelligence is proposed, identifying the essence of human intelligence not in isolated individuals but in participation within social symbol systems. The book concludes by reconsidering the question: What does it mean to be human? It explores how we might design a society that can symbiotically coexist with generative AI, embracing both our technological future and our symbolic nature.

Toward a New Scientific Framework

This book goes far beyond the academic coverage of any single department or discipline. Yet it is not a random collection of keywords. Each entry has been carefully selected either because it is essential for understanding the symbol emergence systems theory as it has developed so far or because it illuminates the scope toward which the theory is now extending.

In this context, it is important to distinguish between interdisciplinary and transdisciplinary approaches. Interdisciplinary discussions involve collaboration between distinct academic fields that share methods, perspectives, and techniques while maintaining their individual boundaries. In contrast, transdisciplinary integration refers to the genuine synthesis of knowledge from multiple domains to generate entirely new theories, concepts, and research areas. Symbol emergence systems theory aspires to the latter—it seeks transdisciplinary fusion.

This theoretical framework offers a unified perspective for understanding the workings of the human mind, including individual cognition, as well as the dynamics of society and linguistic culture. For over 15 years, I have worked toward creating a coherent intellectual axis that runs through these domains. This book marks a significant milestone in that pursuit.

It is also the first keyword-based refere book dedicated to symbol emergence systems theory. To expand its reach, many scholars contributed entries based on their unique expertise. Each of these contributors is a leading figure in their respective field in Japan. I am sincerely grateful to this outstanding group of authors for making this ambitious volume possible.

Contents

Part I: Foundations of Symbol Emergence Systems

Symbol Emergence Systems: Toward a World Where Humans and AI Co-Discover Meaning

Tadahiro Taniguchi

Where Does the Meaning of "Words" Come From?

Our society is saturated with complexity. Each individual lives with their own thoughts, intentions, and perspectives. When we step back to observe not only our immediate surroundings but also the flow of daily life and the social systems that sustain them, what becomes evident is the extraordinary complexity and stability of the whole. Society, in its current form, functions too coherently—almost miraculously—to have emerged purely through spontaneous processes. And yet, it was not designed by any omnipotent entity. Rather, it is something maintained through the continuous and collective activity of human beings.[1] How, then, is such complexity sustained? The answer lies, in large part, in "words"—that is, symbols, and more specifically, language as one kind of symbol system used in communication.[2]

---

[1] This human society is operated using language and currency. Yet, when it comes to legal rules defined by language and their application, or the pricing and movement of goods, there is no single person who oversees or controls everything. And still, society functions, cultures evolve, and cities are formed. I encourage you to pause and reflect on the strangeness of this phenomenon.

Here, the term "spontaneous" refers to Friedrich von Hayek's concept of spontaneous order. In contemporary systems theory, this corresponds to the notion of self-organization. Hayek was a thinker who, early on, recognized the information-aggregating capacity of markets and how that capacity enables the self-organization of social systems.

[2] The term "symbol" as used in this book, as explained in Chapter "Semiotics and Semiology: Two Perspectives on Capturing Meaning" and Chapters "Symbol Emergence in Robotics: A Constructive Approach to Overcoming the Symbol Grounding Problem," encompasses a broad concept that includes language.

T. Taniguchi (✉)
Graduate School of Informatics, Kyoto University, Kyoto, Japan

Research Organization of Science and Technology, Ritsumeikan University, Kyoto, Japan
e-mail: taniguchi@i.kyoto-u.ac.jp

T. Taniguchi (ed.), *Symbol Emergence Systems*,
https://doi.org/10.1007/978-981-95-1327-7_1

Words are indispensable for human coordination. We use them to express our intentions, share schedules, exchange opinions, convey emotions, and collaborate in both informal and professional contexts. Words form the backbone of contracts in business, laws in governance, and policies in politics. Even gestures and body language—though often seen as separate—are in fact forms of symbols.

In what follows, drawing from semiotic theory, we use the term symbol to refer broadly to signs that are produced with the intent to express, and those that are interpreted in the process of meaning-making. These include both linguistic and non-linguistic signs that signify something other than themselves.

Yet despite their central role in our social lives, the fundamental principles governing how symbols acquire meaning remain unresolved. While physics has given us quantum mechanics for the microscopic world and classical mechanics for the macroscopic, we still lack an equivalent framework for explaining how symbolic meaning emerges and stabilizes in human societies. To clarify these principles, we must draw from a wide range of disciplines—not only the human and social sciences, such as linguistics and psychology, but also AI, robotics, systems theory, pragmatism, and phenomenology. This kind of transdisciplinary inquiry—which seeks not just collaboration across fields but genuine theoretical integration—is the very ambition of symbol emergence systems theory.

In communication, a symbol functions as a sign that stands in for something other than itself. When a receiver interprets that symbol, it gains meaning from the receiver's perspective. As semiotics teaches us, symbols are not limited to communication between individuals; they emerge whenever an observing subject assigns meaning to a phenomenon beyond its immediate appearance.

At the heart of symbolic communication lie two fundamental mysteries: the operational closure of the agents involved, and the arbitrariness of the symbols themselves.

Operational closure refers to the fact that each of us is limited to our own sensory-motor experience; in communication, this means we cannot directly access the internal thoughts of others.[3] At the same time, symbols are arbitrary—they point to something beyond themselves, but what they point to is determined by social or contextual agreement between sender and receiver.

This raises a crucial question: How is communication even possible, given this closure and arbitrariness? Symbolic communication requires mechanisms to align meaning across individuals, both within social systems and cognitive architectures. Without such mechanisms, meaningful coordination would collapse. I cannot directly know what meaning you assign to a word—unless we share some common ground.

It is precisely these mechanisms of alignment that are addressed by the theory of symbol emergence. And the larger socio-cognitive structures that support them constitute what we call a symbol emergence system.

Language as a Dynamic Equilibrium System

Symbol systems in society function as dynamic equilibrium systems grounded in the ongoing activities of humans, who collectively form an autonomous and decentralized system. When we speak of language, we often imagine static structures—grammar as found in textbooks, or vocabulary listed in dictionaries. However, these are merely synchronic snapshots: representations of a system caught in a moment, reflecting only explicit, formalized knowledge. In reality, language and meaning are constantly evolving—historically and in everyday life—and our ability to interpret language depends largely on tacit knowledge.[4]

Defining the meaning of a word using other words quickly reaches its limits. Take "apple": describing it as "red" or "fruit" only creates a network of symbol-to-symbol associations, disconnected from embodied experience. Meaning often arises through our interaction with the real world. Moreover, it is not only shaped by personal experience, but also by shared social norms and collective agreements. To account for both, we need a systems-theoretical framework that connects bottom-up meanings emerging from embodied cognition with top-down meanings shaped by society.

A symbol emergence system is such a framework—an autonomous, decentralized (or multi-agent) system that generates and sustains symbol systems. Figure 1

---

[4]The distinction between explicit knowledge and tacit knowledge was introduced by Michael Polanyi and became more widely known through the work of management scholar Ikujiro Nonaka, who incorporated it into his SECI model in the context of knowledge management.

See:

Polanyi, Michael. "The tacit dimension." Knowledge in organisations. Routledge, 2009. 135–146.

Nonaka, Ikujiro. "The knowledge-creating company." The economic impact of knowledge. Routledge, 2009. 175–187.

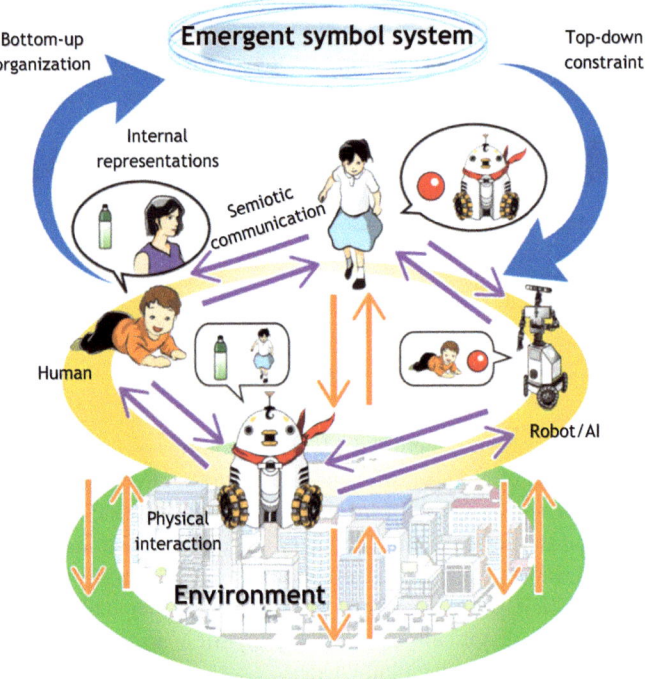

Fig. 1 Overview of the symbol emergence system involving humans and robots. Through physical interactions with the environment (orange arrows), people gradually form internal representations. Through semiotic communication (purple arrows) among them, emergent symbol systems are progressively organized in a bottom-up manner. Once formed, the emergent symbol systems impose top-down constraints on people, influencing their behaviors, interpretations, and communications. The interplay between top-down constraints from these emergent systems and bottom-up organization from embodied experiences jointly shapes internal representations and semiotic communication

illustrates this concept.[5] The primary constituents of such systems are humans. However, this does not mean that biological humanness is required. Rather, any entity that can participate in semiotic communication—using arbitrary symbols to contribute to societal functions—qualifies as a member of the system.

The robot depicted in the figure should not be taken to represent current machines of the early 2020s, but rather envisioned as future agents—or even fictional beings from science fiction and anime—that can naturally collaborate with humans in society. This inclusion underscores the theoretical stance of symbol emergence systems theory: it aims to reveal the cognitive and social competencies that support human

---

[5] Taniguchi, T., Ugur, E., Hoffmann, M., Jamone, L., Nagai, T., Rosman, B., Matsuka, T., Iwahashi, N., Oztop, E., Piater, J., and Wörgötter, F. "Symbol Emergence in Cognitive Developmental Systems: A Survey." *IEEE Transactions on Cognitive and Developmental Systems* 11, no. 4 (2019): 494–516. https://doi.org/10.1109/TCDS.2018.2867772.

symbolic communication, while also specifying the necessary conditions for robots to engage meaningfully with us and contribute to the shaping of future societies.

Symbol emergence systems also rest on the assumption that each constituent agent possesses operational closure in its cognition.[6] That is, agents lack a God-like perspective and cannot directly access the inner mental states of others.

Dynamics of Symbol Emergence Systems

When we understand the word "apple," we recall its appearance, its taste, and the range of experiences associated with it. Although the symbol "apple" is arbitrary in its linguistic form, its meaning is grounded in the sensory and embodied experiences we have accumulated—its redness, its sweetness, the tactile sense of biting into it. These experiential foundations are made possible by our bodies, equipped with sensory and motor systems that mediate our interactions with the world.

The same applies to action words such as the verb "walk." Without having physically experienced walking, or at least observed others doing so, it is difficult to intuitively grasp what the word means. Bodily interaction thus serves as the foundation for the formation of internal representations, which in turn underpin our capacity to interpret symbols.

However, internal representations are not yet symbols in themselves. They are the raw material—the substrate—of symbol formation. Words, as external representations, derive their meaning not solely from the individual, but through interpretation by others within a social context. This interpretation is not fixed; it involves ongoing processes of negotiation, adjustment, and shared coordination. Through the accumulation of such interactions over time, emergent symbol systems—such as language—become structured.

While all symbol systems are, by nature, emergent, we explicitly call them emergent symbol systems to emphasize this point. Emergence is not an exceptional case—it is the norm.

As humans, we possess not only the capacity but also the agency to adapt and creatively transform the symbol systems that structure our world. For example, if you and your family decide to give an object in your home a new name and reach consensus on its use, that name becomes a functional symbol for that object. The rise of idioms, neologisms, and viral slang in everyday life vividly illustrates the dynamic, ever-evolving character of language.

In this way, symbol systems are not only inherited—they are continuously recreated. The dynamics of symbol emergence lie at the intersection of individual cognition and collective negotiation.

---

[6] The term "cognitive closure" is sometimes used in this context. However, please note that the informal usage of the term in symbol emergence in robotics may differ somewhat from its theoretical usage in autopoiesis and neo-cybernetics.

Micro–Macro Loops and Emergent Properties

Our symbolic communication and our perception of the world are shaped by the symbol systems—such as language—that structure the societies to which we belong. Even if you personally grow tired of distinguishing between "apple" and "pear" and casually ask your friend to hand you an "apple," they are unlikely to bring you a pear. Conversely, if your friend has never encountered a "quince," they might classify it together with pears. While this is a simple example, it illustrates how shared emergent symbol systems shape both our semiotic interactions (like speech and interpretation) and our physical interactions (like perception and action).[7]

Such influences are known as constraints. And it is precisely because of these constraints that we are able to suppress the inherent arbitrariness of symbols, allowing language to function reliably as a medium of communication.

Symbol emergence systems exhibit emergent properties, a hallmark of complex adaptive systems. Emergent properties arise when micro-level interactions among agents generate macro-level structures—systems of order—that in turn exert top-down constraints on the agents themselves. This recursive, bidirectional relationship is known as a micro–macro loop.

The systems-theoretical implication of symbol emergence systems is that it is this very structure—the micro–macro loop of symbolic activity in human society—which gives rise to symbolic meaning itself. In other words, the emergent property of human social systems and the cognitive and social adaptability that sustains them constitute the foundational source of meaning in language.

---

[7] Here, the term "internal representations" can also be interpreted as referring to internal representations in the brain, but it does not imply a literal copy of the external world, as assumed in classical representationalism.

Semiotics and Semiology: Two Perspectives on Capturing Meaning

Noburo Saji

What Is a Symbol?

A symbol is something which is determined by something else for someone. For example, the sound /crow/ evokes the image of a crow, a large, black bird. Words are typical examples of symbols, but symbols are not limited to words. For example, the cawing of a crow signifies the approach of evening, and scattered garbage at a dump suggest that crows have scavenged there. These are all examples of symbols. The nature of symbols has long attracted the interest of psychologists, linguists, and philosophers because it explains the process of generating meanings. The study of symbols has traditionally been developed through two theoretical frameworks: *semiotics*, grounded in the work of Charles Sanders Peirce, and *semiology*, developed by Ferdinand de Saussure. This chapter provides an overview of these two approaches to symbols and discusses their relevance to symbol emergence systems theory.

Semiotics

Semiotics aim to theorize logical norms governing reasoning processes. In this sense, semiotics possesses qualities akin to logic. Given its capacity to analyze the dynamics of thought and communication, as well as its systematic classification of symbols, semiotics has found contemporary applications in empirical disciplines such as linguistics and psychology.

N. Saji (✉)
Waseda University, School of Human Sciences, Saitama, Japan

© The Author(s) 2026
T. Taniguchi (ed.), *Symbol Emergence Systems*,
https://doi.org/10.1007/978-981-95-1327-7_2

Semiotic processes are understood through a triadic relationship comprising a *sign* (the signifying objects[1]), an *object* (what the sign signifies), and an *interpretant* (the understanding of the relationships between signs and objects). Viewing symbolic processes through this triadic relationship effectively explains the flexible process by which humans assign meaning to the world. For instance, the sound /crow/ (sign) signifies a crow (object) because the linguistic conventions in English mediate this connection (interpretant). Importantly, these relationships are not fixed across situations. Suppose a caregiver and a child see a crow and pigeon, and the caregiver says, "See, that's a crow!" If the child responds with "Oh, pigeon," this suggests that the child associates the sound /crow/ with a pigeon. This demonstrates that the meaning of linguistic signs is fluid, as it is mediated by the speaker's knowledge and thought within a specific context. Furthermore, the interpretant itself can be a new sign, triggering a chain reaction of symbolic processes. For example, the child's utterance may prompt the caregiver to respond, "No, pigeon is not black" continuing the exchange. The child's utterance, which was previously an interpretant, immediately becomes a new sign. In this way, signs constantly generate new interpretants, perpetuating an ongoing semiotic process.

Peirce classifies symbols with exceptional precision based on his universal categories of existence: *Firstness*, *Secondness*, and *Thirdness*. Firstness refers to entities existing independently of any relationships (something that exists itself); Secondness describes entities existing in relation to others but not mediated by a third party (something must be related to something else); and Thirdness involves mediation by a third entity (something requires more complex relationships). Based on these categories, Peirce categorizes signs, relationships between signs and objects, and relationships between signs and interpretants.[2] Let us consider the classification of signs themselves. Imagine encountering a crow in the darkness. Even if the crow is invisible to you, its potential color and shape exist as possibilities independent of you. This potential sign is termed a *qualisign*, representing the Firstness of a symbol. Next, suppose your hand accidentally touches the crow's feathers. You perceive tactile feedback resulting from your movement. Each instance of touch invokes different sensation by time is termed a *sinsign*. Finally, when the lights are turned on, you finally identify the bird as a crow. This identification relies on conventional knowledge that distinguishes a crow from a sparrow or a pigeon; even if the crow flies away, the relationships can be maintained. Such conventionally understood symbols are termed *legisigns*, based on Thirdness. These three types of signs are interdependent: legisigns require the existence of sinsigns to function, and sinsigns must involve qualisigns to represent potential properties.[3]

---

[1] In Peirce's early discussions, the term "representamen" was also used.

[2] Peirce's classification of signs encompasses not only the triadic components but also their combinations and variations, ultimately identifying 66 types of signs.

[3] "Nomenclature and Divisions of Triadic Relations, as Far as They Are Determined," in Peirce, Charles Sanders. Edited by the Peirce Edition Project, 1998. "Essential Peirce: Selected Philosophical Writings, Vol. 2 (1893–1913)," pp. 289–299. Indiana University Press.

How does semiotics contribute to symbol emergence systems theory? Symbol emergence systems theory assumes a dynamic cycle in which agents collectively organize emergent symbol systems through symbolic interaction with their environment while being constrained by these systems. Peirce's model of semiosis, which addresses how humans continuously assign meaning to a constantly changing world, provides an essential foundation for explaining such mechanisms of symbolic interaction. For example, the classification of signs elucidates levels of interaction within symbol emergence systems: the environment as a source of potential symbols (qualisigns), real-time interactions between agents and their surroundings (sinsigns), and collectively emergent symbolic systems as legisigns. Thus, the semiotic approach effectively captures the triadic relationship between these components.[4]

Semiology

Saussure's semiology, summarized in his lecture notes "Course in General Linguistics," seeks the foundation of symbols in the structure of relationships between symbols.[5] This approach has been particularly successful in capturing the nature of linguistic symbols, providing a critical theoretical foundation for linguistics. Semiology explains the functioning of symbols as a coupling of the *signifier* (signifiant: the form of the symbol) and the *signified* (signifié: what the symbol represents). A critical characteristic of linguistic symbols is their *arbitrariness*, which can be understood from two perspectives.

First, the relationship between the signifier and the signified is assumed to be arbitrary. For instance, the English term "crow" conventionally refers to a crow, but in other languages, the equivalent might be "karasu" or "corbeau" in Japanese and French. Second, the delineation of the signifier and signified is also arbitrary. From the perspective of the signifier, English speakers distinguish the sound /crow/ from /brow/. This phonetic distinction is valuable within the English phonological system because it generates different meanings. Similarly, from the perspective of the signified, the delineation of the referent involves arbitrariness. For example, English distinguishes between small urban "crows" and large rural "ravens," while Japanese typically refers to both as a single word, "karasu." Thus, the form and meaning of a

---

[4] The classification of signs in semiotics has also garnered attention in developmental psychology, particularly in the study of language acquisition. For example, children's acquisition of symbolic signs like language builds upon iconic signs, such as ideophones, and indexical signs, such as pointing gestures. This suggests that the meaning of symbolic signs, like language, relies on multimodality, a perspective relevant to the multimodality emphasized in the theory of symbol emergence systems.

[5] De Saussure, Ferdinand. (1966). Course in General Linguistics (Edited by Charles Bally and Albert Sechehaye, Translated by Wade Baskin). New York, Toronto, London: McGraw-Hill Book Company.

symbol are determined by differences within the internal structure of a language system. This may be easier to understand if we use an example from a dictionary. Saussure termed this shared linguistic system among native speakers as *langue*, distinguishing it from actual speech acts (*parole*). According to Saussure, our ability to communicate with others through symbols arises from adhering to the shared conventions of langue while producing specific parole. Due to the arbitrariness of signs, the meaning of linguistic elements is determined by their differential relations with other elements within the langue. A useful analogy to understand the point is to imagine a dictionary. Looking up "crow" in a dictionary might reveal its relationships with other potential substitutes (paradigmatic sides, e.g., sparrow, pigeon) and its co-occurrence with other terms (syntagmatic sides, e.g., black, fly, scavenger). Such relationships describe the meaning of symbols based on their position and difference within the system.

The synchronic approach of semiology abstracts time to elucidate the structure of langue at a given moment. This perspective is highly effective for depicting the vast symbolic systems emerging from collective human interactions. For example, paradigmatic differences underpin semantic networks and thesauri, while syntagmatic differences inform distributional semantics.

Pragmatism: What Is the Meaning of Symbols?

Takafumi Kato

Explaining the Meaning Through Pragmatism

Pragmatism, a philosophical movement established in the USA during the late nineteenth century, underpins the conceptual foundation of the symbol emergence systems theory described in Chapter "Symbol Emergence Systems: Toward a World Where Humans and AI Co-Discover Meaning". This theory adopts Charles Sanders Peirce's conception of symbol, which is integral to his pragmatist philosophy. For a detailed discussion of Peirce's semiotics, see Chapter "Semiotics and Semiology: Two Perspectives on Capturing Meaning". This chapter takes a broader view to examine why the pragmatist philosophy underlying Peirce's semiotics is particularly suitable for understanding symbols within the framework of the symbol emergence systems theory.

From a pragmatist perspective, how is the meaning of symbols such as words understood? To address this question, let us first consider how analytic philosophy,[1] often seen as contrasting with pragmatism, approaches the meaning of symbols. Analytic philosophy traditionally clarifies meaning by providing necessary and sufficient conditions. For instance, consider the symbol "bachelor."[2] If (1) "A is a

---

[1] Analytic philosophy emerged in Europe in the late nineteenth century and gained prominence in the English-speaking world by the 1930s. It traditionally aimed to clarify the meanings of concepts and logical relationships between propositions using tools from mathematical logic.

[2] This example of "bachelor" is based on the discussion in Quine's "Two Dogmas of Empiricism" (Quine, W. V. O. 1953. "Two Dogmas of Empiricism." In *A Logical Point of View*. Harvard University Press, pp. 20–46).

T. Kato (✉)
Osaka Seikei University, Osaka, Japan

T. Taniguchi (ed.), *Symbol Emergence Systems*,
https://doi.org/10.1007/978-981-95-1327-7_3

bachelor," then (2) "A is an unmarried man," and vice versa, there seems to exist a necessary and sufficient relationship between (1) and (2). According to this analytic approach, the meaning of "bachelor" can be defined as "unmarried man."

However, this approach encounters problems. In reality, even if A is an unmarried man, A is not necessarily called a "bachelor." For example, male children, though unmarried, are not typically referred to as "bachelors." Thus, the term "bachelor" implicitly carries the connotation of adulthood. Consequently, any necessary and sufficient condition between (1) and (2) does not hold. One might refine the analysis to define "bachelor" as "an unmarried adult man." While such refinements are possible, they overlook an essential point: the implicit connotations of "bachelor" are culturally loaded and can change with the accumulation of practical usage of the symbol. For example, if the term "bachelor" were deemed socially undesirable due to its reinforcement of binary gender norms, its gender-related implications might diminish over time. The analytic approach's reliance on necessary and sufficient conditions would thus lead to an endless cycle of attempting to explicate these evolving social connotations.

From a pragmatist standpoint, on the other hand, the situation seems less problematic. Pragmatism explains the meaning of symbols by considering the actions they are associated with. For example, the meaning of "cup" can be described as "something that allows you to carry liquid" or "something that enables you to drink beverages," linking the term to actions like carrying liquid or drinking. Furthermore, the meaning of "cup" can also encompass a broader range of actions derived from social practices. For instance, a personal cup placed in a shared office kitchen may imply that its owner regularly visits that place and belongs to the community associated with the place. Pragmatism emphasizes that symbol users continuously update the meaning of each symbol based on the accumulated practices within their environment. By focusing on actions, pragmatism offers a flexible approach to understanding symbols, extending beyond dictionary-like definitions to include the dynamic process of symbol emergence as users adapt to their environment.

Peirce's Pragmatism and Symbol Emergence Systems

The symbol emergence systems theory describes how new meanings for symbols emerge within systems consisting of diverse agents. Pragmatism, which emphasizes the dynamic processes through which agents create meanings, aligns more closely with the symbol emergence systems theory than the analytic philosophy, which focuses on necessary and sufficient conditions. As discussed in Chapter "Semiotics and Semiology: Two Perspectives on Capturing Meaning", Peirce's semiotics incorporates plasticity into the concept of symbol by introducing the interpretant as a third element of a triadic relationship. The interpretant encompasses a wide range of things, such as conventions and practices associated with the symbol's use and the users themselves. For example, in the case of the linguistic symbol "cat," the conventions of English usage, cultural practices related to the concept of "cat," and the users of the word can all serve as interpretants. This suggests that Peirce's philosophy considers the communities that use these conventions and practices, as well as the individuals who belong to these communities.

In order to illustrate the pragmatist approach to the meaning of symbols, let us consider an example provided by Peirce himself. The meaning of "hard" in the statement "A is hard" can be explained as "A would not be scratched if various objects were rubbed against it."[3] This explanation connects the meaning of "hard" to the action of experimentally testing whether A can be scratched. Notably, this highlights Peirce's consideration of scientific procedures. His pragmatism aims to ensure the sound and reliable progress of scientific inquiry within the scientific community. Peirce further argues that scientific inquiry requires the establishment of "regulative assumptions" within the community, such as "there exists a solid reality unaffected by individual subjective thoughts."[4] While such an idealized view of the scientific community might seem naive to contemporary readers, it can be generalized as a vision of diverse communities, each governed by its own regulative assumptions and engaged in reconfiguring these assumptions through ongoing inquiry. This view aligns with the conception of symbol emergence systems, wherein both individual agents and their communities collectively adapt their practices to create new meanings and revise regulative assumptions.

---

[3] Peirce's 1878 paper "How to Make Our Ideas Clear" Peirce, C. S. 1992. In N. Houser & C. Kloesel (Eds.), *Essential Peirce: Selected Philosophical Writing, vol. 1 (1867–1893)*, pp. 124–141. Indiana University Press) is the basis for this discussion. In this paper, Peirce introduces the famous "pragmatic maxim."

[4] For a detailed explanation of regulative assumptions, see Misak, Cheryl. 2013. *The American Pragmatists*. Oxford University Press, Ch. 3.

The Past and Future of Pragmatism

To provide context for readers from various backgrounds, the rest of this chapter briefly describes the historical development of pragmatism.[5] While Peirce left a vast array of unpublished manuscripts, the term "pragmatism" gained public recognition through William James, who was then a professor of philosophy at Harvard University. John Dewey later solidified pragmatism's status within American academia. As a result, pragmatism became associated primarily with James and Dewey, while Peirce's contributions were largely overlooked for much of the twentieth century.

During the 1930s, as philosophers from Europe sought refuge in the USA amidst the political turmoil preceding World War II, their ideas emphasized mathematical logic and aimed to clarify the meanings of philosophical terms and concepts. This movement, known as analytic philosophy, came to dominate American philosophy.

This trend was reversed by Richard Rorty, a leading figure of "neo-pragmatism." Starting in the 1970s, Rorty championed the revival of James' and Dewey's pragmatism in sharp contrast to analytic philosophy. However, Rorty remained indifferent to Peirce's pragmatism. Since around 2000, scholars like Cheryl Misak have taken steps to distance themselves from Rorty. Misak highlights the overlaps and collaborations between analytic philosophy and pragmatism from the outset and praises Peirce's accurate depiction of the scientific community's pursuit of truth. Misak further develops Peirce's theory of inquiry, and suggests that sincere pragmatist inquiry into "truth" can extend beyond science to include ethics and politics.[6] Today, Peirce's pragmatism is undergoing renewed evaluation, attracting interest from fields as diverse as artificial intelligence design and anthropology.[7] This chapter represents an effort to respond to these multidisciplinary interests from the perspective of a philosophical scholar.

---

[5] For further discussion of the historical context of pragmatism and analytic philosophy, see Misak (2013).

[6] Misak, Cheryl. 2000. *Truth, Politics, Morality: Pragmatism and Deliberation*. Routledge.

[7] For example, see Kohn, Eduardo. 2013. *How Forests Think: Toward an Anthropology Beyond the Human*. University of California Press.

Uexküll's Theory of Umwelt: The Worlds as Seen by Living Beings

Yohei Nishida

Umwelt

The term *Umwelt* refers to the world experienced by living beings of a particular species—the world they perceive and act within. It is not an objective environment, but rather a subjective world constructed from the organism's own meanings.[1]

Jakob von Uexküll, a biologist born in Estonia in 1864 who worked primarily in Germany, introduced this concept within a biological framework. Even at that time, the natural sciences predominantly treated organisms as objective entities, often likening them to machines.[2] In contrast, Uexküll argued that organisms are not mere objects, but *subjects*, functioning more as operators than as machines. He proposed that biology should focus on understanding the meaningful world of these subjects, which led to the development of his Umwelt theory.

The Umwelt of a female tick after mating is one of the most well-known illustrations of this concept.[3] A tick lacks vision but can detect butyric acid emitted from

---

[1] Although Uexküll gave this specific meaning to the word Umwelt, the German word Umwelt is commonly used to mean "environment" in English. Uexküll used the term Umgebung (surroundings) to refer to the objective environment.

[2] Uexküll critically refers to this perspective, which represents the viewpoint of a physiologist or a zoologist. See von Uexküll, J., & Kriszat, G. 1934; 1956 Streifzüge durch die Umwelten von Tieren und Menschen. Rowohlt Taschenbuch Verlag. and von Uexküll, J. 1950 Das allmächtige Leben. Christian Wegner Verlag.

[3] von Uexküll, J., & Kriszat, G. 1934; 1956 Streifzüge durch die Umwelten von Tieren und Menschen. Rowohlt Taschenbuch Verlag. For English translations, see, for example, von Uexküll, J. 1992 A stroll through the worlds of animals and men: A picture book of invisible worlds. Semiotica, 89, pp.319–391.

Y. Nishida (✉)
Tokai University, Hiratsuka, Kanagawa, Japan
e-mail: nishida.yohei.h@tokai.ac.jp

© The Author(s) 2026
T. Taniguchi (ed.), *Symbol Emergence Systems*,
https://doi.org/10.1007/978-981-95-1327-7_4

the sebaceous follicles of mammals. This butyric acid serves as a mark or *sign* prompting the tick to drop from its perch. Upon landing, the tick senses contact and begins to move around. When it perceives warmth, indicating bare skin, it burrows in and consumes liquid (blood).

The tick's Umwelt consists of three perceptions—the smell of butyric acid, touch, and warmth—and three actions—falling, moving, and sucking liquid. The tick's Umwelt is thus extremely simple. The other characteristics that mammals are objectively thought to possess are not so much ignored as nonexistent in this world. The tick lives within such a world. However, this simplicity ensures the tick's survival. The tick's Umwelt is simple, yet it is complete.

Functional Cycle

Each organism has its own unique Umwelt. Unlike an objective environment, the Umwelt varies among species, which is why the concept is often referred to in the plural as Umwelten.[4]

Uexküll diagrammatically represented the shared fundamental structure of diverse Umwelten as *functional cycle* (Funktionskreis) (see Fig. 1).[5] This

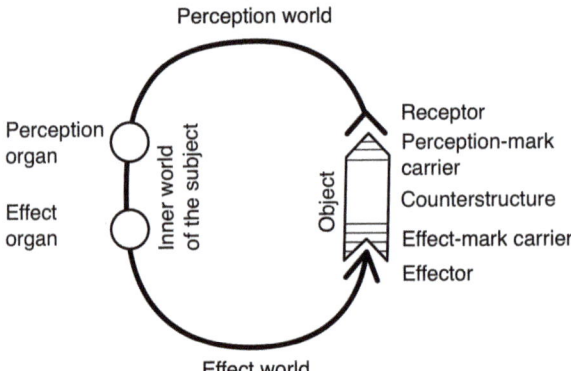

Fig. 1 The functional cycle of perception and action. The diagram illustrates how the subject's inner world engages with the object via perception and effect organs. The object is structured in three layers—the perception-mark carrier, counterstructure, and effect-mark carrier—enabling feedback between the subject's perception world and the effect world

---

[4] For further details on diverse Umwelten, see von Uexküll, J. 1909 Umwelt und Innenwelt der Tiere. Verlag von Julius Springer. (Boettcher, R. tr. 2021 Environment and Inner World of the Animals. Independently Published.)

[5] Functional cycle diagrams vary slightly across sources. Here, we present a new translation of the 1956 German version, note 3.

closed-loop diagram illustrates the connection between the organism and the objects within its Umwelt. The completeness of an Umwelt is captured through this structure.

For example, in the tick's Umwelt, the smell of butyric acid functions as a perception-mark signaling the presence of a mammal. Through the tick's *inner world* (Innenwelt), this mark triggers the action of falling and projects the effect-mark of shock onto the mammal as the tick's object. This, in turn, erases the first perception-mark, the smell of butyric acid, and the next functional cycle, which consists of a new perception-mark—touch—follows. The tick's three perceptions and three actions are thus understood through these successive functional cycles.

The *perception world* (Merkwelt) of the tick comprises all domains accessible through its receptors, while its *effect world* (Wirkwelt) encompasses all domains accessible through its effectors. These two worlds together form a unified Umwelt through one or more functional cycles.[6]

Thus, simple animals correspond to simple Umwelten, and complex animals correspond to complex Umwelten, but any animal is completely fitted into its respective Umwelt. Uexküll called this "the first fundamental theorem of Umwelt theory."[7]

Approaching Umwelt

Since the Umwelt is the subjective world of organisms, accessing it is challenging. Care must be taken to avoid anthropomorphizing an animal's unique meaning world by overly analogizing it to human subjectivity. Uexküll consciously confronted this pitfall, maintaining a cautious distance from psychological approaches.

Instead, he focused on animal behavior. While an organism's subjective state cannot be directly accessed, it can be inferred from its behavior. For example, a tick will pierce a membrane to extract liquid if the temperature is appropriate, regardless of whether the liquid is blood. This implies that ticks lack a sense of taste, a conclusion reached by constructing appropriate experimental conditions and observing their behavior. Umwelt theory is thus often regarded as a precursor to modern *ethology*.[8]

---

[6] Umwelt is thus a world created or constructed in response to the subject, and it is connected to the constructivist perspective of I-5. Piaget's genetic epistemology can be regarded as a theory that focuses on the human Umwelt, particularly its developmental aspect.

[7] See note 3, 1956, p.27.

[8] According to Adolph Portmann, there are in fact multiple sources of animal behavior research, and it seems that this cannot be attributed solely to Uexküll. His son, Thure von Uexküll, also states that the subjectivity of organisms has been overlooked in recent behavioral research and that Umwelt studies have regressed. For more details, see the commentary in 1970 Streifzüge durch die Umwelten von Tieren und Menschen (Conditio humana series). S. Fischer Verlag.

While focusing on behavior, Uexküll did not neglect internal states. For instance, a sea anemone may serve both as a dwelling and as food for a hermit crab, depending on the crab's internal state. Uexküll referred to this as the organism's *mood* (Stimmung).[9]

Additionally, interacting Umwelten are described as being in *counterpoint* (Kontrapunkt). Similar to the harmonization of independent melodies in musical counterpoint, each organism's Umwelt remains distinct yet interwoven with others. Such musical metaphors are prominent in Uexküll's later works.[10]

The Human Umwelt

Uexküll's Umwelt theory significantly influenced philosophers like *Max Scheler* and *Martin Heidegger* within the tradition of *phenomenology*. While these contemporaries focused on humans as distinct from animals, Uexküll sought to position humans and animals on the same plane by applying Kantian *epistemology* to biology.[11] Thus, Umwelt theory also serves as a precursor to *post-anthropocentric* perspective and remains relevant in contemporary humanities.

It must be emphasized that, while Umwelt theory is certainly not anthropocentric, it does take into account the perspective of the human being as *observer*. The fact that living organisms exist in a world of subjective meaning also applies to us as humans, as a type of living organism. In other words, the objective environment is nothing more than the Umwelt unique to human beings.[12] Moreover, descriptions of the Umwelten of other organisms always require the clarification that they are the result of such human observation. In this sense, Umwelt theory also anticipates the concept of *observation* in neo-cybernetics, which will be discussed in "Neo-Cybernetics and Information: What Is Information?".

In addition, Umwelt theory is fundamental to *biosemiotics*, which interprets life as a semiotic process (semiosis). This approach aligns more with Peircean semiotics than with Saussurean semiology, focusing on micro-level semiotic processes.

---

[9] See note 3, 1956, p.66.

[10] von Uexküll, J. 1940; 1970 Bedeutungslehre. S. Fischer Verlag. (1982 The Theory of Meaning. Semiotica, 42(1), pp.25–79.) and von Uexküll, J. 1950 Das allmächtige Leben. Christian Wegner Verlag.

[11] von Uexküll, J. 1920 Theoretische Biologie. Paetel. (Mackinnon, D. L. tr. 1926 Theoretical biology. K. Paul, Trench, Trubner & co. ltd.; Harcourt, Brace & company, inc.)

[12] See note 3, 1956, pp.30–31.

However, biosemiotics often overlooks the inherent observer's perspective within itself.[13]

The Robot's Umwelt

Symbol emergence systems theory examines how symbolic communication emerges at a social level, assuming that each agent's perspective is inherently closed. This suggests that the concept of Umwelt forms the foundation of this framework for exploring symbolic issues.[14]

What might a robot's Umwelt look like as a future member of a symbol emergence system? Within the structure of functional cycles, a robot's camera and microphone serve as receptors, while its arms, wheels, and speakers act as effectors. A *robot's Umwelt* can thus be imagined as the unified domain of its potential perceptions and actions.[15] Symbol emergence systems theory explores the symbolic interactions emerging from such sensorimotor systems.

However, Umwelt theory applies to robots only if they are considered subjects. Uexküll emphasized the necessity of a subject for time and space to exist[16] and distinguished between organisms and machines, considering only the former as subjects. Of course, modern robots were beyond Uexküll's purview, and he did not explicitly deny the possibility of machines as subjects. He even acknowledged the mechanistic nature of organisms, but he also argued that organisms possess *supermachine* (übermaschinelle) properties in their self-formation and constant reconstruction.[17]

This view of organisms as both mechanical and yet exceeding machines recalls the concept of *autopoiesis* (discussed in Chapter "Neo-Cybernetics and Information: What Is Information?"), which suggests that robots can become subjects when they achieve organizational closure in the manner of autopoiesis.

---

[13] Nishida, Y. 2011 "The Relationship between Autopoiesis Theory and Biosemiotics: On Philosophical Suppositions as Bases for a New Information Theory," tripleC, 9(2), pp.424–433.

[14] As will be outlined in Chapter "Neo-Cybernetics and Information: What Is Information?", the concept of information must likewise be considered within the premise of a closed system.

[15] The robot's Umwelt can be imagined as corresponding to its world model (see Chapter World Models: Agents That Learn About the World from Subjective Experience).

[16] See note 3, 1956, p.30.

[17] See note 4, 1909, p.12.

Developmental Psychology and Constructivism: From Piaget to Contemporary Theory

Yusuke Moriguchi

Piagetian Theory: Schema and Adaptation

Jean Piaget is a pioneer of children's cognitive development. As discussed in Chapter "Language Acquisition: Statistical Learning and Social Cognitive Skills", while there is often debate about whether experiential or innate factors are more crucial in child development, Piaget emphasized the interaction between both factors and highlighted children's active role in knowledge construction. As will be detailed later, Piaget is known as a constructivist.

Schema (or sheme) represents the fundamental unit of cognitive framework in Piaget's theory and is a core concept in his constructivism. Specifically, it encompasses a series of actions, memories, thoughts, and strategies for understanding and predicting the environment. Importantly, as mentioned in Chapter "Symbol Emergence Systems: Toward a World Where Humans and AI Co-Discover Meaning" on symbol emergence systems theory, schemas are constructed through the interaction between the subject's sensorimotor system and the environment.[1] Consider, for example, the grasping schema: while the manner of grasping differs depending on an object's size and weight, the meaning of grasping remains constant for the actor. Thus, schema represents a unit that characterizes the equivalence of various actions.

---

[1] Piaget, J. 1970 Piaget's theory. In P. H. Mussen (Ed.), Carmichael's Manual of Child Psychology (Vol.1, third ed.) (pp.703–732). John Wiley & Sons.

Y. Moriguchi (✉)
Kyoto University, Kyoto, Japan
e-mail: moriguchi.yusuke.8s@kyoto-u.ac.jp

T. Taniguchi (ed.), *Symbol Emergence Systems*,
https://doi.org/10.1007/978-981-95-1327-7_5

According to Piaget, children adapt to their environment through schemas, particularly through two processes: assimilation and accommodation. Assimilation, derived from biological concepts, refers to how organisms incorporate environmental elements. In Piaget's theory, it describes how children transform and incorporate new information to fit their existing schemas. Accommodation refers to how organisms modify their existing schemas to match new experiences. In other words, it involves adjusting one's cognition based on new experiences. Using grasping behavior as an example, when an infant encounters a new object and applies their existing grasping method, this represents assimilation. When the usual grasping method proves ineffective and the infant explores different approaches to successfully grasp the object, this process represents accommodation.

Genetic Epistemology

Piaget is recognized as the founder of genetic epistemology, a theoretical framework that attempts to explain the development of knowledge, particularly scientific knowledge, based on its historical and psychological origins of its fundamental concepts and operations. Piaget published books of genetic epistemology in 1950 and established the International Center for Genetic Epistemology at the University of Geneva in 1955 to pursue this line of inquiry.

According to Piaget, genetic epistemology relates to knowledge development in both the historical aspect of science (phylogenesis) and individual development (ontogenesis). This theory seeks to explain how knowledge is acquired, organized, and transformed over time.

Genetic epistemology differs from traditional epistemology in several key aspects. Traditional epistemology focuses on the nature of knowledge and methods of acquisition, primarily concerned with logical and conceptual analysis and justification of knowledge. In contrast, genetic epistemology centers on the origins and development of knowledge. The methodological approaches also differ. Traditional epistemology employs philosophical and abstract methods, attempting to answer epistemological questions through logical reasoning, thought experiments, and philosophical argument analysis. Genetic epistemology, however, is more empirical and practical, utilizing experimentation and observation. The role of the individual also differs. Genetic epistemology incorporates Piaget's constructivist perspective, where learners construct knowledge through interaction with the world, while traditional epistemology does not necessarily consider the individual's role in knowledge generation.

Constructivism

Constructivism posits that mental structures, including perception and memory, are not passively acquired but actively assembled or constructed (refer also to Sect. I-6: Neo-cybernetics and Information). This concept was initially introduced by psychologist Frederic Bartlett in memory research. In the field of perception, psychologist Ulric Neisser employed it to explain various visual illusions. Radical constructivism, partially originating from Piaget, was formalized by philosopher Ernst von Glasersfeld in his work "Radical Constructivism." This approach is predicated on the assumption that subjects construct mental structures by observing the effects of their actions on the environment. Social constructivism, based on "The Social Construction of Reality" by sociologist Peter L. Berger and colleagues, focuses on how people come to share interpretations of their social environment.

Piaget and Radical Constructivism

Radical constructivism proposes an alternative perspective on the relationship between knowledge and reality. While traditional epistemology and cognitive psychology view knowledge as corresponding to objective reality, radical constructivism, while not denying the existence of objective reality, argues that we lack direct access to it. Knowledge is considered functional adaptation, reflecting frameworks of the world constructed through subjective experience. In other words, knowledge does not reflect objective reality but rather represents an individual's subjectively constructed understanding of the world. According to this theory, subjects create structures within their stream of experience, and these structures constitute what they experience as reality. While Piaget, one of the pioneers of constructivist theory, is not necessarily considered a radical constructivist himself, his ideas closely align with central aspects of radical constructivism. Radical constructivism can be viewed as an inheritance and refinement of Piaget's constructivist theory.

Development of Constructivism in Developmental Psychology

Piaget's theory faced considerable criticism in the latter half of the twentieth century due to theoretical ambiguities and insufficient empirical support. However, research continues through various approaches, including neo-Piagetian theory, which develops Piaget's ideas from a cognitive science perspective. Regarding constructivism, a new approach called rational constructivism emerged in the 2000s. This theoretical framework integrates elements of constructive developmental explanation with rational statistical inference, particularly probabilistic models and Bayesian approaches to learning. Specifically, this process involves individuals implicitly evaluating and integrating prior beliefs, knowledge, and biases with new evidence from the environment, assessing the prior probabilities of hypotheses and the strength and generation of evidence, and combining these evaluations to generate posterior probabilities of hypotheses. Rational constructivism has successfully explained certain aspects of infant cognitive development.[2]

---

[2] Xu, F., Dewar, K., & Perfors, A. 2009 Induction, Overhypotheses, and the Shape Bias: Some Arguments and Evidence for Rational Constructivism. In B. M. Hood & L. Santos (Eds.), The Origins of Object Knowledge (pp.263–284). Oxford University Press.

Neo-Cybernetics and Information: What Is Information?

Yohei Nishida

Cybernetics and Neo-Cybernetics

Cybernetics is an interdisciplinary field that aims to understand biological organisms and machines from a systems-theoretical perspective. *Systems theory* is an approach to research that focuses on studying systems as wholes, rather than reducing them to individual components.

Cybernetics was introduced in 1948 by mathematician *Norbert Wiener*.[1] However, it did not function as an independent discipline, but rather as an intellectual movement that engaged scholars from diverse fields, playing a pioneering role in the development of knowledge in the latter half of the twentieth century with key concepts such as control, communication, and information.

The origins of cybernetics lie in *feedback mechanisms* that adjust inputs based on outputs to approach desired states and in the *McCulloch-Pitts neural network model*, which conceptualized mental processes as mechanical operations of the nervous system. These foundations paved the way for a mechanistic understanding of biological bodies and minds, leading to the development of cybernetics, which treats organisms and machines as analogous systems.

---

[1] Wiener, N. 1948, 1961. Cybernetics: Or Control and Communication in the Animal and the Machine. John Wiley.

Y. Nishida (✉)
Tokai University, Hiratsuka, Kanagawa, Japan
e-mail: nishida.yohei.h@tokai.ac.jp

T. Taniguchi (ed.), *Symbol Emergence Systems*,
https://doi.org/10.1007/978-981-95-1327-7_6

31

Neo-cybernetics,[2] a term used to refer to theories that emerged in the 1970s, represents an *epistemological turn* in cybernetics.[3] Heinz von Foerster referred to it as the "cybernetics of cybernetics" or *second-order cybernetics*, emphasizing that if cybernetics discusses humans as cybernetic systems, then it must include cybernetics itself, because it is the discussion that the very cybernetic systems discuss.[4]

Unlike conventional cybernetics, or first-order cybernetics, which is limited to an objective scientific theory and described from a third-person perspective, second-order cybernetics incorporates the observing system, which observes in a cybernetic manner, into its discourse. In other words, it requires the observation of cybernetic observation itself. This means that observed phenomena do not simply exist as they are; they must always be recognized as existing as such because they are observed by an *observer*.

This perspective is consistent with *constructivist* approaches to reality (see I-5), which hold that reality is constructed by us. This neo-cybernetic view of reality was further developed by Ernst von Glasersfeld into *radical constructivism*, combining it with Giambattista Vico's philosophy and Jean Piaget's genetic epistemology.[5]

Autopoiesis

Neo-cybernetics also theorizes biological and artificial systems as distinct from each other. This distinction was formalized in the concept of *autopoiesis*, introduced by Humberto Maturana and Francisco Varela.[6]

Autopoiesis, derived from the Greek words for "self" (auto) and "creation, production" (poiesis), refers to the characteristic organization of living systems, describing a mechanism by which the system continuously creates and sustains itself. The *components* of an autopoietic system generate a network of processes

---

[2] This term was introduced by Bruce Clarke, a scholar of literature, and Mark Hansen, a media scholar, in their 2009 paper "Neocybernetic Emergence: Retuning the Posthuman," Cybernetics and Human Knowing, 16(1–2), pp.83–99. Although the same term is used in some areas of engineering, it is unrelated to that usage.

[3] For an overview of the "turn" from cybernetics to neo-cybernetics and the theories that constitute the latter—second-order cybernetics, autopoiesis theory, and radical constructivism—see Nishida, Y. 2023 Ningen Hi-Kikai Ron (Anti-Mechanical Philosophy of Man). Kodansha (in Japanese).

[4] von Foerster, H. 2003 Understanding Understanding. Springer.

[5] The term "radical constructivism" directly refers to a radical acceptance of Piaget's theory. It asserts that the cognitive subject does not assimilate or accommodate to the objective environment, but instead perceives and acts subjectively based on schemas that they have constructed. Accommodation is not the reverse of assimilation; it is a phenomenon that occurs only when a schema fails to produce the expected result. See von Glasersfeld, E. 1995 Radical Constructivism: A Way of Knowing and Learning. Routledge.

[6] Maturana, H. R., & Varela, F. J. 1980 Autopoiesis and Cognition: The Realization of the Living. D. Reidel Publishing Company.

through mutual interaction, and it is through this very network of processes that the components themselves are produced.[7]

Such systems are *autonomous*, continuously self-producing to define their own existence. In contrast, artificial machines are heteronomous, *allopoietic* systems, externally directed and organized for the production of other entities.[8]

Autopoiesis theory, originally developed with cellular systems in mind, has since been extended to mental and social systems, most notably by *Niklas Luhmann*.[9] Luhmann argued that social systems are not composed of humans but of *communications*. *Social systems* are autopoietic networks in which the production of communication processes both sustains and is sustained by the network itself.

Fundamental Informatics

Cybernetics is inherently tied to the concept of information. From its early stages, it has supported fields ranging from computer science and communication engineering to cognitive and life sciences, all of which have been regarded as disciplines that treat "information" as an objective scientific concept.

However, the concept of information underwent a fundamental shift following the "turn" to neo-cybernetics, evolving into something entirely different from what it was before. Since living systems are autonomous, the objective "information" that governs them is not provided as input from the outside. Autonomous systems are *informationally closed*. Information exists inseparably as subjective meaning generated within the system itself.

The concept of information, based on neo-cybernetics, is clearly presented in Toru Nishigaki's *fundamental informatics*.[10] In fundamental informatics, *information* is defined as "something that brings about significance to a living thing." Focusing on the carriers of such information, that is, the medium of information, it is "a pattern by which a living thing generates patterns."

---

[7] This can be specifically imagined as the interdependence between the cell's metabolic processes and the cell membrane. For more on the autonomy of such systems, refer to Chapter "Enactivism: Cognition as Non-representational, Embodied Action."

[8] In autopoiesis theory, living systems are also considered a type of machine, but their mechanisms are those of autopoiesis, which is a super-mechanical (see Chapter "Uexküll's Theory of Umwelt: The Worlds as Seen by Living Beings").

[9] Luhmann, N. 1984 Soziale Systeme. Suhrkamp.

[10] Nishigaki, T. 2004, 2008, 2021 Kiso Johogaku (Fundamental Informatics) vol.1–3. NTT Publishing (in Japanese). and Nishigaki, T. 2007 "For the Establishment of Fundamental Informatics on the Basis of Autopoiesis: Consideration on the Concept of Hierarchical Autonomous Systems," https://digital-narcis.org/nishigaki_pdf/FI-English-01.pdf (Revised and translated by Toru Nishigaki from original Japanese version, in Shiso, no.951, July 2003, pp.5–22).

Life Information, Social Information, and Mechanical Information

In fundamental informatics, all information is essentially considered *life informa-tion* tied to significance for living beings.[11] To an observer, it corresponds to some-thing that aids the organism's survival, shaped by processes such as evolution and learning. These iterative processes generate semantic structures as patterns, which in turn enable further pattern generation. This aligns with Peircean semiotics, par-ticularly the *biosemiotics* of *Jesper Hoffmeyer*, which frames the internal processes of living systems as *semiosis* (semiotic processes).[12] Thus, life information emerges self-referentially within the organism.

A subset of life information is explicitly observed and described by humans, transforming into *social information*. Social information consists of signs or *sym-bols*, such as words or images that are used within human societies. All information exchanged within human societies is considered social information.

Social information presupposes the society in which it is used. For example, the use of the Japanese language presupposes the existence of a *linguistic community* that uses it. As Ferdinand de Saussure pointed out, universal conceptual structures do not exist beyond such communities. Furthermore, as Charles Sanders Peirce dis-cussed, the meanings of individual signs dynamically transform through semiosis.

When the dynamic aspect of signs is abstracted, leaving only their representam-ina (the plural of representamen) or signifiers, the narrowest definition of informa-tion emerges: *mechanical information* Mechanical information separates symbols from their meanings, enabling efficient processing and transmission. Computers primarily handle this form of information, as do *written characters*, which are assumed to convey meaning accurately when transcribed correctly.

HACS

Focusing solely on the carriers of information, such as mechanical information, allows for the transmission of information. However, fundamental informatics argues that if genuine information is understood as life information emerging within the internal processes of informationally closed autonomous systems, it cannot be transmitted.

Rather, the issue lies in a mechanism that creates the illusion of social informa-tion transmission. The concept of the *Hierarchical Autonomous Communication System (HACS)*, as proposed by fundamental informatics, offers a way to

---

[11] Nishigaki, T. 2013 The Wisdom to Bridge the Gap between Lives and Machines: An Introduction to Fundamental Informatics. (Can be freely downloaded from: https://digital-narcis.org/toru-nishigaki/?lang=english) (Translated by Toru Nishigaki and Nami Ohi from original Japanese ver-sion, 2012, Koryosha).

[12] Hoffmeyer, J. (Danish version 1993) 1996 Signs of Meaning in the Universe. Indiana University Press.

understand the fiction of information transmission through a systems-theoretical mechanism.

The key point is that observers can dynamically shift their viewpoints to grasp the constraints between autonomous systems (see Fig. 1). While social and *mental systems* are autonomous in themselves (from the viewpoint of their internal mechanisms) to an observer of the social system as the higher-level HACS, mental systems, as the lower-level HACS, appear as heteronomous allopoietic systems, constrained by the operation of the social system. When communication that constitutes the social system continuously occurs, based on the material of descriptions produced by the mental systems, observers perceive this as "information transmission." Information cannot be transmitted in principle, but the very fact that the social system, which is at a higher level than the mental system, is continuously maintained gives rise to the fiction of information transmission.

Symbol emergence systems theory, which assumes cognitive closure for each agent, aligns with this neo-cybernetic tradition.[13] Currently, artificial systems like robots are non-autopoietic and, therefore, cannot be positioned as the lower-level HACS like mental systems. However, at the social system level, even autonomous mental systems can appear constrained. This opens up possibilities for exploring artificial systems that, despite their heteronomous allopoietic nature, function in a way that is equivalent to humans within social systems.[14] Symbol emergence systems theory investigates how the mechanisms of individual systems contribute to the realization of symbolic communication at the social level.

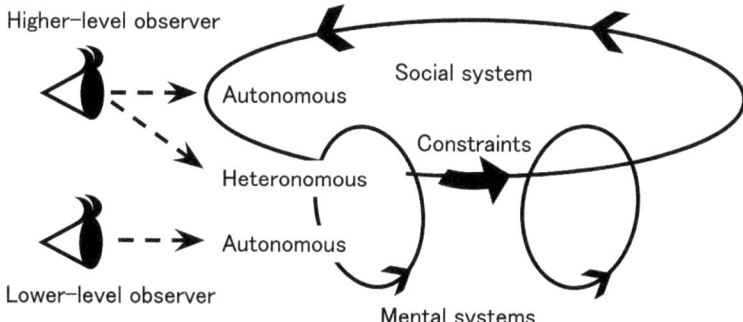

Fig. 1 A hierarchical view of social and mental systems based on Hierarchical Autonomous Communication System (HACS). Mental systems operate autonomously in themselves, but they are observed as heteronomous by observers at the social system level. The figure contrasts the perspectives of higher-level and lower-level observers, illustrating how autonomy and heteronomy can coexist within the same systems without contradiction

---

[13] However, the understanding of systems in Symbol Emergence Systems theory and fundamental informatics does not perfectly align. For a comparison of their differences and similarities, see Chap. 3 of Taniguchi, T. et al. 2023 Miraishakai to Imi no Kyokai (Future Society and the Boundaries of Meaning). Keiso Shobo (in Japanese).

[14] Nevertheless, if it remains a heteronomous machine in its own right, it should be distinguished from autopoietic autonomous beings like ourselves.

Part II: Symbol Emergence in Robotics

Symbol Emergence in Robotics: A Constructive Approach to Overcoming the Symbol Grounding Problem

Tadahiro Taniguchi

Constructive Approach to Symbol Emergence Systems

How can we design artificial intelligence and robotics systems that are capable of forming internal representational structures, learning vocabulary and usage patterns, engaging in linguistic (i.e., symbolic) communication, and ultimately living alongside us in the real world? In the vision presented earlier in Chapter "Symbol Emergence Systems — Toward a World Where Humans and AI Co-Discover Meaning" (see Fig. 1, revisited), both humans and artificial agents participate in a symbol emergence system capable of generating language. But what kinds of cognitive and interactive capabilities must AI and robots possess in order to become constituents within human-driven symbol emergence systems?

Symbol emergence in robotics is a constructive approach that addresses these questions through engineering-based methodologies. At its core, this field seeks to deepen our understanding of human cognition and communication by constructing artificial agents that learn language through real-world experience and interaction.

Specifically, symbol emergence in robotics aims to develop robots that acquire language grounded in sensory-motor interaction. This research involves studying how robots can form concepts, acquire vocabulary, and engage in diverse communication strategies—by actually building such systems. Central to this approach is the idea that a robot, equipped with sensory and motor systems, can achieve symbolic interaction through embodied engagement with the environment, thereby offering insights into the mechanisms underlying human cognition.

The term "Symbol Emergence Robotics" was first introduced during the organized session "Symbol Emergence Robotics and Multimodal Semantic Interaction"

T. Taniguchi (✉)
Graduate School of Informatics, Kyoto University, Kyoto, Japan

Research Organization of Science and Technology, Ritsumeikan University, Kyoto, Japan
e-mail: taniguchi@i.kyoto-u.ac.jp

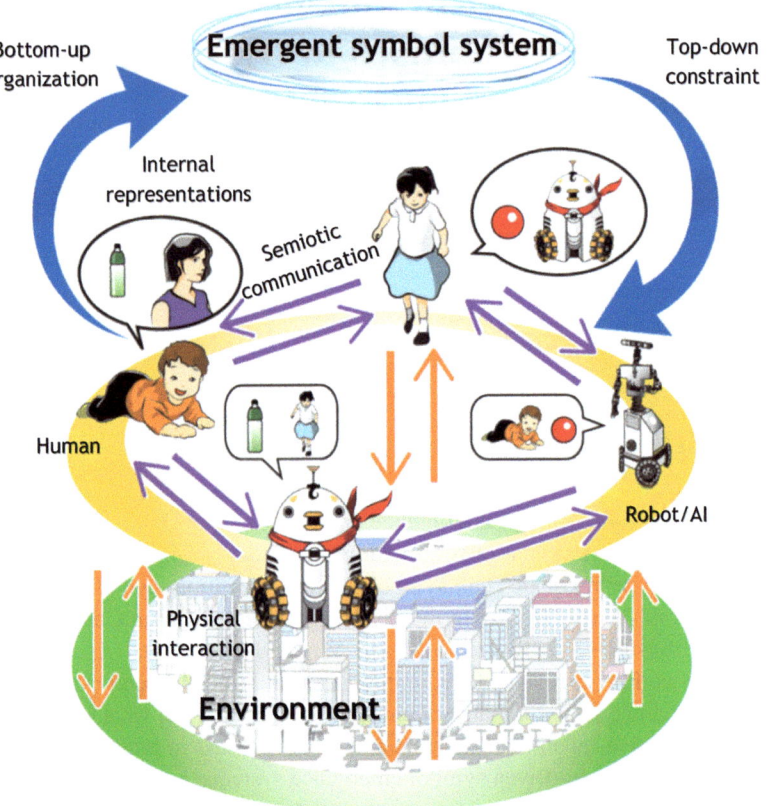

Fig. 1 Overview of the symbol emergence system involving humans and robots. (See the caption of Chapter "Symbol Emergence Systems: Toward a World Where Humans and AI Co-Discover Meaning", Fig. 1 for details)

at the Japanese Society for Artificial Intelligence (JSAI) conference in 2011.[1] The foundational ideas and early research were later compiled into the Japanese volume "Symbol Emergence Robotics: An Introduction to the Mechanisms of Intelligence, which contributed to the expansion of research in this field, especially within the Japanese academic community. But what does it mean to deepen our understanding of humans by creating robots?

The constructive approach—in contrast to the traditional analytical approach—seeks to understand by building. Although its philosophical underpinnings are still under discussion, the method has become increasingly prominent since the late twentieth century, particularly in complex systems science, due to advances in

---

[1] Organized session summary: Taniguchi, T., Iwahashi, N., Nitta, T., Okada, H., & Nagai, T. 2011. "Symbol Emergence Robotics and Multimodal Semantic Interaction." Proceedings of the Japanese Society for Artificial Intelligence Annual Conference, 25, 2B2OS22a1.

computation and simulation. In the context of symbol emergence in robotics, the focus lies in constructing models that imitate human cognitive processes. These models enable empirical investigation into phenomena such as concept formation and vocabulary acquisition by asking whether robots can reproduce human-like behavior.

Of course, the question of whether robotic cognition is truly equivalent to human cognition remains open. However, the goal is not to claim equivalence, but rather to propose new models of human cognition, and to test and refine these models through implementation in robots—offering empirical and falsifiable evidence for their validity.

In this view, AI and robots become cognitive models of the human mind. The concept of "model" itself is essential not only in cognitive science and linguistics but also in physics, chemistry, and even in our everyday reasoning. We use models to extract and isolate relevant phenomena from the world, and we study those models to better understand what we cannot directly observe. Human cognitive systems, for example, are fundamentally inaccessible to direct observation; therefore, modeling becomes a key scientific strategy for conceptualizing and understanding their dynamics and adaptive properties.

Robots as Models in Science

Among the most frequently asked questions in the field of symbol emergence in robotics are:

Why robots?

Why do we need to build robots to understand the human mind, language, and meaning in symbol emergence systems?[2]

To answer this, we must consider the role of models in science. Scientific modeling can be understood in terms of four progressively more concrete and operational forms:

1. Linguistic Models

    These rely on natural language to describe systems or phenomena. While flexible and rich in interpretation, they tend to be vague, speculative, and often lack falsifiability—a critical criterion in empirical science. They are common in philosophy but frequently remain at the level of untestable theorizing.

2. Schematic Models

    These use diagrams to illustrate relationships, structures, or processes in a system. Although more logically structured than linguistic models, their operational viability is typically untested. A schematic model may look plausible, but whether it actually behaves as theorized remains unknown.

---

[2] Detailed discussion of model levels: Taniguchi, T. 2020. Artificial Intelligence for Understanding Minds: Symbol Emergence Robotics as Cognitive Science. Kyoritsu Shuppan.

3. Simulation Models

Enabled by advances in computational power, simulation models allow schematic structures to be operationalized using mathematical and algorithmic representations. These models can be executed, measured, and tested in silico. They have contributed greatly across disciplines, especially since the late twentieth century. However, they remain disembodied, confined within computational environments.

4. Robotic Models

These go beyond simulations by introducing embodied interaction with the real world. A robot, by definition, is a computational system with a physical body—a sensory-motor apparatus that enables direct environmental interaction. This embodiment allows for the integration of real-world sensory data and physical action, which are essential for studying symbolic and bodily interactions in the context of human-like cognition.

In symbol emergence systems, the agents involved are operationally closed entities whose cognition develops through interactions with their environment—both physically and semiotically. To model such systems effectively, it is not enough to simulate them mathematically; the system must be embedded in the world. Only when an AI system has a body and interacts with the real world can it be said to participate meaningfully in a symbol emergence system.

In this sense, robotic models are not just an option—they are a necessity. The formal, diagrammatic model of symbol emergence systems inherently demands agents that engage in self-organizing, embodied, symbolic interaction. It is precisely this necessity that leads us—logically and methodologically—to the use of robots as scientific models.

Beyond the Symbol Grounding Problem

In discussing the concept of symbols in this book, it is important to clarify how it differs from the notion of "symbols" that gained prominence in AI and cognitive science from the mid to late twentieth century. The school of symbolic AI, based on symbolism and computationalism, was built upon the physical symbol system hypothesis formulated by Allen Newell and others.[3] In this framework, "symbols" referred not to signs in the semiotic sense used in everyday communication but to abstract, discrete tokens defined within symbolic logic and computer science.

Throughout this book, we distinguish between symbols (semiotically grounded, meaning-bearing signs) and "symbols" (logically defined tokens in symbolic AI). The quotation marks serve to emphasize this conceptual separation.

---

[3] Newell, A., & Simon, H. A. 2007. "Computer Science as Empirical Inquiry: Symbols and Search." Communications of the ACM, 19(3), 113–126.

In symbolic AI, knowledge is represented as a set of logical expressions composed of fixed symbolic tokens—"symbols"—manipulated by formal rules within a system designed by humans. This atomistic approach treats intelligence as the manipulation of predefined "symbols." However, from a constructivist perspective, the validity of such a system has largely collapsed in light of advances in the 2010s and 2020s—particularly with the rise of deep learning and the breakthrough of large language models capable of distributed representation and inference.

Simply put, symbolic AI based on "symbols" has failed to produce intelligent systems capable of adapting flexibly to real-world contexts. In contrast, AI systems grounded in learning from data have exceeded symbol systems in a wide array of tasks, often achieving human-level performance.

Yet, the deeper mystery—the source of meaning in the symbols we use—remains unresolved.

The symbol grounding problem, introduced by Stevan Harnad in 1990,[4] pointed to this limitation in symbolic AI: even if a system encodes that "apples are red," it cannot understand redness without grounding it in sensorimotor experience. While some have argued that deep learning has "solved" this issue through distributed representation, the original problem was framed within the context of symbolic AI itself, and its limitations.

Indeed, Luc Steels, a pioneer in research on language evolution and symbol emergence, argued as early as 2008 that the symbol grounding problem was either already resolved or fundamentally misframed.[5] The real issue, he suggested, was not grounding per se, but a misguided obsession with logical "symbols," disconnected from the social and embodied nature of meaning.

From the perspective of symbol emergence in robotics, it is not the symbol grounding problem that lies at the core of artificial intelligence. Rather, the essential challenge is the symbol emergence problem—that is, how meaningful symbols arise, evolve, and become organized through social and embodied interaction.

What truly matters are the mechanisms of language understanding and generation, rooted in lived experience and collective negotiation—not the artificial grounding of formal tokens.[6]

---

[4] Harnad, S. 1990. "The Symbol Grounding Problem." Physica D: Nonlinear Phenomena, 42(1–3), 335–346.

[5] Steels, L. 2008. "The Symbol Grounding Problem Has Been Solved. So What's Next?" In Symbols and Embodiment: Debates on Meaning and Cognition. Oxford University Press, pp. 223–244.

[6] Taniguchi, T., Ugur, E., Hoffmann, M., Jamone, L., Nagai, T., Rosman, B., Matsuka, T., Iwahashi, N., Oztop, E., Piater, J., and Wörgötter, F. "Symbol Emergence in Cognitive Developmental Systems: A Survey." *IEEE Transactions on Cognitive and Developmental Systems* 11, no. 4 (2019): 494–516. https://doi.org/10.1109/TCDS.2018.2867772.

Language Acquisition: Statistical Learning and Social Cognitive Skills

Noburo Saji

Nativism and Empiricism in Language Development

The mechanism of human development is believed to be explained by empirical factors, innate factors, and their interactions. Empirical factors refer to the influences from experiences in physical and social environments after birth, while innate factors pertain to genetically endowed characteristics. The interaction between these factors varies by domain, but since the mid-twentieth century, nativism has been particularly influential in the field of language acquisition. This perspective, strongly shaped by Noam Chomsky's argument regarding the impossibility of language acquisition through experience alone, posits that humans are uniquely endowed with innate symbolic-logical rules for language. This idea aligned with the early cognitive science framework that conceptualized human intelligence as information processing and was widely embraced by researchers.

However, as cognitive science shifted from a computationalism (or symbolism) to an perspective of embodied and situated cognition, the understanding of empirical and innate factors in language acquisition research also evolved. A new focus emerged: the unique features of human language acquisition might lie in learning strategies derived from experience. This chapter explores two key aspects of this perspective: *statistical learning* and *social cognitive skills*.

N. Saji (✉)
Waseda University, School of Human Sciences, Saitama, Japan
e-mail: saji@waseda.jp

T. Taniguchi (ed.), *Symbol Emergence Systems*,
https://doi.org/10.1007/978-981-95-1327-7_8

Statistical Learning and Language Acquisition

One of the significant discoveries influencing language acquisition research since the 1990s is that human beings are highly sensitive to stable distributional patterns of information in their environment and can use this ability for new activities. Jenny R. Saffran and colleagues pioneered this discussion in language acquisition by demonstrating that 8-month-old infants use transitional probabilities—the likelihood of one sound following another—to segment continuous streams of sounds into words.[1] This ability to detect patterns in the distribution of environmental information is remarkably robust, extending beyond word segmentation to various levels of language, including semantics and syntax. For example, studies by Linda B. Smith and others have shown that statistical learning can detect mappings between auditory signals (sounds) and visual referents (objects) across sensory modalities.[2] In cross-situational learning experiments, children rapidly identified patterns linking auditory inputs with visual objects across multiple scenarios.[3]

Computational simulations have further examined the mechanism of statistical learning. In one remarkable study, Jeffrey L. Elman used simple recurrent networks to investigate how syntactic knowledge could be extracted from linguistic input.[4] By inputting sequences of words, the network learned to predict grammatical categories that might follow (e.g., nouns after adjectives or verbs after nouns). This demonstrated partial learning of syntactic rules through exposure to input patterns.

The discovery of statistical learning has significant implications for language acquisition research. It suggests that mechanisms previously assumed to be innate could, at least in part, be explained by experience. Related to this, usage-based models of language acquisition have gained attention by proposing that linguistic knowledge can be learned by abstracting relationships between linguistic forms and their meanings from input. According to this view, various forms of linguistic knowledge—even syntactic knowledge—can be acquired as symbolic relations linking word sequences (e.g., noun-verb-noun structures) to their meanings (e.g., transitive events). This perspective aligns with the *symbolic view of grammar*, which frames grammatical knowledge as learned symbolic associations.[5]

---

[1] Saffran, J. R., Aslin, R. N., & Newport, E. L. 1996. Statistical Learning by 8-Month-Old Infants. Science, 274, 1926–1928.

[2] Smith, L. B., & Yu, C. 2008. Infants Rapidly Learn Word-Referent Mappings via Cross-Situational Statistics. Cognition, 106, 333–338.

[3] Modality refers to sensory modes, such as vision, hearing, smell, and touch, processed through respective sensory organs. In language acquisition, integrating multiple modalities to construct linguistic meaning is a critical issue. For example, associating the sound "apple" with a red fruit that smells sweet and sour requires integration of auditory, visual, and olfactory modalities.

[4] Elman, J., Bates, E., Johonson, M. H., Karmiloff-Smith, A., Parisi, D., & Plunkett, K. 1998. Rethinking Innateness: A Connectionist Perspective on Development. MIT Press.

[5] Langacker, R. W. 1987. Foundations of Cognitive Grammar, vol. 1: Theoretical Prerequisites. Stanford University Press.

Social Cognitive Skills and Language Acquisition

While statistical learning likely represents an evolutionarily ancient ability, social cognitive skills may reflect a more recently evolved and uniquely human capability. Children exhibit a strong response to inputs from conspecifics, and the discovery of robust social cognitive skills in pre-linguistic infants during the 1990s and 2000s has had a profound impact on language acquisition research.

One foundational area in this research is the study of intention reading. Michael Tomasello introduced the concept of the "9-month revolution," referring to the developmental milestone when infants begin recognizing others as intentional agents acting to achieve goals.[6] This realization transforms caregiver-child communication qualitatively. Before this stage, infants primarily engage in dyadic interactions, focusing either on toys or caregivers. After about 9 months, infants start following others' gazes to identify what they are attending to and use pointing gestures to direct others' attention to shared objects of focus, establishing *joint attention*. This triadic interaction—involving self, other, and object—is a foundation for symbolic communication and *role-reversal imitation*, which Tomasello argues is uniquely human beings[7]. Following the emergence of this communicative form, children begin imitating speech sounds and using language to influence others' intentions.

The uniqueness of human cultural learning, including language acquisition through communication, is further explored in Gergely Csibra and György Gergely's *natural pedagogy theory*.[8] Human communication often involves teaching and learning from others, a practice unparalleled among other species. For instance, caregivers frequently provide "ostensive cues" to signal their intent to initiate communication, such as making eye contact or calling the child's name. Following these cues, caregivers convey "informative intent" by showing objects or telling stories. Infants are particularly sensitive to ostensive cues and tend to imitate and learn from the ensuing interactions, enabling human-specific cultural learning.[9] Chibra and Gergely point out that the transition to a mode of communication in which caregivers and children engage in both teaching and learning through explicit intentional cues facilitates the uniquely human capacity for cultural learning.

The debates surrounding social cognitive skills have significantly broadened the scope of language acquisition research, framing linguistic knowledge as part of

---

[6] Tomasello, M. 2003. Constructing a Language: A Usage-Based Theory of Language Acquisition. Harvard University Press.

[7] This imitative learning involves reproducing others' actions while understanding their intentionality, distinguishing it from mimicry, which lacks this intentional context. For example, a child pointing at an object to manipulate a caregiver's attention demonstrates an understanding of the caregiver's intent to direct attention, embodying role-reversal imitation—a foundation for all social learning, including language.

[8] Csibra, G., & Gergely, G. 2009. Natural Pedagogy. Trends in Cognitive Sciences, 13, 148–153.

[9] This uniqueness may reflect the distinctive cognitive structures of humans as social animals and the specific characteristics of their Umwelt.

human symbolic communication and the transmission of cultural knowledge. However, discussions continue regarding the extent to which these mechanisms are innate or unique to humans. The mechanism of language acquisition was once framed as a question of innate symbolic-logical rules during the early days of cognitive science is now reexamined as a question of the uniqueness of human social cognitive skills.

Vocabulary Acquisition by Robots: Modeling Vocabulary Learning Using Probabilistic Generative Models

Tomoaki Nakamura

Introduction

Language acquisition is a crucial challenge in symbol emergence robotics.[1] While cognitive science seeks to uncover mechanisms of language acquisition through human observation, symbol emergence robotics aims to elucidate the process by constructing mathematical models that replicate phenomena and validate their plausibility. This approach, which aims to clarify phenomena by constructing models, is called the constructive approach and strives to unravel the complex mechanisms underlying human language acquisition by developing mathematical models. Since word meanings are acquired through interactions with the environment, they are closely tied to sensory and motor experiences. In symbol emergence robotics, robots as embodied agents engage with their environments to acquire language, offering insights into the integration of multimodal information.

Many studies in symbol emergence robotics use probabilistic generative models to model phenomena. These models describe how real-world information obtained via sensors is generated from internal representations using probability distributions. By treating internal representations as latent variables, such models enable inference of these variables solely from observable information. Consequently, probabilistic models can represent the process of constructing internal representations through interaction with the environment.

---

[1] Taniguchi, T., Nagai, T., Nakamura, T., Iwahashi, N., Ogata, T., & Asoh, H. 2016. Symbol Emergence in Robotics: A Survey. *Advanced Robotics*, 30(11–12), 706–728.

T. Nakamura (✉)
Graduate School of Informatics and Engineering, The University of Electro-Communications, Chofu, Japan
e-mail: tnakamura@uec.ac.jp

© The Author(s) 2026
T. Taniguchi (ed.), *Symbol Emergence Systems*,
https://doi.org/10.1007/978-981-95-1327-7_9

49

To replicate vocabulary acquisition, four main phenomena illustrated in Fig. 1a must be modeled: speech recognition, word segmentation, concept formation, and the association of concepts with words. Speech recognition involves extracting phonemes or syllables as the smallest units of sound from patterns of air vibrations caused by human speech. Word segmentation identifies individual words from sequences of phonemes or syllables. Concepts must then be formed and linked with words to acquire meaning. Additionally, from sensory observation, humans evoke multiple concepts simultaneously, such as objects, colors, shapes, and smells. Words spoken by others can thus refer to a range of concepts, necessitating the estimation of word concept associations. Notably, these four phenomena do not occur in isolation; their learning processes interact and complement one another. Probabilistic generative models have been proposed to reproduce these intertwined phenomena in symbol emergence robotics. This section describes the essential components of such learning and introduces research on vocabulary acquisition using robots.

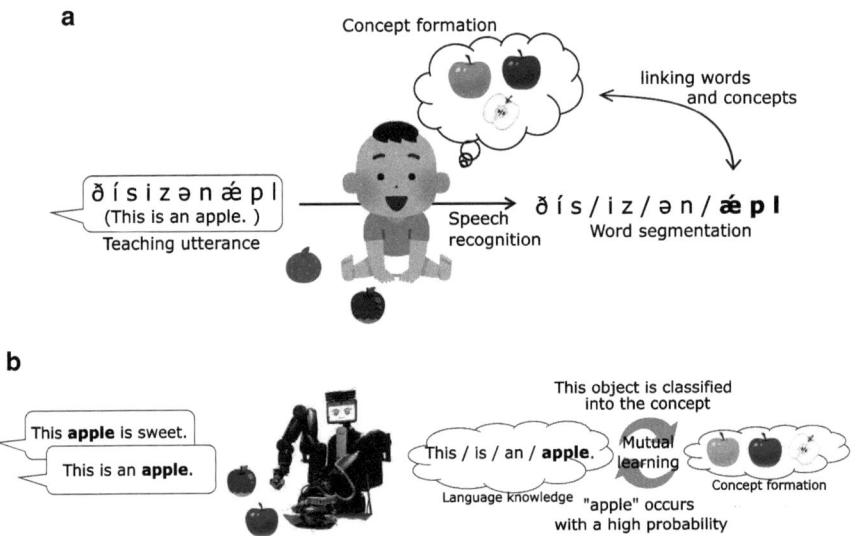

Fig. 1 (a) A developmental model of concept formation in infants. The child segments a spoken utterance (e.g., "This is an apple") into word units through speech recognition and associates the segmented word "apple" with the visual object. The process leads to the formation of a concept and the linking of linguistic input to perceptual categories. (b) A robot learning model for grounding language in perception. Through exposure to multiple utterances and co-occurring objects, the robot segments language (e.g., "This is an apple") and identifies the word "apple" as reliably associated with a specific object. Mutual learning between conceptual categorization and linguistic structure supports the acquisition of grounded meaning

Simultaneous Learning of Concepts and Words

Imagine an apple placed in front of a learner while a teacher says, *"ko re wa ri n go de su."* ("This is an apple." in Japanese) The learner extracts words from the utterance and links them to the object's concept to acquire meaning. However, if the learner lacks lexical knowledge, it becomes challenging to extract words from the teaching utterance. One solution involves word segmentation based on patterns of character occurrences. For example, given the phrases *"ko re wa ri n go da yo"* ("This is an apple." in Japanese) and *"ko no ri n go wa a ma i"* ("This apple is sweet." in Japanese), the substring *"ri n go"* ("apple" in Japanese) appears consistently, and preceding and following characters differ. By leveraging such patterns, *"ri n go"* can be identified as a word. This process, known as unsupervised morphological analysis, segments unstructured text into words. An example is the Nested Pitman-Yor Language Model (NPYLM),[2] which segments words from text without requiring ground-truth labels. Figure 2 demonstrates how NPYLM extracts words from the English text of Alice in Wonderland with spaces removed.

For a robot to acquire vocabulary, it must also recognize sounds. Without linguistic knowledge, recognizing sounds can be difficult. A teacher's utterance of *"ri n go"* ("apple" in Japanese) might be misheard as *"ri n bo"* or *"ri n do"* due to noise. Humans typically use linguistic knowledge and context to resolve such misrecognitions. Linguistic knowledge includes probabilities of word occurrences, such as *"ri n go"* being more likely than *"ri n bo"* in Japanese. Context encompasses conversational flow and environmental cues, such as the likelihood of *"ri n go"* being mentioned near an apple tree. By integrating these factors, humans can correct misheard words. Similarly, research has focused on enabling robots to learn vocabulary by associating linguistic knowledge with sensory information. For example, models combining the Multimodal Latent Dirichlet Allocation (MLDA) framework with speech recognition and NPYLM enable robots to jointly learn words and concepts by leveraging contextual information to reduce errors.[3]

Vocabulary Learning from Continuous Speech

Humans learn words by segmenting continuous speech into phonemes (e.g., /a/, /i/, /u/ in Japanese or /æ/, /ʌ/, /ɑː/ in English) and then segmenting phoneme sequences into words. This two-step segmentation extracts meaningful words from speech,

[2] Mochihashi, D., Yamada, T., & Ueda, N. 2009. Bayesian Unsupervised Word Segmentation with Nested Pitman-Yor Language Modeling. In Proceedings of the Joint Conference of the 47th Annual Meeting of the ACL and the fourth International Joint Conference on Natural Language Processing of the AFNLP, 100–108.

[3] Nishihara, J., Nakamura, T., & Nagai, T. 2017. Online Algorithm for Robots to Learn Object Concepts and Language Models. *IEEE Transactions on Cognitive and Developmental Systems*, 9(3), 255–268.

lastly,shepicturedtoherselfhowthissamelittlesisterofhersw
ould,intheafter-time,beherselfagrownwoman;andhowshe
wouldkeep,throughallherriperyears,thesimpleandlovingh
eartofherchildhood:andhowshewouldgatheraboutherothe
rlittlechildren,andmaketheireyesbrightandeagerwithmany
astrangetale,perhapsevenwiththedreamofwonderlandoflo
ngago:andhowshewouldfeelwithalltheirsimplesorrows,an
dfindapleasureinalltheirsimplejoys,rememberingherownc
hild-life,andthehappysummerdays.

(a) Training data (in part).

last ly , she pictured to herself how this same little sis-
ter of her s would , inthe after - time , be herself agrown
woman ; and how she would keep , through allher ripery
ears , the simple and loving heart of her child hood : and
how she would gather about her other little children ,and
make theireyes bright and eager with many a strange tale
, perhaps even with the dream of wonderland of longago
: and how she would feel with all their simple sorrow s ,
and find a pleasure in all their simple joys , remember ing
her own child - life , and thehappy summerday s .

(b) Segmentation result. Note we used no dictionary.

Fig. 2 Example of input data and segmentation result for lexical acquisition (Referenced from Mochihashi et al. 2009[2]). (**a**) A training text excerpt used for learning, displaying a passage with typical language structure. (**b**) Corresponding segmentation output showing how the system identifies word boundaries without using any predefined dictionary

and this two-level speech structure is known as the double articulation structure. Research on autonomous vocabulary acquisition in robots focuses on modeling this process using probabilistic frameworks.[4, 5]

These models assume that phonemes are generated from words and speech waveforms are generated from phonemes. Learning involves inferring both words and phonemes as well as their lengths from observed waveforms. For instance, the word "this" consists of three phonemes, while "apple" consists of four. In other words, in order to infer a word, it is necessary to estimate the length of the phonemes that make up the word. Similarly, the word "apple" remains "apple" whether spoken slowly or quickly. Therefore, it is also necessary to infer the duration of each sound. Although the model is complex, inference can be performed by calculating the probability of these multiple hidden variables being generated under the given observed speech signals.

[4] Taniguchi, T., Nagasaka, S., & Nakashima, R. 2015. Nonparametric Bayesian Double Articulation Analyzer for Direct Language Acquisition from Continuous Speech Signals. *IEEE Transactions on Cognitive and Developmental Systems*, 8(3), 171–185.

[5] Nagano, M., & Nakamura, T. 2023. Unsupervised Structural Learning of Continuous Speech Using a GP-HSMM-Based Dual Articulation Model. *Journal of the Robotics Society of Japan*, 41(3), 318–321.

Learning Word Meanings through Cross-Situational Learning

Consider a learner observing an apple and an orange while hearing the word "red." If the learner does not know the word "red," the learner cannot clearly determine what it refers to. There are countless possibilities: "Red" could refer to the apple, the orange, the color red, the round shape common to both objects, or many other possibilities. Humans resolve such ambiguities using various pieces of information and cognitive biases and learn word meanings efficiently.

Robotic vocabulary acquisition tackles this issue through cross-situational learning. For instance, if "red" is taught in situations depicted in Fig. 3a, b. In each situation, it is ambiguous what the word refers to, making it difficult to determine its meaning. However, by statistically analyzing both instances, one can infer that whenever the word "red" is spoken, there is a high likelihood that a red object is present. This allows for the conclusion that the word represents the characteristic of being red. This process is known as cross-situational learning. Taniguchi et al. proposed a probabilistic generative model for cross-situational learning.[6] Nagano et al. proposed a model incorporating joint attention mechanisms, enabling robots to focus on objects indicated by the teacher's attention .[7]

Fig. 3 Grounding color words through multimodal teaching utterances. The robot receives the word "red" as a teaching utterance in different contexts—first with red fruits (left) and then with red vehicles (right)—allowing it to associate the term "red" with visual features shared across distinct object categories

[6]Taniguchi, A., Taniguchi, T., & Cangelosi, A. 2017. Cross-Situational Learning with Bayesian Generative Models for Multimodal Category and Word Learning in Robots. *Frontiers in Neurorobotics*, 11, 66.

[7]Nagano, M., & Nakamura, T. 2021. Learning Word Meanings Using Joint Attention and MLDA in Environments with a Plurality of Objects. Journal of the Robotics Society of Japan, 39(6), 549–552. (in Japanese).

Probabilistic Generative Models: Foundational Theory for Cognitive Modeling Based on Bayesian Inference

Akira Taniguchi

Probabilistic Generative Models and Bayesian Inference in Cognitive Modeling

As discussed in Chapter "Vocabulary Acquisition by Robots: Modeling Vocabulary Learning Using Probabilistic Generative Models", probabilistic generative models (PGMs) play a crucial role in mathematically representing human cognitive functions. PGMs are mathematical models designed to capture latent structures and patterns underlying observed data. The advantages of PGMs include their ability to handle uncertainty, incorporating prior knowledge, and adapting flexibly to new data. These characteristics make them highly useful for mimicking human cognition and decision-making processes.

Generative models describe the process of generating observed data and capture latent structures or patterns underlying them. PGMs introduce probability distributions into the generative process, enabling the representation of uncertainty and variability in data. This capability allows for accurate predictions when encountering new data while enhancing the understanding of the overall characteristics of an observed dataset.

The concepts of PGMs and Bayesian inference extend beyond cognitive modeling for symbol emergence in robotics and are widely applied in constructing world models[1] and computational neuroscience.[2] PGMs can mathematically define internal representations that generate and predict observed data as brain and

---

[1] See Chapter "World Models: Agents That Learn About the World from Subjective Experience".

[2] For an explanation of the Bayesian brain hypothesis, see: Doya, K., Ishii, S., Pouget, A., & Rao, R. P. N. (2007), Bayesian Brain: Probabilistic Approaches to Neural Coding, MIT Press.

A. Taniguchi (✉)
Ritsumeikan University, College of Information Science and Engineering, Osaka, Japan
e-mail: a.taniguchi@em.ci.ritsumei.ac.jp

© The Author(s) 2026
T. Taniguchi (ed.), *Symbol Emergence Systems*,
https://doi.org/10.1007/978-981-95-1327-7_10

cognitive models. Additionally, Bayesian inference facilitates the computation of arbitrary probability distributions under given model definitions, functioning as a concrete processing mechanism for cognitive functions.

Fundamentals of Probability Theory

Fundamental concepts of probability play a crucial role in numerous applications, including probabilistic statistics and inference in PGMs. Probability expresses the likelihood of an event occurring as a numerical value between 0 and 1, where the sum of probabilities of all possible events equals 1. A function that represents the probability of a given event (random variable) is called a probability distribution. Probability distributions can be classified into discrete and continuous distributions, represented by probability mass functions and probability density functions, respectively. When multiple events occur simultaneously, the probability is represented as a joint probability, such as P(A, B), which denotes the probability of events A and B occurring together. Given that event B has already occurred, the probability of event A occurring is expressed as P(A | B), known as conditional probability.

Key formulas for computing the probability of multiple events include the multiplication rule of probability, which expresses the joint probability of two events as the product of one event's probability and the conditional probability of the other event. The multiplication theorem is represented as:

$$P(A,B) = P(B|A)P(A) = P(A|B)P(B).$$

In the joint distribution P(X, Y) of variables X and Y, the summation of probabilities over all possible values of Y is known as marginalization, integrating out. Here, P(X), as the distribution of the variable X, can be derived by integrating out Y from the joint distribution P(X, Y), also referred to as the marginal probability (marginal likelihood). Marginalization (Integrate out) is represented as:

Discrete random variable Y:

$$P(X) = \sum_y P(X, Y = y),$$

Continuous random variable Y:

$$P(X) = \int_{-\infty}^{\infty} P(X, Y = y) \, dy.$$

Bayes' theorem, an important theorem in probability theory, can be derived from the multiplication rule of probability as follows:

$$P(A|B) = \frac{P(B|A)P(A)}{P(B)}.$$

Bayes' theorem can be interpreted as a mechanism for updating posterior beliefs (posterior distribution) by combining prior beliefs (prior distributions) and the likelihood of new data. The prior distribution represents existing beliefs or knowledge about model parameters before data is observed. The likelihood function quantifies how likely/probable the observed data is under a given model. In other words, the likelihood expresses the probability that the data is generated under the parameters. The posterior distribution expresses updated beliefs after data is observed.

When making predictions based on new observations, a predictive distribution is used as follows:

Discrete random variable θ:

$$P(X'|X) = \sum_{\theta} P(X'|\theta) P(\theta|X),$$

Continuous random variable θ:

$$P(X'|X) = \int_{-\infty}^{\infty} P(X'|\theta) P(\theta|X) d\theta.$$

The predictive distribution describes the probability distribution of new observations conditioned on past observations obtained to date and learned model parameters. When the set of all past observation data to date is denoted as X, new observations X', and the set of model parameters θ, the predictive distribution is expressed as $P(X'|X)$. Here, $P(X'|\theta)$ represents the likelihood function under parameter θ, and $P(\theta|X)$ represents the posterior distribution of the parameter θ under data X.

Bayesian Inference (Bayesian Estimation)

Bayesian inference is a statistical framework that estimates and updates probability distributions to compute posterior and predictive distributions when new data or information is introduced. By treating the posterior distribution obtained through Bayes' theorem as the prior distribution for subsequent steps, this approach enables iterative learning and inference, facilitating a sequential adaptation process with each new data point.

Bayesian inference is broadly classified into two main approaches:

1. Sampling-based methods:
   These include Sampling-Importance-Resampling (SIR) and Markov Chain Monte Carlo (MCMC) methods. MCMC methods, which enable sampling from posterior distributions. Many of these sampling methods are based on the idea of approximating a probability distribution using a large number of sample points. Widely used MCMC algorithms include Gibbs sampling and the Metropolis-Hastings algorithm, which are particularly effective in obtaining representative samples from complex posterior distributions.

2. Approximate inference methods:

   Variational inference (also known as variational Bayes) provides computationally efficient alternatives when it is difficult to solve the true posterior distribution analytically. Here, another approximate posterior distribution that is
   relatively easy to calculate is used. Variational inference introduces an analytically manageable approximation to the posterior distribution and minimizes the
   Kullback-Leibler (KL) divergence between the true posterior and its approximation. KL divergence measures the difference between two probability distributions. Since minimizing KL divergence directly is computationally intractable,
   an alternative optimization objective, the Evidence Lower Bound (ELBO), is
   maximized instead. The negative ELBO is also known as variational free energy.[3] Variational inference is known as a powerful method for efficiently computing posterior distributions in large-scale data and complex models.

Graphical Model Representation for PGMS

Graphical models serve as visual representations of dependencies between random
variables in PGMs, using graph structures to clarify relationships within the model
(Fig. 1). Nodes in these graphs correspond to random variables, with edges (solid
lines) signifying conditional dependencies between connected variables.
Additionally, dotted edges represent inference models,[4] which are separately defined
from the generative model. Observed variables are typically shaded/gray, while

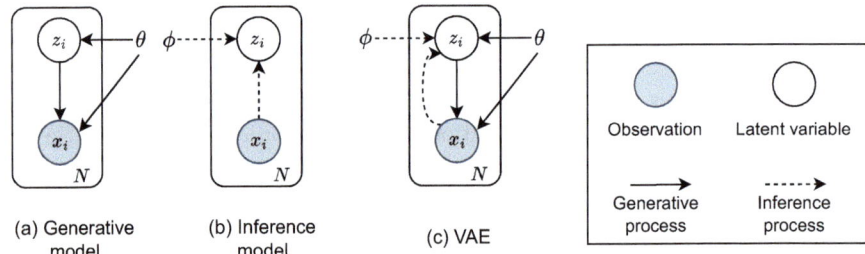

(a) Generative model (b) Inference model (c) VAE

Fig. 1 Graphical models representing (**a**) the generative model, (**b**) the inference model, and (**c**)
the variational autoencoder (VAE). Circles denote latent variables z_i, and shaded circles represent
observations x_i. Solid arrows indicate the generative process governed by parameters θ, while
dashed arrows indicate the inference process parameterized by φ. The VAE jointly models both the
generative and inference processes for efficient approximation of the posterior

---

[3] See Chapter "Free-Energy Principle and Predictive Coding: A Computational Theory Explaining
Varios Brain Functions".

[4] Also referred to as a recognition model, it is expressed as an approximate posterior distribution in
variational inference.

unobserved (latent) variables remain white. Plates, depicted as rounded rectangles[5] enclosing groups of nodes, collectively represent variables indexed by subscripts.[6]

Two primary forms of graphical models exist: Bayesian networks and Markov networks. Bayesian networks are directed acyclic graphs (DAGs) that effectively model probabilistic dependencies in generative processes. In contrast, Markov networks use undirected graphs and are particularly well-suited for representing mutual relationships and interactions among variables.

A key concept in graphical models is conditional independence, which specifies that under given conditions, a particular variable becomes independent of others. This concept is often illustrated using the Markov blanket, which consists of a variable's parents, children, and co-parents in the graph structure. Within a Bayesian network, conditioning on a variable's Markov blanket ensures its independence from all other variables outside this set.[7]

Representing PGMs through graphical models not only provides a clear depiction of dependencies between variables but also facilitates the integration of different models under a unified theoretical framework. This capability is essential for constructing sophisticated cognitive systems, enabling the seamless combination of models with distinct functionalities.[8,9] Additionally, graphical models unify various machine learning paradigms—such as supervised, unsupervised (self-supervised), and reinforcement learning—under a probabilistic inference perspective, allowing the realization of diverse cognitive models.

Cross-Modal Inference and Deep PGMs

In PGM learning and inference, the goal is to determine the posterior distribution $P(Z, \theta \mid X)$, where Z represents unknown variables[10] and θ denotes model parameters, based on the observed data X. Here, let consider a case of multimodal data by adding another sensory observed data Y. The multimodal PGMs can inference across different modalities—a process known as cross-modal inference (Fig. 2).[11]

---

[5] Sometimes simply represented as a rectangular frame.

[6] Graphical model representations may vary depending on references. Factor graphs are another representation used in free energy principle and active inference research.

[7] The Markov blanket assumes that all other variables besides X are known. If unknown variables exist, conditional independence may be violated.

[8] For a framework integrating different generative models, see: Taniguchi, T. et al. (2020), Neuro-SERKET: Development of Integrative Cognitive Systems through Deep Probabilistic Generative Models, New Generation Computing, 38(1), 23–48.

[9] On whole-brain PGMs, see: Taniguchi, T. et al. (2022), A Whole Brain Probabilistic Generative Model, Neural Networks, 150, 293–312.

[10] Also called hidden or latent variables.

[11] See Chapter "Multimodal Object Concept Formation: Concept Modeling Based on Probabilistic Models" for concrete examples.

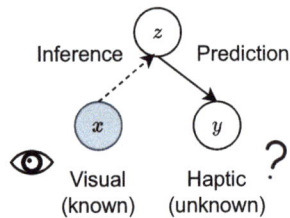

Fig. 2 A graphical model illustrating cross-modal inference and prediction. The visual observation x (known) is used to infer the latent variable z, which is then used to predict the haptic modality y (unknown). Solid arrows represent the generative process, and the dashed arrow represents the inference process

This approach allows for predictions such as estimating the tactile properties of an object from its visual appearance or predicting an object's visual characteristics based on its sound.

PGMs can also be effectively combined with deep learning to create deep PGMs (deep generative models), which facilitate modeling and inference in tasks involving large datasets and complex latent structures. A notable example of such a model is the Variational Autoencoder (VAE) (Fig. 1c), which leverages variational inference techniques to enable efficient probabilistic modeling and representation learning.

By integrating PGMs with graphical models, a powerful framework for cognitive modeling emerges, allowing for more comprehensive representations of uncertainty and complex relationships in observed data. These models unify different learning paradigms and facilitate cross-modal inference, paving the way for advanced AI systems that more closely approximate human cognition.

Multimodal Object Concept Formation: Concept Modeling Based on Probabilistic Models

Tomoaki Nakamura

What Is a Concept?

A concept is an internal representation of a category, which encompasses a set of similar experiences. Concepts allow humans to classify experiences, enabling various cognitive processes. One such process is prediction. Even for unknown phenomena, if they are identified as a subset of a certain category, it is possible to predict unobserved aspects based on the shared characteristics of that category. For example, if an unknown bird can be classified into the category "bird," one can predict it is likely capable of flight, a common feature of birds. Furthermore, concepts can be combined to generate new ones, such as imagining a golden bird by combining the concepts of "gold" and "bird."

Concepts also exhibit hierarchical structures. For instance, the category "bird" belongs to the more abstract category "animal" and includes more specific subcategories, such as "sparrow." Abstract categories are termed superordinate categories, while more specific ones are called subordinate categories. Subordinate categories inherit features from their superordinate counterparts.

Numerous theories have explored how concepts form. Classical theories, such as defining feature theory, propose that concepts are structured by defining features—for instance, the category "even number" is defined by divisibility by two. However, not all concepts adhere to clear definitions, limiting this theory's applicability. Later, the prototype model emerged, suggesting that concepts are organized around a central prototype representing the average features of a category. The degree of similarity between an instance and prototypes determines category membership. Simpler still, the exemplar model posits that concepts are represented by storing individual examples of a category.

T. Nakamura (✉)
Graduate School of Informatics and Engineering, The University of Electro-Communications, Chofu, Japan
e-mail: tnakamura@uec.ac.jp

These models struggle to represent ad hoc categories, which form temporarily based on specific contexts. For example, items like suitcases, clothing, cameras, and chargers form the ad hoc category "things to bring on a trip." The perceptual symbol system addresses this by positing that categories emerge through simulation based on embodiment.[1] In the travel example, simulating the act of traveling brings forth this contextual category.

Despite extensive research, the definition of concepts remains ambiguous. This section explores the engineering realization of robots capable of forming concepts. By simplifying and concretizing concepts, we identify key requirements for their implementation. Let us first consider the concept of an object "apple." When imagining an apple, various associated images come to mind (Fig. 1). These images themselves represent the concept, encompassing abstracted information such as "red," "sweet," "round," "some are green," "like/dislike," and so on—covering aspects like appearance, taste, and personal preference.

In other words, one defining characteristic of a concept is that it is an abstract representation integrating multiple types of information. Moreover, this image varies from person to person. For instance, preferences such as liking or disliking apples differ among individuals, and the image of an apple held by someone from a

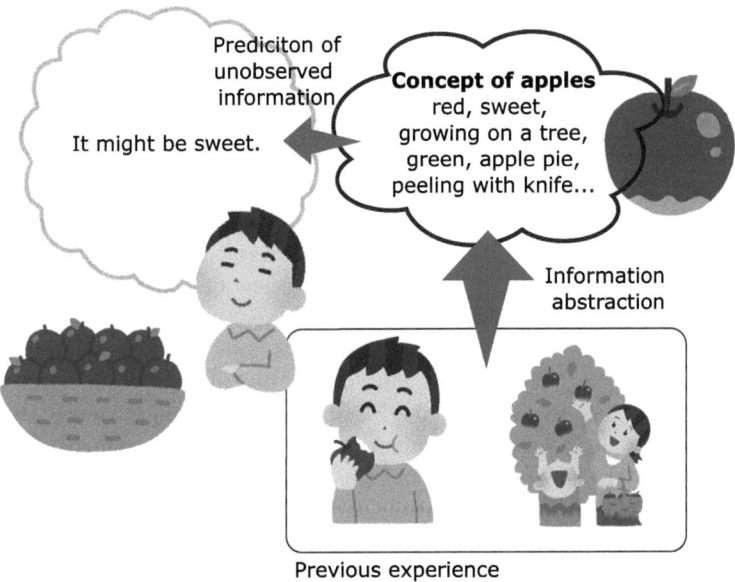

Previous experience

Fig. 1 Illustration of concept-based prediction grounded in previous experience. Abstraction from past experiences allows a child to form a concept of apples, which includes features such as color, taste, and usage. This concept enables the prediction of unobserved information, such as inferring that an unfamiliar apple might be sweet

[1] Barsalou, L. W. 1999. Perceptual Symbol Systems. *Behavioral and Brain Sciences*, 22(4), 577–660.

region known for apple production likely differs from that of a person from an area where apples are rarely eaten. These differences arise due to variations in individual experiences. Therefore, another defining characteristic of a concept is that it is shaped by personal experience.

Finally, let us consider the function of concepts. Since a concept is an image that integrates multiple types of information, it allows us to predict unobserved information. As you read this section, you are likely predicting various details about apples, even though no actual apple is present. Simply seeing the word "apple" enables you to infer associated information such as its taste, shape, and color. This predictive function of concepts is crucial, as it allows people to anticipate various types of information that they cannot directly observe.

In summary, the requirements for a concept, simplified and concretized for engineering implementation, are as follows:

1. Abstraction of diverse types of information.
2. Formation through experience.
3. Ability to predict unobserved information.

Mathematical Representation of Concepts

To implement concept formation in robots, we must mathematically formalize concepts following the requirements defined in the previous section. First, multiple types of information refer to sensory data obtained through different modalities. For humans, this includes visual, olfactory, and taste information acquired through sensory organs. For robots, it corresponds to data obtained from various sensors about an object. Such information collected from multiple sensors is called multimodal information. In general, multimodal information obtained from sensors is represented as a high-dimensional vector. Let each of these vectors be denoted as w_1, w_2, w_3, ..., where the subscript indicates the type of sensor. Furthermore, let's consider the image as a low-dimensional vector z that compresses high-dimensional multimodal information w_1, w_2, w_3, ..., and consider a probabilistic generative model as shown in Fig. 2. To facilitate interpretation, we assume three sensor inputs, with w_1,

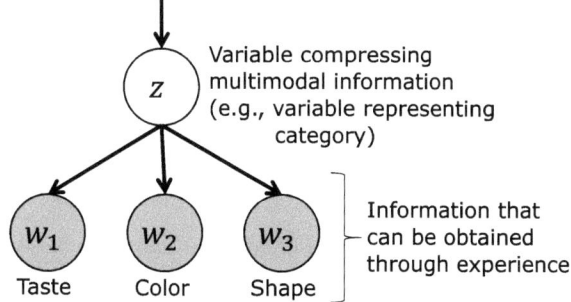

Fig. 2 A schematic diagram of a latent variable model that compresses multimodal information. The latent variable z represents a category inferred from experiential features such as taste (w_1), color (w_2), and shape (w_3), which are obtained through sensory experience

Variable compressing multimodal information (e.g., variable representing category)

Information that can be obtained through experience

w_2, and w_3 representing taste, color, and shape, respectively. The low-dimensional vector z can be any variable that compresses w_1, w_2, and w_3, but for intuitive understanding, we consider it a discrete variable representing categories. In other words, in this probabilistic generative model, by providing a numerical vector representing an apple to z, we can recall various associated information such as taste, color, and shape, indicating that z is an image that abstracts multiple types of information. This satisfies the first requirement of the concept in the previous section.

Furthermore, the second requirement of the concept is that it must be formed through experience. Here, experience refers to the acquisition of multimodal information through the robot's actions. In the apple example, this means obtaining shape and color information from the visual sensor by seeing the apple, and taste information from the gustatory sensor by eating it. In other words, the variables represented by the gray nodes shown in Fig. 2 are known variables that can be obtained through experience.

In a probabilistic generative model, the process by which observable variables are generated is modeled, which corresponds to modeling the joint probability:

$$p\left(w_1,w_2,w_3,z\right) = p\left(w_1|z\right)p\left(w_2|z\right)p\left(w_3|z\right)p\left(z\right).$$

By formulating it in this way, we can obtain the posterior probability, which is the probability that variable z is generated from observed variables w_1, w_2, and w_3:

$$p\left(z|w_1,w_2,w_3\right) \propto p\left(w_1,w_2,w_3,|z\right)p\left(z\right).$$

In a probabilistic generative model, determining unknown parameters and random variables is called inference, and the parameters of the posterior probability distribution can be inferred by methods such as the variational Bayes method and the Markov chain Monte Carlo method. That is, the robot can learn a low-dimensional vector (a variable representing an object category) that compresses the multimodal information w_1, w_2, and w_3 obtained through experience.

The third requirement for a concept was the ability to predict unobserved information. Here, prediction is defined as calculating the probability that an unobserved variable will be generated from observed variables. For example, when the visual features of an object, color w_2 and shape w_3, are obtained by seeing it, calculating the probability $p(w_1|w_2,w_3)$ of its unobserved taste w_1 is the prediction of unobserved information. In a probabilistic generative model, this probability can be calculated as follows:

$$p\left(w_1 | w_2,w_3\right) \propto \sum_z p\left(w_1,w_2,w_3 | z\right)p\left(z\right).$$

Note that such prediction between modalities (senses or sensors) is called cross-modal inference.

Although this is a simplified definition, it can be seen that the requirements of the concept described in the previous section are satisfied by this model.

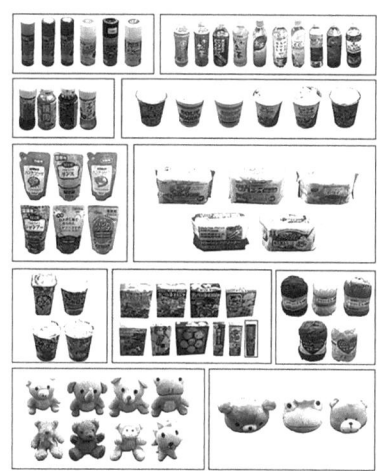

Fig. 3 Example of object recognition and categorization by a robot. The robot manipulates a bottle while visually processing various daily objects grouped into categories such as beverages, instant noodles, and stuffed toys, enabling learning of visual features and category structures through interaction

Multimodal Object Concept Formation by Robots

Research has validated the feasibility of robot-based concept formation using the probabilistic model described above.[2] Experiments employed a robot equipped with sensors mimicking human perception: cameras for vision, pressure sensors for touch, and microphones for hearing (Fig. 3a). The robot collected data on 67 objects (Fig. 3b) by observing, grasping, and shaking them to generate multimodal information.

As a concept model, we utilized the Multimodal Latent Dirichlet Allocation (MLDA), represented by the graphical model shown in Fig. 4. In this model, w^v, w^h, and w^a represent visual, auditory, and tactile information, respectively, while z represents the object category variable. The other variables are parameters of the probability distributions that generate these, and although they are somewhat complex, they are fundamentally the same as the model introduced in the previous section. Using this model, we verified whether it is possible to learn object categories from only the multimodal information that the robot obtained through its own experience.

Figure 3b shows the categories classified by humans. When the robot's classifications were evaluated using these human classifications as the correct answers, it was able to classify with an accuracy of 95.5%. This means that a variable representing the categories was successfully learned. Furthermore, this research also conducted evaluations using fewer modalities. As a result, it was found that using all

---

[2] Nakamura, T., Araki, T., Nagai, T., & Iwahashi, N. 2012. Grounding of Word Meanings in LDA-Based Multimodal Concepts. *Advanced Robotics*, 25, 2189–2206.

Fig. 4 Graphical model of a multimodal topic model incorporating visual (v), auditory (a), and haptic (h) modalities. The shared latent topic z generates modality-specific observations w^v, w^a, and w^h based on modality-dependent parameters ϕ and Dirichlet priors β. The model allows joint representation learning across heterogeneous sensory inputs

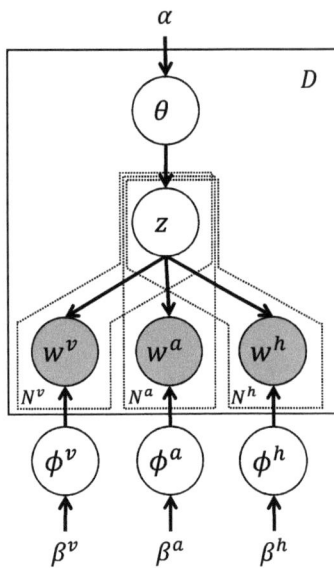

three modalities formed categories closest to those of humans, compared to using only a part of the three modalities. In other words, the configuration closest to human sensory organs can form categories closest to those of humans. This result suggests the importance of embodiment in concept formation. Concepts are rooted in the body, and to have concepts similar to humans, a body similar to humans is necessary; different bodies will lead to the formation of different concepts.

Furthermore, cross-modal inference is possible by using the MLDA learned in this way. That is, this robot can predict the sound, hardness, etc., of an object by looking at it.

Experiments using this robot have shown that it can form categories, which are abstracted images of multimodal information, based on its own experience, and that it can also predict unobserved information through cross-modal inference. This means that it has satisfied the requirements of the concept defined at the beginning of this section.

Extending Concept Models

Furthermore, various concept models are being constructed by developing based on this MLDA.

Ando et al. showed that a hierarchical structure of object concepts,[3] as shown in Fig. 5, can be acquired by using a model that introduces a hierarchical structure into

---

[3] Blei, D., Griffiths, T., & Jordan, M. 2010. The Nested Chinese Restaurant Process and Bayesian Nonparametric Inference of Topic Hierarchies. *Journal of the ACM*, 57, 1–30.

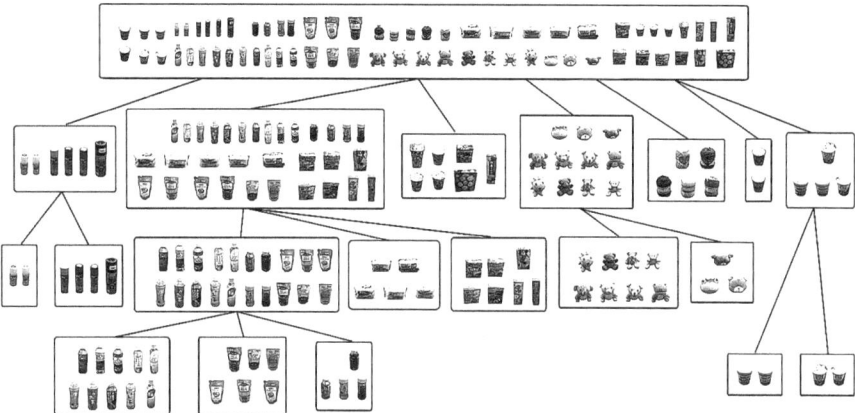

Fig. 5 Hierarchical clustering of everyday objects based on visual similarity. Objects such as bottles, cups, food packages, and stuffed toys are grouped recursively into clusters and subclusters, revealing a tree-like structure that reflects feature-based categories learned by the robot

the generative process.[4] By combining categories such as plastic bottles and glass bottles, a higher-level category of liquid containers can be formed. While humans can gain various experiences regarding objects, robots can only obtain information from vision, hearing, and touch. Therefore, there are categories that do not necessarily match human senses. However, considering the hierarchy constructed only from visual, auditory, and tactile information, it can be said that a reasonable hierarchical structure has been learned.

The research introduced so far has focused on the formation of object concepts. However, humans possess not only object concepts but also concepts associated with specific modalities, such as color concepts and sound concepts. Concept models aimed at acquiring such concepts have also been proposed.[5] In this model, humans teach the robot the features of objects using language. For example, when the robot is observing a plastic bottle, a person teaches the object's features by saying, "This is a plastic bottle. When you shake it, it makes a splashing sound." The robot forms concepts that can represent the words included in the given teaching sentence by combining its modality information with various degrees of importance. As a result, it was able to form the concept of a plastic bottle using visual, auditory, and tactile information and also acquire the concept representing the splashing sound by emphasizing auditory information. In this way, it realized the acquisition of concepts related not only to objects but also to color, sound, and touch. Furthermore, it was also learned that words like "this" included in the

[4] Ando, Y., Nakamura, T., Araki, T., & Nagai, T. 2013. Formation of Hierarchical Object Concept Using Hierarchical Latent Dirichlet Allocation. *IEEE/RSJ International Conference on Intelligent Robots and Systems*, 2272–2279.

[5] Nakamura, T., & Nagai, T. 2018. Ensemble-of-Concept Models for Unsupervised Formation of Multiple Categories. *IEEE Transactions on Cognitive and Developmental Systems*, 10(4), 1043–1057.

teaching sentence cannot be represented by the currently obtained modality information.

As we have seen so far, various engineering concept models are being researched. However, the definition of concepts in these studies is highly simplified, and it cannot explain all the properties and functions of concepts. In the future, in order to clarify concepts constitutively, it is necessary to further advance research and construct mathematical models that can explain various phenomena related to concepts.

Multimodal Spatial Concept Formation: Spatial Cognition and Semantics for Mobile Robots

Akira Taniguchi

Spatial Cognition in Robots

Robots that coexist with humans in real-world environments must interact with their surroundings to perform various tasks. Robots acquire multimodal information about their environment through sensors such as depth sensors, RGB cameras, microphones, and wheel encoders. By processing this multimodal observation data, robots can learn environmental maps, recognize object positions, classify place categories, and estimate their state within the environment. Such spatial cognition abilities are essential for robots operating in real-world settings.

Simultaneous Localization and Mapping (SLAM)[1] is a fundamental technology for mobile robots, enabling them to simultaneously estimate their position and construct maps of their surroundings. In probabilistic generative models, SLAM is expressed as a time-series model in the form of a Partially Observable Markov Decision Process (POMDP), incorporating latent variables representing self-location, observations, and actions. SLAM-based maps can be categorized into:

- Metric maps: Capturing precise geometric structures of the environment.
- Topological maps: Representing abstract relationships between locations as graph structures.[2]

---

[1] Thrun, S., Burgard, W., & Fox, D. 2005. Probabilistic Robotics. MIT Press.
[2] Biologically inspired SLAM approaches offer alternatives to purely engineering-based methods.

A. Taniguchi (✉)
Ritsumeikan University, College of Information Science and Engineering, Osaka, Japan
e-mail: a.taniguchi@em.ci.ritsumei.ac.jp

© The Author(s) 2026
T. Taniguchi (ed.), *Symbol Emergence Systems*,
https://doi.org/10.1007/978-981-95-1327-7_12

An extension of SLAM, semantic mapping, associates environmental maps with semantic information, such as place labels, categories, and object placements, making them comprehensible to both robots and humans.[3, 4]

Spatial Concept Formation from Multimodal Information

Navigation and path planning based on human verbal instructions, such as "Go to the living room and bring a cup," are crucial functionalities for robots. To achieve this, robots must possess spatial concepts,[5] which define what constitutes a specific place, its boundaries, and its name. The definition of a place can vary depending on context, environment, or user perception, making manual design of place boundaries and labels difficult. Therefore, as illustrated in Fig. 1 (upper section), it is desirable for robots to autonomously form and acquire spatial concepts based on their experiences.

The SpCoSLAM[6] framework was proposed as a probabilistic generative model integrating map construction, self-localization, speech recognition (word segmentation), and multimodal spatial categorization within a nonparametric Bayesian framework (Fig. 2).[7]

Without prior knowledge of the environment or vocabulary, SpCoSLAM enables robots to incrementally learn spatial extents, place categories, and associated words in unknown environments.[8] Furthermore, SpCoSLAM supports many-to-many associations between locations and words, allowing robots to acquire vocabulary

---

[3] Garg, S., Sünderhauf, N., Dayoub, F., Morrison, D., Cosgun, A., Carneiro, G., Wu, Q., Chin, T.-J., Reid, I., Gould, S., Corke, P., & Milford, M. 2020 Semantics for Robotic Mapping, Perception and Interaction: A Survey. Foundations and Trends® in Robotics, 8 (1–2), 1–224.

[4] For example, there is an extension to a topometric semantic map, which is a hierarchical semantic map that integrates topological maps and metric maps.

[5] Here, the concept of place refers to the category knowledge of places that is formed by unsupervised learning based on the robot's own experience (multimodal sensor information obtained from the environment) regarding places and spaces.

[6] Taniguchi, A., Hagiwara, Y., Taniguchi, T., & Inamura, T. 2017 Online Spatial Concept and Lexical Acquisition with Simultaneous Localization and Mapping. In Proceedings of the IEEE/RSJ International Conference on Intelligent Robots and Systems (IROS), 811–818.

[7] By assuming a mathematically infinite number of model parameters, it is possible to automatically adjust the complexity of the model according to the complexity and uncertainty of the observation data. Typical examples include Dirichlet processes and Gaussian processes. In SpCoSLAM, a Dirichlet process is used, and the number of place categories and vocabulary are made variable according to the observations. Nonparametric Bayesian does not require setting an upper limit on the number of categories to be learned in advance and can be expressed as a more natural cognitive model.

[8] This is achieved by an online unsupervised learning algorithm using Rao-Blackwellized Particle Filters.

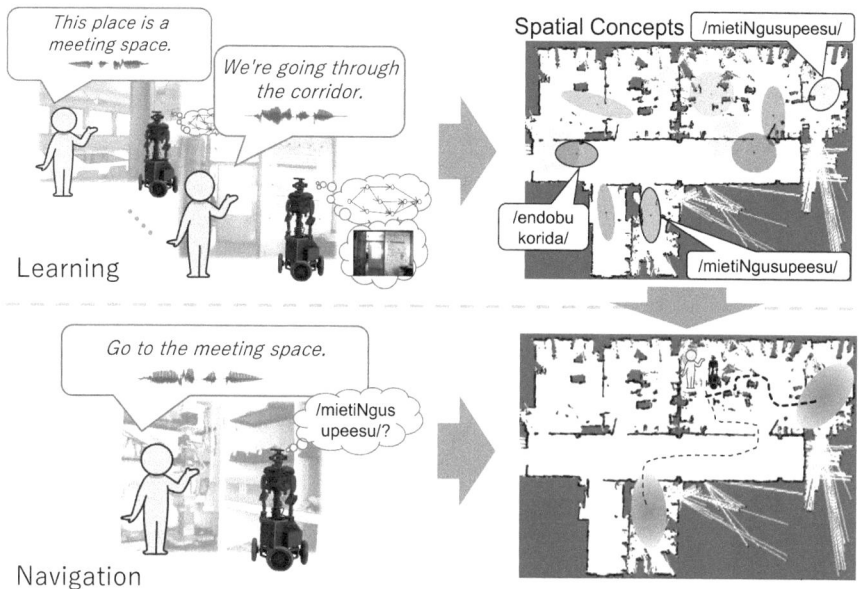

Fig. 1 An overview of spatial concept formation and language-guided navigation. In the learning phase (top), a robot associates speech utterances with locations through interaction and builds spatial concepts such as "Robot storage area," " Emergent Systems Laboratory," and "meeting space." In the navigation phase (bottom), the robot interprets spoken commands and navigates to the corresponding conceptual area on the map using the learned associations

and learn unknown words through the co-occurrence of specific phoneme sequences in speech and observed locations.[9]

To actively explore the environment and acquire new knowledge, a robot must autonomously select actions that allow it to make observations in new locations. Learning through active exploration is realized by maximizing information gain or minimizing expected free energy.[10] The probabilistic generative model framework for selecting actions to reduce uncertainty is known as active inference. In spatial concept formation models, active exploration is achieved by treating movement to a specific location and asking, "What kind of place is this?" as an action.[11]

---

[9] This is related to Chapter "Vocabulary Acquisition by Robots: Modeling Vocabulary Learning Using Probabilistic Generative Models."

[10] Information gain is formulated as the expected value of the Kullback-Leibler divergence between the current state's probability distribution and the posterior probability distribution based on the observation that would be predicted if a certain action were taken. For more information on free energy, please refer to Chapter "Free-Energy Principle and Predictive Coding: A Computational Theory Explaining Various Brain Functions," and for more information on active search, please refer to Chapter "Curiosity and Exploration: Why Do We Want to Learn?."

[11] Taniguchi, A., Tabuchi, Y., Ishikawa, T., Hafi, L. El, Hagiwara, Y., & Taniguchi, T. 2023 Active Exploration based on Information Gain by Particle Filter for Efficient Spatial Concept Formation. Advanced Robotics, 37(13), 840–870.

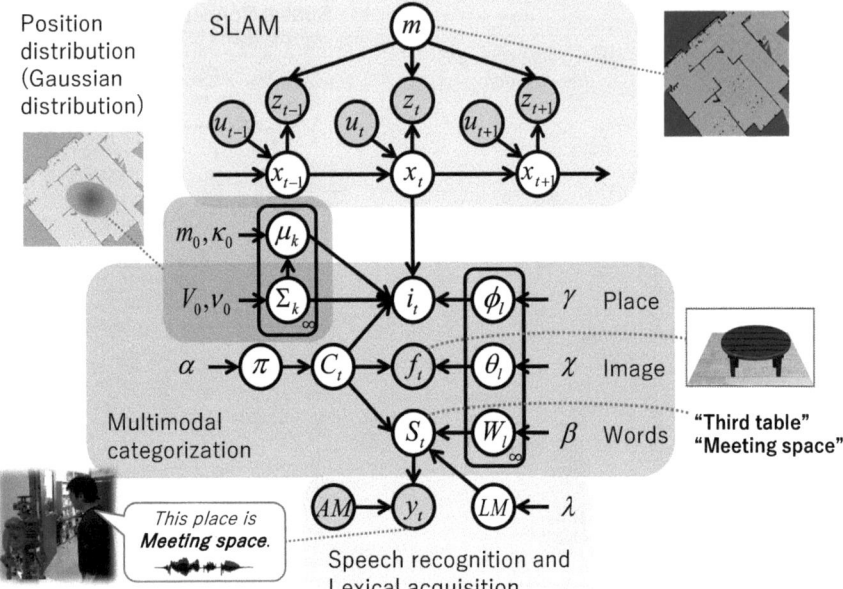

Fig. 2 A generative model of SpCoSLAM integrating SLAM, multimodal categorization, and lexical acquisition. The system combines spatial information, object features, and spoken utterances to form concepts grounded in both linguistic and perceptual modalities. Latent variables govern the generative processes for place, image, and word observations, enabling concept formation such as "meeting space" through interaction

Humans generalize spatial experiences across different environments and adapt to new surroundings. Similarly, robots can achieve knowledge transfer and adaptive learning by forming generalized spatial concepts from multi-environmental information.[12] The transfer of spatial concept knowledge can be modeled using a hierarchical Bayesian model, which consists of both generalized parameters applicable to multiple environments and environment-specific parameters.[13] By utilizing image features and other information from a known environment, robots can transfer spatial knowledge to new layouts, enabling real-time spatial concept formation without explicit linguistic input. From the perspective of a symbol emergence system, the diverse environments created by multiple people may be seen as a kind of emergence system for spatial functions and structures.

---

[12] Hagiwara, Y., Taguchi, K., Ishibushi, S., Taniguchi, A., & Taniguchi, T. 2022 Hierarchical Bayesian Model for the Transfer of Knowledge on Spatial Concepts Based on Multimodal Information. Advanced Robotics, 36(1-2), 33–53.

[13] There are also attempts to integrate common sense knowledge and field knowledge by utilizing base models such as large-scale language models that have been pre-trained using large data sets.

Additionally, further advancements are progressing in computational models that replicate human-like spatial cognition, including relative spatial relationships, hierarchical spatial structures, and adaptation to temporal environmental changes.

Real-World Applications of Spatial Concepts

Models for spatial concept formation are also applied in robotics competitions such as RoboCup@Home and World Robot Summit (WRS), which focus on developing service robots for real-world environments. Because spatial concept formation models probabilistically associate locations, image features,[14] and words, they facilitate cross-modal inference. For example, when given the command "Bring me a water bottle," a robot can infer that a bottle is likely located in the kitchen and navigate accordingly.

One application of spatial concepts in service robots is navigation and path planning. SpCoNavi,[15] built upon SpCoSLAM, introduces the Control as Inference (CaI) framework for trajectory planning based on spoken instructions. As illustrated in Fig. 1 (lower section), given a command such as "Go to the meeting space," SpCoNavi determines the appropriate route from its current position to the target location. If multiple meeting spaces exist, the robot considers factors such as distance from its current location and past usage frequency to select the most suitable destination. By leveraging autonomously acquired spatial concepts and vocabulary, robots can perform path planning based on human verbal commands, distinguishing this approach from traditional engineering-based methods that require specifying goal coordinates on a map. This has made it possible to perform reasoning based on abstract and conceptual representations of places.

Utilizing spatial concepts derived from object location information also enables efficient tidy-up tasks. After learning the probability of object locations in a tidy environment, robots can use probabilistic inference to determine the most likely items to be tidied first and their appropriate placements in a cluttered setting. Consequently, robots prioritize tidying items with more apparent placement locations while deferring uncertain cases for human confirmation.

---

[14] Pre-trained models are used to extract scene features. In some cases, image features, recognition probabilities, and labels of observed objects are used.

[15] Taniguchi, A., Hagiwara, Y., Taniguchi, T., & Inamura, T. 2020 Spatial Concept-Based Navigation with Human Speech Instructions via Probabilistic Inference on Bayesian Generative Model. Advanced Robotics, 34(19), 1213–1228.

Hippocampal Formation-Inspired Probabilistic Generative Models

Brain-inspired AI (Brain Reference Architecture)[16] is thought to be effective in constraining the design spaces for developers while realizing human-like functionality. The hippocampal formation, responsible for spatial cognition, place recognition, the processing of episodic memory, and the consolidation of memory, includes neural structures such as the hippocampus, dentate gyrus, and entorhinal cortex. In the hippocampal formation, place and grid cells, and so on, which fire at specific locations, encode spatial representations.

The Hippocampal Formation-Inspired Probabilistic Generative Model (HF-PGM)[17, 18] mimics hippocampal formation processing by integrating egocentric (self-centered) and allocentric (environment-centered) perspectives through a structured encoder–decoder model. HF-PGM is a brain-inspired model that refers to the function and structure of the hippocampal formation. HF-PGM focuses on the differences in processing in the medial and lateral entorhinal cortices, which are mainly connected to the hippocampus and dentate gyrus. Projections from the medial entorhinal cortex are thought to be involved in allocentric (environment-centered perspective/objective coordinate system) information processing, while projections from the lateral entorhinal cortex are thought to be involved in egocentric (self-centered perspective/subjective coordinate system) information processing. The hippocampus integrates these two types of information and uses them to predict the state of the next moment and observations. Implementing HF-PGM in robots enables novel spatial cognition processing distinct from conventional engineering approaches.

---

[16] Yamakawa, H. 2021 The Whole Brain Architecture Approach: Accelerating the Development of Artificial General Intelligence by Referring to the Brain. Neural Networks, 144, 478–495.

[17] Taniguchi, A., Fukawa, A., & Yamakawa, H. 2022 Hippocampal Formation Inspired Probabilistic Generative Model. Neural Networks, 151, 317–335.

[18] It was constructed using the structure-constrained interface decomposition (SCID) method, a methodology for constructing a brain reference architecture by mapping the functions and structures of brain regions and the generation-inference process allocation (GIPA) method, which is a task that expresses a brain reference architecture as a prpbabilistic generative model. In GIPA, the feedforward pathway (bottom-up pathway from the observed signal) in the brain is divided into the inference process, and the feedback pathway (top-down prediction pathway) is divided into the generation process. These two pathways correspond to the predictive coding explained in Chapter "Free-Energy Principle and Predictive Coding: A Computational Theory Explaining Various Brain Functions".

Enhancing Spatial Semantics with Large Language and Foundation Models

Recent advancements integrate large language models (LLMs) and foundation models to improve spatial semantics in robotics. For instance, the SayCan[19] framework leverages LLMs for context-aware action selection, combining language-based planning with external sensory data to determine robot actions. Research is also progressing on task planning based on the fusion of spatial concept models and LLM-derived commonsense knowledge.

Approaches combining vision-language models (VLMs) with semantic maps, such as CLIP-Fields[20] and VLMaps,[21] enable robots to associate language with spatial understanding, facilitating navigation based on diverse natural language instructions. While LLM-based methods provide an open vocabulary covering a wide range of terms, handling environment-specific terms (e.g., "Alice's room") remains a challenge. Integrating spatial concept models capable of acquiring environment-specific vocabulary may provide a robust solution.

From the perspective of knowledge transfer from multiple environments, a large-scale foundation model trained on a large dataset of images, including spatial appearances, may be seen as capturing visual features related to location acquired by various devices and robots, and as performing collective concept formation through integration with language.

[19] Ahn, M., Brohan, A., Brown, N., Chebotar, Y., Cortes, O., David, B., et al. 2022 Do As I Can, Not As I Say: Grounding Language in Robotic Affordances. arXiv preprint.

[20] Shafiullah, N. M. M., Paxton, C., Pinto, L., Chintala, S., (Mahi) Shafiullah, N., et al. 2023 CLIP-Fields: Weakly Supervised Semantic Fields for Robotic Memory. Robotics: Science and Systems.

[21] Huang, C., Mees, O., Zeng, A., & Burgard, W. 2023 Visual Language Maps for Robot Navigation. In Proceedings of the IEEE International Conference on Robotics and Automation (ICRA).

Part III: Cognitive Development in the Environment

Cognitive Developmental Robotics: A Constructive Approach to Understanding and Designing Cognitive Development

Yukie Nagai

Cognitive Developmental Robotics for Understanding and Designing Intelligence

Cognitive developmental robotics is a research field focused on uncovering the mechanisms underlying cognitive development.[1,2,3] By creating computational models and robots that simulate the human brain and body, researchers investigate human intelligence and, as a result, establish new principles for designing artificial intelligence. While the concept of symbol emergence in robotics, discussed in Part II, specifically addresses the acquisition and manipulation of symbols, such as language, cognitive developmental robotics encompasses a broader range of cognitive functions, including self-recognition, object manipulation, imitation, emotion, and more.

This field has a rich history. In the early 2000s, the first international conferences on developmental robotics[4] and epigenetic robotics[5] were held, bringing together

---

[1] Asada, M., Hosoda, K., Kuniyoshi, Y., Ishiguro, H., Inui, T., Yoshikawa, Y., Ogino, M., and Yoshida, C. 2009. Cognitive Developmental Robotics: A Survey. IEEE Transactions on Autonomous Mental Development. 1(1):12–34.

[2] Cangelosi, A. and Schlesinger, M. 2015. Developmental Robotics: From Babies to Robots. The MIT Press.

[3] Cangelosi, A. and Asada, M. (Eds) 2022. Cognitive Robotics. The MIT Press.

[4] Lungarella, M., Metta, G., Pfeifer, R., and Sandini, G. 2003. Developmental robotics: a survey. Connection Science. 15(4):151–190.

[5] Berthouze, L., and Ziemke, T. 2003. Epigenetic robotics – modelling cognitive development in robotic systems. Connection Science. 15(4):147–150.

Y. Nagai (✉)
International Research Center for Neurointelligence, The University of Tokyo, Tokyo, Japan
e-mail: nagai.yukie@mail.u-tokyo.ac.jp

© The Author(s) 2026
T. Taniguchi (ed.), *Symbol Emergence Systems*,
https://doi.org/10.1007/978-981-95-1327-7_13

Fig. 1 Interaction between a humanoid robot and a human in a structured environment. The image highlights the distinction between the robot's internal structures (brain and body) and the external environment, including objects and human agents that shape the robot's perception and behavior

researchers from diverse disciplines, including robotics, developmental science, cognitive science, and neuroscience. In 2001, Asada et al.[6] proposed the concept of cognitive developmental robotics, sparking numerous large-scale research initiatives, particularly in Japan and Europe. Since then, the field has grown into a dynamic interdisciplinary area influencing both artificial and natural intelligence.

A key distinction between cognitive developmental robotics and traditional artificial intelligence (AI) is that the former focuses on exploring the principles of intelligence by providing only the minimal mechanisms required for learning, whereas the latter typically aims to perform predefined tasks using engineered architectures and large-scale data. In cognitive developmental robotics, robots are equipped with learning capabilities and undergo sensorimotor experiences akin to those of human infants. Researchers investigate the process of acquiring cognitive functions, rather than merely focusing on the outcome, in order to uncover the underlying principles of intelligence. Two essential factors in designing such systems are the robot's internal mechanisms (corresponding to the brain and body) and its external environment (including objects and other individuals), as illustrated in Fig. 1.

Another important distinction is that while conventional AI aims to optimize intelligence, cognitive developmental robotics explores the diversity of intelligence. For instance, neurodiversity—the variations in cognitive functions observed in individuals with developmental disorders—can emerge from changes to internal and/or external structures. Researchers in cognitive developmental robotics study how

---

[6]Asada, M., MacDorman, K. F., Ishiguro, H., and Kuniyoshi, Y. 2001. Cognitive developmental robotics as a new paradigm for the design of humanoid robots. Robotics and Autonomous Systems. 37:185–193.

different brain, body, and environmental factors influence the emergence of intelligence, offering insights into the fundamental principles of cognitive development.

Designing Internal Structures of Robots

The first critical step in replicating cognitive development is designing learning mechanisms for robots. Among the various machine learning models explored in artificial intelligence, the theory of predictive processing (or predictive coding)[7,8] has gained significant attention in cognitive developmental robotics.

Predictive processing, initially proposed by neuroscientists and philosophers, offers a unified framework for understanding a wide range of brain functions, including perception and action. The theory suggests that the brain operates by minimizing prediction errors—discrepancies between bottom-up sensory signals received through the sensory organs and top-down prediction signals generated by internal models. While originally introduced to explain adult brain functions, the theory has since been extended to address developmental mechanisms in infants. The central hypothesis posits that the acquisition of internal models through prediction error minimization underpins the development of sensorimotor and social abilities. Numerous studies have been conducted in cognitive developmental robotics to validate this hypothesis.[9,10]

For instance, self-recognition can be acquired by minimizing prediction errors between proprioceptive and exteroceptive signals. Through motor babbling, a robot receives visual feedback from various postures and movements, learning a representation of its own body by updating its internal model. Similarly, emotions such as joy and sadness can be learned through minimizing prediction errors between external stimuli (e.g., objects and others) and interoceptive responses (e.g., heartbeat and respiration). Importantly, these internal models not only shape the robot's own actions but also enable prosocial behaviors. In early developmental stages, the boundary between self and others is not clearly defined, allowing the robot to apply its own internal model to others. As a result, primitive prosocial behaviors such as imitation, empathy, and altruism emerge, much like the function of the mirror neuron system. Furthermore, predictive processing serves as a foundation for intrinsic motivation. Minimizing prediction errors acts as a positive reward for exploration and learning, fostering more human-like, open-ended development. Further details

[7] Friston, K. and Kiebel, S. 2009. Predictive coding under the free-energy principle. Philosophical Transactions of the Royal Society B. 364:1211–1221.

[8] Clark, A. 2013. Whatever next? Predictive brains, situated agents, and the future of cognitive science. Behavioral and Brain Sciences. 36(3):181–204.

[9] Nagai, Y. 2019. Predictive learning: its key role in early cognitive development. Philosophical Transactions of the Royal Society B. 374:20180030.

[10] Friston, K, Moran, R. J., Nagai, Y., Taniguchi, T., Gomi, H., and Tenenbaum, J. 2021. World model learning and inference. Neural Networks. 144:573–590.

on predictive processing and its applications are provided in Chapters "Free-Energy Principle and Predictive Coding: A Computational Theory Explaining Various Brain Functions" and "Neurorobotics: Controlling Robots with Neural Systems".

Another crucial aspect of robot design is the body itself. Unlike adults, infants have smaller bodies and less developed sensorimotor functions, which were traditionally seen as disadvantages in learning. However, developmental psychologists suggest that these constraints could actually aid in structuring information, thereby facilitating learning.[11] For example, the development of visual acuity controls the complexity of incoming signals, allowing the acquisition of better-organized internal models that are more adaptable. Similarly, in motor learning, gradually increasing the degrees of freedom allows learning to progress by expanding the exploration space incrementally. Importantly, these developmental constraints extend beyond the body to the brain, such as memory capacity. The synchronized development of both body and brain is expected to mutually enhance learning and cognitive development.

Designing External Environment Including Other Individuals

The second crucial step in investigating cognitive development is designing the robot's external environment. As observed in infants, both physical and social environmental factors play significant roles in shaping learning and development. A well-known concept in developmental psychology is the zone of proximal development (ZPD),[12] which emphasizes the importance of scaffolding—support from caregivers or the environment—in fostering development. According to this idea, learning progresses more smoothly when infants are presented with challenges that are slightly beyond their current abilities, rather than tasks that are either too easy or too difficult.

This concept has been computationally explored in cognitive developmental robotics. Researchers seek to better understand the role of environmental factors while also improving the learning efficiency of robots. For example, gradually increasing the quality and/or quantity of training data can accelerate the learning of, for example, object manipulation and joint attention. The complexity of the physical environment and the strategy for social feedback can be adjusted so that a robot first learns simpler tasks and, as learning progresses, gradually tackles more complex ones.

This principle has recently been applied in machine learning. Curriculum learning—a training approach in which tasks are introduced in a structured, stepwise manner—has become widely used in various applications. This is a successful

---

[11] Newport, E. L. 1990. Maturational constraints on language learning. Cognitive Science. 14(1):11–28.

[12] Vygotsky, L. S. 1978. Interaction between learning and development. Mind in Society. Harvard University Press.

example of how principles from cognitive developmental robotics have contributed to the development of new AI technologies.

Diversity in Cognitive Development

Understanding the individual diversity and temporal dynamics of cognitive behaviors is essential for uncovering the principles of development. While traditional AI research primarily focuses on optimizing intelligence, cognitive developmental robotics aims to explore how the diversity of intelligence emerges through the interactions between the brain, body, and environment.

For example, some computational studies have examined how neural modifications contribute to conditions, such as autism spectrum disorder (ASD) and schizophrenia, which are often associated with challenges in sensorimotor and social abilities.[13] Researchers have investigated the impacts of these neural mechanisms on cognitive development by introducing modifications to neural networks. Studies based on predictive processing theory have shown that aberrant precision in prediction and sensory signals can cause robots to struggle with environmental perception and object manipulation. These disruptions may also limit the ability to generalize learned behaviors. Additionally, research has demonstrated that changes in external teaching or reward structures can hinder the development of social skills in robots. These findings suggest that both typical and atypical development can result from subtle modifications within shared neural models and that imbalances between the brain, body, and environment can lead to diverse developmental trajectories.

Future Directions of Cognitive Developmental Robotics

Since its introduction in 2001, cognitive developmental robotics has driven the creation of numerous computational models and robots. These models, designed to replicate and predict behaviors observed in infants, have demonstrated the potential of this approach not only for engineering applications but also for addressing the fundamental scientific challenge of understanding human intelligence.

Despite these advances, achieving truly human-like intelligence remains a significant challenge. Several critical issues must still be addressed, including uncovering the evolutionary and genetic origins of the neural mechanisms underlying cognitive development and designing robots with bodies that grow and evolve alongside their cognitive processes.

---

[13] Lanillos, P., Oliva, D., Philippsen, A., Yamashita, Y., Nagai, Y., and Cheng, G. 2020. A review on neural network models of schizophrenia and autism spectrum disorder. Neural Networks, 122:338–363.

Overcoming these challenges requires cognitive developmental robotics to extend beyond traditional disciplines, such as psychology, cognitive science, and neuroscience. This expansion could drive a paradigm shift, fostering the emergence of a new scientific field. Such a transformation is expected to deepen our understanding of intelligence and inspire novel design principles for artificial intelligence, grounded in insights from cognitive development.

Free-Energy Principle and Predictive Coding: A Computational Theory Explaining Various Brain Functions

Shingo Murata

Free-Energy Principle

The free-energy principle,[1] proposed by neuroscientist Karl Friston in 2006, is a theory of brain information processing. In simple terms, it explains various brain functions, including perception, action, and learning, as different solutions to the minimization of a cost function called variational free energy.[2] The explanatory scope of this principle extends beyond brain function to encompass topics, such as cellular self-organization, emotions, consciousness, and neurodevelopmental disorders. It represents an ambitious attempt to unify existing theories into a single overarching framework.

The starting point of the free-energy principle is the minimization of an information-theoretic measure called surprise, which quantifies the improbability of sensory inputs. Surprise is low when an organism receives desirable sensory inputs (e.g., a comfortable ambient temperature, stable body temperature, or a desired state) and increases when deviations from these conditions occur. Thus, it serves as

---

[1] There are numerous related references, including the following:

  - Friston, K., Kilner, J., & Harrison, L. (2006). A free energy principle for the brain. Journal of Physiology-Paris, 100(1–3), 70–87.

  - Friston, K. (2009). The free-energy principle: A rough guide to the brain? Trends in Cognitive Sciences, 13(7), 293–301.

  - Friston, K. (2010). The free-energy principle: A unified brain theory? Nature Reviews Neuroscience, 11(2), 127–138.

[2] It should be noted that the free energy in the free-energy principle is not the Helmholtz free energy from thermodynamics but rather the variational free energy used for performing variational Bayesian inference in machine learning.

S. Murata (✉)
Keio University, Yokohama, Kanagawa, Japan
e-mail: murata@elec.keio.ac.jp

T. Taniguchi (ed.), *Symbol Emergence Systems*,
https://doi.org/10.1007/978-981-95-1327-7_14

a measure of an organism's adaptation to both external and internal states. However, computing surprise directly requires complex integral calculations that are likely infeasible for neural circuits in the brain. To address this, the free-energy principle posits that biological systems approximate surprise by computing its upper bound, known as variational free energy. By minimizing variational free energy through perception, action, and learning, the brain indirectly minimizes surprise.[3]

Minimization of Variational Free Energy

The free-energy principle assumes that the brain maintains a generative model (also called a forward model or world model) that represents the joint distribution of observable sensory inputs and their unobservable hidden states. Variational free energy is expressed as the Kullback–Leibler (KL) divergence between an approximate posterior distribution (the recognition model), which serves as a tractable substitute for the true but computationally intractable posterior, and the generative model. By reformulating this KL divergence, it can be shown that the difference between surprise and variational free energy is itself a KL divergence between the approximate posterior and the true posterior. Additionally, variational free energy can be decomposed into the sum of accuracy (negative log-likelihood) and complexity (the KL divergence between the approximate posterior and the prior).

In the free-energy principle, perception contributes to minimizing variational free energy by inferring hidden states that generate sensory predictions closely matching the sensory input. Action minimizes variational free energy by actively interacting with the environment to obtain sensory inputs that align with sensory predictions. Learning contributes by updating the parameters of the generative model in the brain to refine it. For example, consider the case where visual information indicating "red and round" is received as sensory input. Perception corresponds to inferring the hidden state that caused this visual input using a recognition model. Suppose the system infers that the hidden state corresponds to "a fruit, specifically an apple." This inference process is referred to as (Helmholtzian) unconscious inference or perceptual inference. Through this process, the KL divergence between the approximate posterior and the true posterior can be minimized. When this minimization is successfully achieved, the variational free energy becomes equal to surprise. However, action can further reduce this value to achieve additional

---

[3] Surprise and variational free energy correspond to the negative values of evidence and the evidence lower bound (ELBO) in machine learning, respectively. Therefore, learning based on minimizing variational free energy is equivalent to learning based on maximizing the variational lower bound, as seen in variational autoencoders (VAEs).

minimization. For instance, by moving closer to the object and acquiring new visual information, the system may revise its inference to conclude that the object is actually "a toy apple." Moreover, learning can refine the generative model by incorporating this newly obtained sensory input. In this process, based on the relationship between accuracy and complexity, the generative model tends to learn to represent the acquired sensory input as simply as possible.

This cycle of perception and action is referred to as active inference,[4] in which an agent minimizes variational free energy by modifying its internal interpretation (internal states) and acting upon the environment (external states). Consequently, this leads to the minimization of surprise.

Minimization of Expected Free Energy

Variational free energy is a cost function computed based on past and present sensory inputs. However, extending active inference to include future sensory inputs enables long-term planning of actions. The variational free energy computed in this way—accounting for yet-to-be-observed sensory inputs—is termed expected free energy. In this framework, past and present sensory inputs are used to infer the current hidden state, and a set of possible future action sequences (policies[5]) is considered. For each policy, the generative model predicts the sensory inputs that would result from executing those actions. Expected free energy is then computed for each policy, and the policy that minimizes expected free energy is selected.

Expected free energy can be decomposed into the sum of negative intrinsic value and negative extrinsic value. Since minimizing negative intrinsic value is equivalent to maximizing intrinsic value, it promotes exploratory behavior to reduce uncertainty. Likewise, minimizing negative extrinsic value is equivalent to maximizing extrinsic value, leading to goal-directed and exploitative behaviors. This formulation naturally derives the exploration–exploitation trade-off found in conventional reinforcement learning, allowing for policy selection through the minimization of expected free energy.

---

[4] Parr, T., Pezzulo, G., & Friston, K. J. (2022). Active inference: The free energy principle in mind, brain, and behavior. MIT Press.

[5] It should be noted that policies in active inference differ from functions that map states to actions or probability distributions over actions conditioned on states in standard reinforcement learning. Instead, policies in active inference represent entire sequences of actions.

Predictive Coding

Predictive coding,[6] proposed by Rajesh Rao and Dana Ballard in 1999, is a hierarchical model of visual information processing in the brain and is closely related to perceptual inference in the free-energy principle. More recently, the concept has been generalized beyond visual information processing to encompass broader brain functions and is often referred to as predictive processing[7] (see Chapter "Cognitive Developmental Robotics: A Constructive Approach to Understanding and Designing Cognitive Development").

Predictive coding assumes a hierarchical neural network in which each layer contains state units and error units. The system operates through repeated cycles of top-down prediction and bottom-up recognition. In the top-down prediction process, higher levels predict the neural activity of lower levels, with the lowest level predicting sensory input. The bottom-up recognition process computes prediction errors—the differences between top-down predictions and the actual neural activity (or sensory input at the lowest level)—and uses them to refine predictions at each level. Thus, in predictive coding, mutual interaction occurs between top-down predictive signals and bottom-up prediction error signals, based on the computational principle of prediction error minimization.

By applying a Laplace approximation to the free-energy principle, assuming a Gaussian distribution for the approximate posterior—predictive coding can be derived,[8] positioning the free-energy principle as a more general framework that encompasses predictive coding.

Connections to Related Fields

Thus far, we have discussed the theoretical aspects of the free-energy principle and predictive coding. Finally, we summarize their connections to related fields, such as psychology, neuroscience, and deep learning.

For instance, Ryan Smith and colleagues have used computational models based on the free-energy principle (active inference) to analyze behavioral data from human participants, enabling parameter estimation and future behavior prediction.[9] Similarly, Isomura et al. have demonstrated that the free-energy principle can

[6] Rao, R. P., & Ballard, D. H. (1999). Predictive coding in the visual cortex: A functional interpretation of some extra-classical receptive-field effects. Nature Neuroscience, 2(1), 79–87.

[7] Clark, A. (2013). Whatever next? Predictive brains, situated agents, and the future of cognitive science. Behavioral and Brain Sciences, 36(3), 181–204.

[8] Friston, K., & Kiebel, S. (2009). Predictive coding under the free-energy principle. Philosophical Transactions of the Royal Society B: Biological Sciences, 364(1521), 1211–1221.

[9] Smith, R., Friston, K., & Whyte, C. (2022). A step-by-step tutorial on active inference and its application to empirical data. Journal of Mathematical Psychology, 107, 1–60.

predict the self-organization of cultured neural circuits derived from the rat cortex.[10] Additionally, Zenas Chao et al. have identified hierarchical predictive and prediction error signals by analyzing electrocorticography (ECoG) recordings from monkeys exposed to auditory stimuli.[11] These studies illustrate ongoing experimental applications and validations of the free-energy principle and predictive coding.

Conventional proof of concept for the free-energy principle has been demonstrated mainly with simplified low-dimensional data. Recently, scalability improvements have been pursued by representing probability distributions (such as generative and recognition models) using deep neural networks (see Chapter "Deep Learning and Representation Learning: Foundational Theories Underpinning Modern AI"). These efforts have led to the development of deep active inference,[12] which integrates deep learning techniques to scale up the free-energy principle for more complex applications. At the current stage, many studies utilize high-dimensional data obtained in simulation environments; however, it is also expected that deep active inference will be extended to real robots and demonstrated in real-world environments.

[10] Isomura, T., Kotani, K., Jimbo, Y., & Friston, K. (2023). Experimental validation of the free-energy principle with in vitro neural networks. Nature Communications, 14(4547), 1–15.

[11] Chao, Z., Takaura, K., Wang, L., Fujii, N., & Dehaene, S. (2018). Large-scale cortical networks for hierarchical prediction and prediction error in the primate brain. Neuron, 100(5), 1252–1266.

[12] Mazzaglia, P., Verbelen, T., Çatal, O., & Dhoedt, B. (2022). The free energy principle for perception and action: A deep learning perspective. Entropy, 24(2), 1–22.

Curiosity and Exploration: Why Do We Want to Learn?

Takato Horii

Curiosity

Curiosity is the desire to collect information that is novel to oneself. Psychologist William James described curiosity as "an impulse towards better cognition," viewing it as an instinct that motivates approach and exploration of novel objects while counteracting anxiety that motivates avoidance of novel objects.[1] He also asserted that there exists curiosity as a motivating factor that seeks to resolve differences or contradictions in scientific and philosophical knowledge, not merely responses to novel stimuli. Daniel Berlyne categorized curiosity into perceptual curiosity, which is motivation toward novel sensory stimuli, and epistemic curiosity, related to intellectual activities, such as the desire to understand objects.[2] Perceptual curiosity is a primary motivation for exploratory behavior in organisms and serves as the driving force for exploratory behavior not only in adults but also in infants. Conversely, epistemic curiosity is explained as not only collecting stimuli with information to eliminate uncertainty but also as the driving force for acquiring knowledge. Berlyne further divides this epistemic curiosity into diversive curiosity and specific curiosity.[3] Diversive curiosity is a motivation that supports the exploration of novel

---

[1] James, W. 1983 Talks to Teachers on Psychology and to Students on Some of Life's Ideals (Vol.12). Harvard University Press.

[2] Berlyne, D. E. 1954 A theory of human curiosity. British Journal of Psychology. General Section, 45, 180–191.

[3] Berlyne, D. E. 1966 Curiosity and Exploration: Animals Spend Much of Their Time Seeking Stimuli Whose Significance Raises Problems for Psychology. Science, 153(3731), 25–33.

T. Horii (✉)
Graduate School of Engineering Science, The University of Osaka, Toyonaka, Osaka, Japan
e-mail: takato@sys.es.osaka-u.ac.jp

© The Author(s) 2026
T. Taniguchi (ed.), *Symbol Emergence Systems*,
https://doi.org/10.1007/978-981-95-1327-7_15

Fig. 1 Overhead view of a naturalistic play environment. A child engages with various toys scattered across a playmat and wooden floor, providing a rich, unstructured context for observing exploratory behavior, motor development, and early learning processes

information to gain various knowledge. In contrast, specific curiosity motivates exploration of specific information to resolve contradictions or inconsistencies in knowledge. Figure 1 shows a scene from a video of an infant exploring the environment based on its curiosity.[4] In the video, the infant can be seen approaching novel objects around it, grasping them, and playing with them. However, the infant does not continue playing with the same object; after playing and gaining knowledge to some extent, it shifts its interest to other objects. This demonstrates how curiosity constantly changes according to previous experiences and knowledge.

Curiosity and Autonomy

Behavior driven by curiosity—the impulse to collect novel information that organisms and humans possess internally—is called exploratory behavior motivated by intrinsic motivation. Conversely, exploratory behavior is driven not only by intrinsic motivation but also by extrinsic motivation, such as rewards given from the external world. While the precise definition and distinction between intrinsic and extrinsic motivation are difficult, Edward L. Deci defines intrinsically motivated behavior as that which has no obvious rewards other than the activity itself and extrinsic

---

[4]Francis Vachon, Time lapse of a baby playing with his toys. https://www.youtube.com/watch?v=8vNxjwt2AqY.

motivation as motivation through rewards that exist beyond the activity.[5] For example, exploratory behavior like paying to learn the probability of winning on a slot machine is triggered by extrinsic motivation to win, not by curiosity. Conversely, behavior such as wanting to touch something despite not knowing exactly what it is is not linked to external rewards and can be considered exploratory behavior driven by intrinsic motivation.

Such exploratory behavior driven by extrinsic or intrinsic motivation forms the foundation of autonomy as biological beings. For instance, exploratory behavior driven by extrinsic motivations like feeding or sleeping is related to maintaining bodily homeostasis, including the realization of life functions. Rewards such as money or praise are also indirectly related to maintaining life functions through the improvement of social standing. Conversely, exploratory behavior based on intrinsic motivations like curiosity does not directly relate to maintaining life functions at that moment, but behavior that collects information from the external world and reduces uncertainty is thought to enhance an individual's environmental adaptability by promoting the acquisition of knowledge and skills.

Information Gain Maximization and Active Inference in Exploratory Behavior

How can exploratory behavior as a foundation of autonomy be explained by theory? In both perceptual and epistemic curiosity, curiosity-driven exploratory behavior can be viewed as the act of collecting information from the external world. This is the act of selecting behaviors that change beliefs $p(z)$ about the external world based on perceptual experiences and knowledge thus far, when observational information o_t is obtained through some exploratory action a_t. Here, the change in belief $p(z)$ due to observational information o_t can be expressed as information gain (or mutual information) in information theory: $I(o\_t;z) = H(z) - H(z|o\_t) = E_{\{p(o\_t)\}}[D_{\{KL\}}(p(z|o\_t)\|p(z))]$, where $D_{\{KL\}}$ represents the Kullback–Leibler divergence. Thus, from an information theory perspective, perceptual and epistemic curiosity can be viewed as exploratory behavior that maximizes information gain.

However, in the free-energy principle,[6] which aims to explain brain information processing in a unified manner, exploratory behavior can be viewed as active inference that minimizes future free energy, that is, expected free energy. Here, expected free energy can be expressed as the sum of negative intrinsic value $-E_{\{p(o\_t)\}}[D_{\{KL\}}(p(z|o\_t)\|p(z))]$ and negative extrinsic value $-E_{\{p(z,o\_t)\}}[\ln p(o\_t)]$,

---

[5] Deci, E. L., & Ryan, R. M. 2013 Intrinsic Motivation and Self-Determination in Human Behavior. Springer Science & Business Media.

[6] See Chapter "Free-Energy Principle and Predictive Coding: A Computational Theory Explaining Various Brain Functions".

where intrinsic value corresponds to information gain obtained under specific actions. That is, maximizing intrinsic value is equivalent to maximizing information gain through action selection, and this behavior can be interpreted as behavior that reduces uncertainty and satisfies perceptual or epistemic curiosity. Turning attention to maximizing extrinsic value, this corresponds to exploring actions where the probability distribution $p(o\_t)$ shows the highest value. If the probability distribution $p(o\_t)$ is viewed as a prior preference, this maximization of extrinsic value represents utility maximization in reinforcement learning, that is, action selection driven by extrinsic motivation.

Such action selection associated with maximizing each of these intrinsic and extrinsic values corresponds to the exploration–exploitation trade-off in reinforcement learning. By adjusting the maximization of each value through the single norm of minimizing expected free energy, it becomes possible to express autonomous action selection in interaction with the environment, considering not only intrinsic motivation due to curiosity but also extrinsic motivation.

Learning Behavior and Concepts through Computational Models of Curiosity

One important research challenge in cognitive robotics is modeling curiosity, that is, the challenge of autonomous knowledge acquisition by robots. Pierre-Yves Oudeyer et al. proposed a reinforcement learning model that introduces not only external rewards given from the environment but also internal rewards generated when robots explore the environment through their own curiosity and satisfy that curiosity.[7] This research introduced a prediction learner that predicts state changes due to the robot's actions and environmental dynamics and a meta-learner that predicts the learning status of the prediction learner, that is, the error between the prediction learner's output and actual environmental state changes, thereby learning the degree of knowledge acquisition about the environment. The meta-learner estimates the learning progress of the prediction learner using the predicted error of the environment by the prediction learner and its own predicted prediction error. The robot then selects actions to obtain environmental states needed to learn prediction learners judged to have low learning progress by the meta-learner, and when learning progress actually improves, it receives internal rewards proportional to the degree of improvement as a result of satisfying curiosity. In their experiments, an AIBO with three action primitives—rotating its head, tapping objects, and biting objects—was

---

[7] Oudeyer, P. Y., Kaplan, F., & Hafner, V. V. 2007 Intrinsic Motivation Systems for Autonomous Mental Development. IEEE transactions on evolutionary computation, 11(2), 265–286.

placed in an environment with various toys, and it was verified what kind of behaviors would emerge. The AIBO gradually exhibited increasingly complex behaviors in the order of looking at the environment, biting objects, and tapping objects, demonstrating that it gathered information from the environment. This result shows that robots can autonomously acquire structured knowledge and behavior through curiosity as an intrinsic motivation.

Taniguchi et al. proposed a method for efficiently exploring the environment in the task of forming concepts about places by robots, based on active inference in the free energy principle.[8] Here, assuming that the prior preference $p(o\_t)$ for observational information is a uniform distribution, the robot's action is selected to maximize information gain, that is, intrinsic value, for the robot's destination in the environment. In a simulated home environment, an exploration method balancing information gain with movement cost outperformed both uniform exploration and pure information gain maximization. It achieved effective results while minimizing the robot's total travel distance.

Yanagida et al. proposed a complementary learning model that simultaneously learns robot actions and object knowledge using internal rewards from satisfying curiosity and external rewards.[9] Robot experiments showed that when using only external rewards given by object grasping, the robot acquired only behaviors to grasp objects with maximum gripping force, but when adding internal rewards, it could acquire grasping behaviors that reduce uncertainty in sensory information effective for object prediction.

---

[8] Taniguchi, A., Tabuchi, Y., Ishikawa, T., El Hafi, L., Hagiwara, Y., & Taniguchi, T. 2023 Active Exploration Based on Information Gain by Particle Filter for Efficient Spatial Concept Formation. Advanced Robotics, 37(13), 840–870.

[9] Yanagida, K., & Horii, T. 2023 "Complementary Learning of Robot's Behavior Acquisition and Concept Formation." Proceedings of the Japanese Society for Artificial Intelligence Annual Conference, 37, 2O4GS805-2O4GS805 in Japanese.

Emotion and Predictive Processing: How Are Emotions Made?

Takato Horii

The Origins of Emotion

Anger, sadness, joy, and other mental states related to human mood and consciousness are called feelings or emotions. Feelings and emotions are deeply involved in human value judgments and decision-making in everyday life and are also used in communication with others. While there are various definitions of feelings and emotions depending on the research field, recent studies in physiology, neuroscience, and psychology often define emotion as the body's reactions or activities themselves and feeling as the state in which these emotions are cognitively perceived by the brain.

The attention to the relationship between the emergence of emotion and embodiment traces back to the research of evolutionary biologist Charles Robert Darwin. He argued for the existence of evolutionary continuity based on the similarities between human and animal facial expressions. In the late nineteenth century, William James proposed the peripheral origin theory of emotion, which suggests that external stimuli are perceived by the brain independently of emotion, and the subjective emotional experience is the subsequent perception of bodily changes, particularly in the viscera and musculoskeletal system.[1] This theory is famous for the phrase "We do not cry because we are sad, we are sad because we cry."

Conversely, physiologist Walter Bradford Cannon criticized James's peripheral origin theory based on his own experimental and clinical research results and proposed the central origin theory of emotion, which considers the brain's information

---

[1] James, W. 1884. What is an Emotion?. Mind, os-IX(34), 188–205.

T. Horii (✉)

Graduate School of Engineering Science, The University of Osaka, Toyonaka, Osaka, Japan
e-mail: takato@sys.es.osaka-u.ac.jp

© The Author(s) 2026

T. Taniguchi (ed.), *Symbol Emergence Systems*,
https://doi.org/10.1007/978-981-95-1327-7_16

97

processing as central to emotional generation.[2] According to the central origin theory, the thalamus in the brain judges the emotional nature of external stimuli, and bodily responses occur based on this nature. Thus, it was thought that emotional experience is independent of bodily responses.

As a hypothesis focusing on both bodily responses and information processing in the brain, Stanley Schachter and Jerome E. Singer proposed the two-factor theory of emotion, which focuses on bodily responses to external stimuli and the cognitive process that attributes their causes.[3] Additionally, neuroscientist Antonio Damasio proposed the somatic marker hypothesis, which focuses on the bidirectional relationship between the body and brain.[4] Stimuli related to emotions from the external world are detected in a brain region called the amygdala, processed through the ventromedial prefrontal cortex to activate emotions, and trigger bodily responses related to emotions. It is believed that emotional experience occurs when these bodily responses are perceived in brain regions called the somatosensory cortex and insular cortex. Damasio also believes that emotions influence decision-making when bodily responses and their evaluation are conveyed to the prefrontal cortex.

Theories and Research on Emotion

Various theories have been proposed about the types and structures of emotions. Paul Ekman claims in his basic emotions theory that culturally universal basic emotions and their response patterns exist innately, based on the fact that emotional expressions of specific races can be recognized by subjects in various regions and cultures and the unique relationship between facial expressions and physiological responses.[5] Conversely, James Russell proposed the dimensional theory of emotion, which states that the subjective experiences we call emotions can be reduced to two dimensions: pleasure–displeasure and arousal–sleep.[6] Russell and Lisa Feldman Barrett call the bodily state definable by these two dimensions "core affect" and regard it as the core of emotional phenomena.[7]

---

[2] Cannon, W. B. 1927. The James-Lange Theory of Emotions: A Critical Examination and an Alternative Theory. The American Journal of Psychology, 39(1/4), 106–124.

[3] Schachter, S., & Singer, J. 1962. Cognitive, Social, and Physiological Determinants of Emotional State. Psychological Review, 69(5), 379.

[4] Damasio, A. R. 1994. Descartes' error: Emotion, Reason, and the Human Brain. Quill Publishing.

[5] Ekman, P. 1999. Basic Emotions. In T. Dalgleish & M. J. Power (Eds.), Handbook of Cognition and Emotion. (pp.45-60). John Wiley & Sons.

[6] Russell, J. A. 1980. A Circumplex Model of Affect. Journal of Personality and Social Psychology, 39(6), 1161.

[7] Russell, J. A., & Barrett, L. F. 1999. Core Affect, Prototypical Emotional Episodes, and Other Things Called Emotion: Dissecting the Elephant. Journal of Personality and Social Psychology, 76(5), 805.

Concepts such as bodily responses and expressions related to emotions, basic emotions, and the dimensional theory of emotions are also used in robotics and affective computing research that focuses on emotions. For example, the communication robot Kismet,[8] developed by Cynthia Breazeal, has desires and emotions that control its internal bodily state, with emotions expressed according to the dimensional theory using three parameters: pleasure–displeasure, arousal level, and attitude. The three-dimensional space of emotion is divided into categories like basic emotions in specific regions, with corresponding emotion-specific facial expression patterns. Kismet generates behaviors and facial expressions through desires and emotions that change in response to external stimuli. In recent years, advances in deep learning technology have made it possible to identify basic human emotions and estimate two-dimensional emotional parameters from facial images, gestures, and voice.

Emotions Born in Society and Culture and the Theory of Constructed Emotion

We have introduced theories and research focusing on emotions that individuals have, such as unique bodily responses and basic emotions, as the origins and structures of emotions. Meanwhile, we understand that there are emotions felt through social interactions with others and emotions dependent on different societies and cultures.

For example, jealousy, pity, and embarrassment are called social emotions, which are emotions perceived based on interpersonal or social interactions. Understanding social emotions requires various cognitive abilities, not limited to information tied to an individual's body, such as bodily responses, but including understanding others' mental states and causal relationships, predicting the future, and so on.

Additionally, the existence of emotion words dependent on society and culture, such as "schadenfreude" and "arigatameiwaku" (unwelcome kindness), suggests that emotions are not confined to individual bodies but are constructed based on social interactions. The existence of emotions and their concepts (or emotion words) perceived through such social interactions indicates that emotions have aspects as emergent symbol systems based on symbolic interactions.[9]

Barrett criticizes the innateness and essentialism of emotions and has developed the theory of constructed emotion, focusing on bodily responses as instances of emotion and humans' ability to form concepts.[10] According to this theory, unlike

---

[8] Breazeal, C. 2004. Designing Sociable Robots. MIT Press.

[9] See Chapter "Symbol Emergence Systems: Toward a World Where Humans and AI Co-Discover Meaning".

[10] Barrett, L. F. 2017. The Theory of Constructed Emotion: An Active Inference Account of Interoception and Categorization. Social Cognitive and Affective Neuroscience, 12(1), 1-23.

Generally, emotion is often defined as bodily response and affection as cognitive state. However, Barrett defines emotion as a concept and affect as a state of bodily response (core affect).

many theories focusing on emotions and bodily responses, humans do not have universal bodily responses unique to each emotion (such as anger or sadness); rather, they form emotion concepts that enable the perception of their own emotional experiences and others' emotions through physical interactions of sensory information inside and outside the body and social interactions with others through language and other means. In other words, the theory of constructed emotion posits that the background of our universal sharing of emotions deeply involves humans' ability to predictively process sensory stimuli and form concepts through physical and symbolic interactions. This is precisely to view emotion concepts as symbols in the symbol emergence systems theory, where the structure of micro–macro loops of embodiment and sociality forms the foundation for the emergence of emotion concepts.

Interoception as a Source of Emotion

The emotions we experience, such as anger and joy, are strongly linked not only to the external situations we are exposed to but also to internal bodily states, such as heartbeat, pain, and hunger. Just as humans perceive external information through exteroception via senses like vision and hearing, they perceive internal information through interoception. Here, interoception refers to the sense of internal bodily states, including the vascular and fluid circulation systems controlled by the autonomic nervous system, starting with the viscera. For humans to survive, they need to acquire predictive models to predict their desired bodily states and maintain those states. Karl John Friston has proposed the free energy principle as a principle for organisms to maintain homeostasis.[11] Within this principle, interoception, like exteroception, is viewed as perception resulting from an inference process. The brain builds generative models of the internal environment through sensory input from within the body, just as it builds generative models of the external environment, and controls bodily states such as blood pressure, body temperature, and blood glucose levels based on errors between current bodily information and model predictions. For example, when one's body temperature rises due to an increase in external temperature, sweating is promoted as a bodily response from the error between bodily information and model predictions, lowering one's body temperature. This function of maintaining bodily states constant regardless of changes in the external environment is called homeostasis. Conversely, the function of changing bodily states in advance and maintaining homeostasis when significant changes in bodily states are predicted due to external environmental influences is called allostasis. Thus, interoception can be said to be the result of active inference through prediction of the external world, not just unconscious inference of internal bodily states. The maintenance of bodily state homeostasis through predictive processing

---

[11] Friston, K. J. 2017. Self-Evidencing Babies: Commentary on "Mentalizing Homeostasis: The Social Origins of Interoceptive Inference" by Fotopoulou & Tsakiris. Neuropsychoanalysis, 19(1), 43-47.

is related to the management of resources (energy) within the body, such as temperature regulation and hunger reduction. Barrett has named this the management of the body budget and views such interoceptive functions as the source of emotions in the theory of constructed emotion. In other words, it is thought that changes in bodily responses toward improving bodily states to maintain homeostasis are experienced as pleasant emotions, and changes in bodily responses that are different or toward disrupting homeostasis are experienced as unpleasant emotions. For the neural basis related to interoception, please refer to note 12.[12]

Computational Models of Interoception and Emotion

Such attempts to understand emotions from internal sensory information and its predictive processing are attracting attention in various fields, including neuroscience and psychology. Here, we introduce computational models of interoception and emotion aimed at constructively understanding emotions.

Mehdi Keramati et al.[13] modeled the homeostatic function of interoception from the perspective of reinforcement learning. In this model, when two bodily states, blood glucose level and body temperature, are given, the difference between each target state and current state is defined as a drive, and the function of maintaining bodily states constant is expressed through reinforcement learning where the change in drive due to behavior is the reward. Also, Klaas E. Stephan et al.[14] reproduced the predictive processing of interoception as a time-series model using the representation of visceral sensations through differential equations and Bayesian learning. Ohira[15] has proposed an interaction model of interoceptive representation through predictive processing of visceral sensations and decision-making through reinforcement learning by integrating and developing these models. This model expresses the function of allostasis, where reward prediction errors from decision-making actively change the target values of bodily states, through a hierarchical structure where rewards from behavior and reward prediction errors influence the predictive model of blood pressure, which is a visceral sensation. In experiments, the phenomenon of allostatic load, where the target value of blood pressure is maintained at a high level due to reward prediction errors that occur because the model cannot learn in gambling tasks, was reproduced. This result is similar to

---

[12] Craig, Arthur D. "How do you feel?: an interoceptive moment with your neurobiological self." How Do You Feel?. Princeton University Press, 2014.

[13] Keramati, M., & Gutkin, B. 2014. Homeostatic Reinforcement Learning for Integrating Reward Collection and Physiological Stability. Elife, 3, e04811.

[14] Stephan, K. E., Manjaly, Z. M., Mathys, C. D., Weber, L. A., Paliwal, S., Gard, T., ... & Petzschner, F. H. 2016. Allostatic Self-efficacy: A Metacognitive Theory of Dyshomeostasis-Induced Fatigue and Depression. Frontiers in Human Neuroscience, 10, 550.

[15] Ohira, H. 2019. "Predictive Coding of Brain and Body and Its Failure" Japanese Psychological Review, 62(1), 132-141 in Japanese.

experimental results by humans and can be a powerful model for explaining interoceptive responses in decision-making tasks.

Research focusing on the acquisition of emotion concepts includes the developmental models of emotion through parent–child interactions by Horii et al.[16] and Hieida et al.[17] Horii et al.'s model shows that emotion concepts are developmentally structured by integrating exteroceptive sensory information from audiovisual and tactile senses and interoceptive information from C-fibers in the tactile sense through predictive processing. Also, it shows that in sensory information integration using a model without C-fibers in the tactile sense for comparison, a structure different from human emotion concepts like basic emotions is formed. This supports the result that human embodiment influences the acquisition of emotion concepts. Also, Hirai et al.[18] have extended Ohira's aforementioned model and proposed a model that integrates exteroception, proprioception, and interoception through predictive processing. This model shows that as robots repeatedly manipulate various objects, sensory concepts corresponding to each object and integrated concepts are gradually formed.

While Ohira[19] has proposed a conceptual model of the process of co-construction of emotions between two individuals, there are still few computational model studies that clarify how emotion concepts are formed and shared within social or cultural interactions. The convergence of conceptual structures through linguistic interactions (improvement of model accuracy in predictive processing) and the process of concept sharing between individuals can be modeled through multimodal concept formation by robots and the collective predictive coding hypothesis introduced in Chapters "Multimodal Object Concept Formation: Concept Modeling Based on Probabilistic Models" and "Collective Predictive Coding Hypothesis: If Language Exists to Help Us Predict the World". Understanding constructively how socially shareable emotion concepts are formed from the perspective of symbol emergence systems will be an important future challenge.

---

[16] Horii, T., Nagai, Y., & Asada, M. 2018. Modeling Development of Multimodal Emotion Perception Guided by Tactile Dominance and Perceptual Improvement. IEEE Transactions on Cognitive and Developmental Systems, 10(3), 762–775.

[17] Hieida, C., Horii, T., & Nagai, T. 2018. "Deep Emotion: A Computational Model of Emotion Using Deep Neural Networks" arXiv preprint arXiv:1808.08447 (2018).

[18] Hirai, Y., Horii, T., & Nagai, T. 2021. "Integration Model of Interoception, Exteroception, and Proprioception Using Predictive Coding" Proceedings of the Annual Conference of the Japanese Society for Artificial Intelligence, 35, 4D3OS4b03-4D3OS4b03 in Japanese.

[19] Ohira, H. 2020. "Co-construction of Emotions in Culture and History" Emotion Studies, 5(1), 4–15 in Japanese.

Neurorobotics: Controlling Robots with Neural Systems

Shingo Murata

Neurorobotics

Neurorobotics refers to a broad field of research that involves controlling robots using biological neural systems or artificial neural systems modeled after biological ones (i.e., computational models). An example of the former is brain–machine interfaces (BMI),[1] which connect human or primate brains with machines. This research aims to apply actual neural systems to engineering applications. In contrast, examples of the latter include studies using reinforcement learning models or control models that mimic brain functions,[2] as well as those utilizing neural networks that simulate the structure of actual neural systems. Among these networks, some employ spiking neural networks (SNN), which closely mimic the behavior of biological neurons, while others use more abstract recurrent neural networks (RNN). While the former research direction focuses on engineering applications, the latter aims to understand human brain and neural system mechanisms through a constructivist approach, aligning closely with fields, such as symbol emergence robotics (see Chapter "Symbol Emergence in Robotics: A Constructive Approach to Overcoming the Symbol Grounding Problem") and cognitive developmental robotics (see Chapter "Cognitive Developmental Robotics: A Constructive Approach to Understanding and Designing Cognitive Development"). This chapter, in particular,

---

[1] Chen, G., Fitzsimmons, N., Morimoto, J., & Lebedev, M. (2007). Bipedal locomotion with a humanoid robot controlled by cortical ensemble activity, Society for Neuroscience 37th Annual Meeting (Neuroscience 2007).

[2] Kawato, M. (2008). From 'Understanding the Brain by Creating the Brain' towards manipulative neuroscience, Philosophical Transactions of the Royal Society B: Biological Sciences, 363, 2201–2214.

S. Murata (✉)
Keio University, Yokohama, Kanagawa, Japan
e-mail: murata@elec.keio.ac.jp

© The Author(s) 2026
T. Taniguchi (ed.), *Symbol Emergence Systems*,
https://doi.org/10.1007/978-981-95-1327-7_17

introduces research examples that use RNN-based approaches to acquire higher cognitive functions through learning, including interaction with others, the integration of language and behavior, and object manipulation.[3]

Integrating RNNs with Robotics

The research group led by Tani has extensively studied the interaction between top–down processes—such as prediction and action generation based on an agent's intention—and bottom–up processes, such as intention modification based on environmental changes (including interactions with others).[4] RNNs are a type of neural network that consists of input, hidden, and output layers, with the hidden layer featuring feedback loops. They have been widely used for the predictive learning of word sequences and time-series sensorimotor data of robots. In the case of predictive learning with time-series data, the input layer receives current information, while the hidden layer processes both this input and feedback from the previous time step. The output layer then generates a prediction for the next time step. By incorporating feedback loops in the hidden layer, RNNs can consider past data history and perform context-dependent learning. As a concrete example, consider a case where the robot's sensorimotor information at the current time step is used as input, and the target for prediction at the output layer is the sensorimotor information at the next time step. In this scenario, the first step is to collect time-series data of sensorimotor information in advance. Then, an RNN is trained to predict the next time step's sensorimotor information based on the current input. Once trained, the RNN can be implemented in the robot, allowing it to generate actions adaptively according to the situation.

RNNPB for Learning Multiple Time-Series Data

While conventional RNNs can perform context-dependent predictive learning using feedback loops in the hidden layer, they cannot inherently distinguish between different time-series data. To address this limitation, Tani et al. proposed an RNN with parametric bias (RNNPB).[5] In addition to conventional neural network parameters (such as synaptic weights and biases), RNNPB incorporates a parametric bias (PB)

---

[3] Regarding the approach based on SNN, refer to the following works by Jeff Krichmar:
  – Krichmar, J. L. (2018). Neurorobotics—A thriving community and a promising pathway toward intelligent cognitive robots. Frontiers in Neurorobotics, 12, 42.
  – Hwu, T. J., & Krichmar, J. L. (2022). Neurorobotics: Connecting the Brain, Body, and Environment. MIT Press.

[4] Tani, J. (2016). Exploring robotic minds: Actions, symbols, and consciousness as self-organizing dynamic phenomena. Oxford University Press.

[5] Tani, J., & Ito, M. (2003). Self-organization of behavioral primitives as multiple attractor dynamics: A robot experiment. IEEE Transactions on Systems, Man, and Cybernetics—Part A: Systems and Humans, 33(4), 481–488.

unique to each time-series data item. Common information shared across all time-series data items is encoded in the synaptic weights and biases, while information specific to each data item is encoded in the PB. As a result, after training, setting a particular PB value enables the generation of predictions corresponding to the encoded sensorimotor patterns. Additionally, by initially assigning random PB values and then optimizing them to minimize prediction error, RNNPB can also recognize different time-series data. This interaction between top–down prediction processes driven by PB and bottom–up recognition processes based on prediction errors aligns with predictive coding (see Chapter "Free-Energy Principle and Predictive Coding: A Computational Theory Explaining Various Brain Functions").

Robot Learning with RNNPB

Using RNNPB, Ito et al. conducted imitative interaction experiments between humans and robots,[6] while Sugita et al. explored integrated learning of language and behavior.[7] In the imitation experiments, sensorimotor time-series data representing paired arm movement patterns of a human experimenter and a robot were used to train the RNNPB. By learning multiple periodic movement patterns, RNNPB self-organized distinct PB representations for each pattern. During testing, the robot compared the experimenter's presented movement with its RNNPB-predicted movement, optimizing the PB to minimize prediction errors and generating its own corresponding actions. When the experimenter suddenly switched movement patterns, the PB changed in discrete steps, leading to corresponding shifts in sensorimotor predictions. Furthermore, when interacting with new participants unfamiliar with the robot's trained patterns, alternating phases of synchronized movement and exploratory behavior dynamically emerged.

In the experiment on integrative learning of language and behavior, two RNNPB models were used: one for predicting simple sentences composed of verbs and nouns (language RNNPB) and another for predicting sensorimotor data (behavior RNNPB). The PB space was shared between the two models and optimized to minimize both language and behavior prediction errors. After training, when a sentence was provided, an appropriate PB value was first computed. This PB was then used in the behavior RNNPB to generate actions corresponding to the given sentence. The learned PB space self-organized to represent both grammatical structure and the semantic space of sensorimotor information. Consequently, the model demonstrated generalization by generating corresponding behaviors for novel sentences composed of learned words.

---

[6] Ito, M., Noda, K., Hoshino, Y., & Tani, J. (2006). Dynamic and interactive generation of object handling behaviors by a small humanoid robot using a dynamic neural network model. Neural Networks, 19(3), 323–337.

[7] Sugita, Y., & Tani, J. (2005). Learning semantic combinatoriality from the interaction between linguistic and behavioral processes. Adaptive Behavior, 13(1), 33–52.

Robot Learning with MTRNN

Yamashita et al. proposed the multiple timescale RNN (MTRNN),[8] which introduces a temporal hierarchy by incorporating multiple time constants into the continuous-time RNN (CTRNN).[9] The MTRNN consists of a higher layer—with a large time constant that produces slow temporal development of neural activity[10]—and a lower layer—with a small time constant that produces fast temporal development. In general, synaptic connections exist between adjacent layers, and only the lowest layer is responsible for receiving sensorimotor inputs and generating predictions.

For example, in object manipulation, a complex sequence of actions can be broken down into simple action primitives, such as reaching for an object, grasping it, and moving it, and the reverse process is also possible. This kind of hierarchical relationship is referred to as a functional hierarchy. Through robot experiments using the MTRNN, Yamashita et al. demonstrated that such a functional hierarchy can be self-organized: specifically, action primitives are acquired in the lower layer (with the small time constant), and the combined representations of these primitives are acquired in the higher layer (with the large time constant).

Expansion to Robot Learning and Computational Psychiatry

Ogata et al. extended the previously mentioned MTRNN by incorporating a convolutional neural network (CNN) and applying it to industrial robot motion generation, thereby enabling the manipulation of flexible objects.[11] In general, flexible objects are difficult to model due to their physical properties, making their manipulation a challenging task. Without relying on explicit modeling, Ogata et al. demonstrated that by collecting demonstration data of robot actions and training a model, it is possible to achieve representation learning of image features necessary for object manipulation (see Chapter "Deep Learning and Representation Learning: Foundational Theories Underpinning Modern AI") and to generate real-time actions that are robust to disturbances.

---

[8] Yamashita, Y., & Tani, J. (2008). Emergence of functional hierarchy in a multiple timescale neural network model: A humanoid robot experiment. PLoS Computational Biology, 4(11), e1000220.

[9] An RNN in which the temporal development of neural activity in the hidden layer is represented by a leaky integrator equation, where activity exponentially decays according to a certain time constant. For such CTRNNs, the conventional RNN used in RNNPB can also be referred to as a discrete-time RNN.

[10] If the time constant of this higher layer is set to infinity, its behavior corresponds to the previously mentioned PB.

[11] Suzuki, K., Mori, H., & Ogata, T. (2018). Motion switching with sensory and instruction signals by designing dynamical systems using deep neural networks. IEEE Robotics and Automation Letters, 3(4), 3481–3488.

Yamashita et al. explored the pathophysiology of schizophrenia by simulating functional disconnection in the MTRNN with PB through the addition of small noise to the synaptic connections between hierarchical layers.[12] This disconnection disrupts information exchange between layers. Consequently, even though no prediction error occurs in the real world, an internal prediction error arises, causing the PB to shift in an attempt to minimize it. When the disconnection is mild, the PB fluctuates but remains functional, making it indistinguishable from actual prediction errors that arise in the real world. This process of internally minimizing prediction errors can explain the perplexing feeling that "something is wrong" which schizophrenia patients often experience. Moreover, when the disconnection becomes severe, the robot's behavior becomes disorganized, resulting in a behavioral breakdown, such as cataleptic or stereotypic behaviors.

---

[12]Yamashita, Y., & Tani, J. (2012). Spontaneous prediction error generation in schizophrenia. PLoS One, 7(5), e37843.

Deep Learning and Representation Learning: Foundational Theories Underpinning Modern AI

Masahiro Suzuki

What Is Deep Learning?

Deep learning has been a major force in contemporary AI research. While the term *deep learning* gained popularity in the past decade,[1] the underlying methodology originated as *artificial neural networks* or *connectionism*.[2] Artificial neural networks, inspired by biological brains, were computational models developed as early as the 1940s. Over time, the focus shifted toward engineering practical models and algorithms that enhance learning efficiency, culminating in the resurgence of neural network research in the 2010s.

The *deep* in deep learning refers to multilayered architectures called *deep neural networks* (DNNs). Modern neural networks predominantly rely on the *backpropagation*[3] algorithm to calculate gradients for parameter optimization. However, early neural networks struggled with vanishing gradients when extending beyond three

---

[1] The term "deep learning" appears to have been used as far back as the 1980s (Dechter, R. 1986. Learning while searching in constraint-satisfaction problems. AAAI, 86, 178–185). However, it is generally regarded as having come into wide use—specifically in the sense of learning through multi-layer neural networks—following the research by Hinton (Geoffrey Hinton) and colleagues in 2006.

[2] Goodfellow, I., Bengio, Y., & Courville, A. 2018. Deep Learning. MIT Press.

[3] Backpropagation origins: Rumelhart, D. E., Hinton, G. E., & Williams, R. J. 1985. Learning Internal Representations by Error Propagation. California University San Diego.

The backpropagation method is an algorithm for obtaining the weight gradients of each layer by using the errors that arise in the output layer of a multilayer neural network, applying the chain rule of differentiation, and propagating these errors backward from the output layer to the input layer. Using this gradient information, the network weights are updated via optimization algorithms, such as stochastic gradient descent, thereby enabling the network to learn.

M. Suzuki (✉)
The University of Tokyo, Tokyo, Japan
e-mail: masa@weblab.t.u-tokyo.ac.jp

T. Taniguchi (ed.), *Symbol Emergence Systems*,
https://doi.org/10.1007/978-981-95-1327-7_18

layers. Advances in initialization, activation functions, regularization techniques, optimization algorithms, and network architectures have overcome these challenges. Simultaneously, the Internet's growth, larger datasets, and enhanced computational power via graphics processing units (GPUs) have significantly advanced the field.

Challenges in Early AI Research

Why are multilayered neural networks necessary? This is because hierarchical structures are essential for acquiring (learning) good *representations* of the world from experience (data). To understand this, let's look at the challenges of early AI research.

During the earliest period of AI research, researchers focused on environments that were extremely simple and formally defined, compared to the real world. In such restricted environments, humans could explicitly describe every possible situation and knowledge pattern, enabling the creation of AI systems that achieved high performance in search and reasoning.

However, for such AI systems to behave like humans in the real world, it is necessary to represent the vast amount of information in the world concisely, which facilitates reasoning by AI. Naturally, it is infeasible to perform this task manually due to the immense workload. More fundamentally, there remains a major challenge of how the information about the world should be represented in the first place. For instance, while we can instantly recognize whether a photo depicts a dog or a cat, it is difficult to explain the exact *features* that underpin such recognition.[4]

Later, AI research introduced *knowledge bases* for describing world knowledge using *formal languages*. While progress was made in *logical reasoning*, encoding real-world information without contradictions proved infeasible, as it became clear that representing the complexity of the real world using a consistent formal system was practically unattainable. Later, advances in *machine learning* made it possible to learn decision-making rules from datasets, but the data representation itself still required manual design.

Learning algorithms based on backpropagation have been "rediscovered" multiple times in different contexts. However, it was in the 1980s—when Rumelhart and colleagues employed backpropagation to train multilayer neural networks—that the method came to be widely recognized (Rumelhart, D. E., Hinton, G. E., & Williams, R. J. 1985. Learning Internal Representations by Error Propagation [Report No. 8506]. California University San Diego La Jolla Institute for Cognitive Science). Nevertheless, as early as the 1960s, Amari had already proposed a method for training multilayer neural networks based on stochastic gradient descent (Amari, S. 1967. A theory of adaptive pattern classifiers. IEEE Transactions on Electronic Computers, EC-16(3), 299–307.).

[4]Of course, if we take the time to think about it, we could list several distinguishing features—for instance, cats' ears are almost always upright, while some dogs' ears droop. However, in practice, we typically distinguish between dogs and cats on an intuitive level, so it is highly likely that we are not actually relying on these consciously identified features as the basis for our judgments.

For instance, classifying dogs and cats necessitated specifying features, such as ear shape or fur texture, with the chosen representation heavily influencing performance. In fields such as image and speech recognition, extensive research was conducted on extracting feature representations from images or audio to facilitate machine learning classification. However, one still had to design the feature extraction process manually.

Representation Learning and Hierarchies

To solve these problems, it has become possible to consider an approach in which the method of acquiring feature expressions from raw inputs like images is itself acquired through learning. This is what we call *representation learning*. Among the various representation learning approaches proposed so far, deep learning assumes that the world is inherently hierarchical and thus aims to acquire representations by employing layered (hierarchical) networks.

Consider images of dogs and cats. First, if we consider how to represent this image, the simplest aspect to note is whether it's a dog or a cat. More specifically, one can consider where the dog or cat is located in the image, what shape its entire body and face take, and—on an even finer level—the shape and position of its nose and ears. Thus, dog or cat images can be viewed as hierarchically structured, from abstract concepts down to specific details. Consequently, to extract a "dog" or "cat" representation, one can decompose the image into edges and contours, then reconstruct ears, noses, faces, silhouettes, and so forth in progressively more abstract layers. The key advantage is that while jumping directly from raw images to "dog" or "cat" is hard, each step of building from concrete to abstract features (e.g., from edges to an ear) is relatively simpler. Deep neural networks exploit this principle by learning under the structural assumption of such stepwise feature extraction.

Figure 1 illustrates how representations evolve across layers in a deep neural network. Circles represent units (neurons), and the enclosing boxes denote network layers. Pixel data enters the input layer, propagates through successive layer connections, and ultimately a dog-or-cat prediction emerges from the output layer. The strength of these connections (called "weights") are learnable parameters, adjusted via training on datasets. A "representation" at each layer refers to the activation values of its units. In the figure, these are depicted by varying shades, with explanatory notes describing what each layer extracts.

The human brain likewise employs hierarchical information processing for perception. In the ventral pathway of the visual cortex (from V1 to V2 to V4, etc.), the brain first recognizes edges (a process known as orientation selectivity) and then builds progressively more abstract object representations at higher levels.[5]

---

[5] Such hierarchical structures can be observed not only in the visual cortex but also in the auditory cortex, motor cortex, and other areas. However, while these biological hierarchical structures typi-

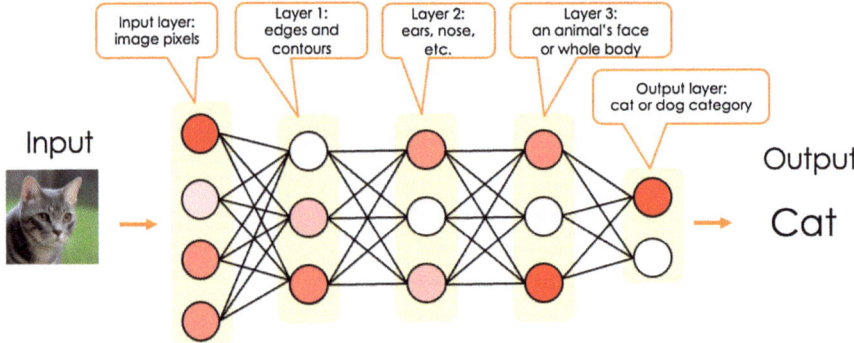

Fig. 1 A simplified illustration of a feedforward neural network for image classification. The input image is processed through multiple hidden layers: Layer 1 detects edges and contours, layer 2 captures features like ears and nose, and layer 3 represents higher-level structures, such as the face or body. The final output layer categorizes the image as either a cat or a dog

Early deep learning research used unsupervised pretraining for feature extraction, then fine-tuned for supervised tasks.[6] Today, *end-to-end*[7] supervised learning predominates, simultaneously optimizing feature extraction and task-specific objectives. Recently, *self-supervised learning*—where parts of the input are predicted by the model itself—has gained widespread adoption for large-scale models.

Changes Brought About by Deep Learning

Thanks to deep learning, it has become possible to directly learn from various types of data (often referred to as different *modalities*)—such as images, audio, and documents—without the need for manual feature extraction. This breakthrough not only dramatically improved performance over earlier methods but also unified fields, such as image recognition, speech recognition, and natural language processing—previously studied through separate approaches—under a common deep learning architecture and training methodology. As a result, *multimodal learning*[8]

cally consist of around four to six layers, modern deep neural networks often contain far more layers than that.

[6] Bengio, Y., et al. 2006 Greedy Layer-Wise Training of Deep Networks. Advances in Neural Information Processing Systems, 19, 153–160.

[7] "End-to-end" refers to learning the target task—such as classification—directly from the input data. In other words, it is a method by which feature extraction and classification are learned simultaneously, optimizing the entire process from input to output in one integrated step.

[8] For more information on multimodal object recognition and spatial cognition, see Chapters "Multimodal Object Concept Formation: Concept Modeling Based on Probabilistic Models" and "Multimodal Spatial Concept Formation: Spatial Cognition and Semantics for Mobile Robots".

(combining different modalities) and *multi-task learning* have become more feasible. While task-specific models once dominated, large-scale transformer-based architectures now command attention.

Deep learning has entered a new phase in recent years. While task-specific models once dominated, large-scale *transformer*-based[9] architectures now command attention. Trained on massive datasets, these models serve as general-purpose systems adaptable to a variety of tasks and modalities by altering the input. Such systems are often referred to as *foundation models*. Recently, *large language models* (*LLMs*), which serve as foundation models for natural language processing, have seen remarkable progress, bringing about significant changes to deep learning research.[10] With the advent of LLM services, such as ChatGPT, Claude, and others, AI has permeated mainstream society and gained widespread attention. At the same time, foundation models for video generation have begun to emerge.[11] By learning temporal dynamics and spatial structures from vast collections of video data, these models can generate realistic or semantically rich sequences of frames—effectively "imagining" how scenes might unfold. This approach is closely linked to the concept of *world models*, which we will explore in the next chapter.

Some researchers believe human-level *artificial general intelligence (AGI)* may soon be realized. Others caution that deploying human-like robots in the real world still comes with numerous challenges. Either way, deep learning remains indispensable to modern AI research, and there is little doubt that its further advancement will continue to drive innovation and greatly expand its impact on society and industry.

---

[9] The transformer is an architecture that uses a self-attention mechanism to effectively capture relationships between different parts of the input data. Through the self-attention mechanism, it calculates the relationship between each element in the input sequence and all other elements, then takes a weighted average of them to obtain a context-aware feature representation. This allows it to effectively handle long-term dependencies in sequential data.

Moreover, unlike conventional architectures for modeling sequences—such as recurrent neural networks (RNNs), which process data in a time-dependent, sequential manner—the transformer processes all elements of the input sequence simultaneously, enabling high-speed parallel computation. In addition, it has been confirmed that the performance of transformers can scale by leveraging large datasets and computing resources.

[10] For more details, please refer to Chapter "Large Language Models and Distributional Semantics: Do Large Language Models Understand Language?".

[11] https://openai.com/index/video-generation-models-as-world-simulators/

World Models: Agents That Learn About the World from Subjective Experience

Masahiro Suzuki

What Are World Models?

We humans constantly observe diverse information from our surroundings. Based on the environmental information accumulated from these experiences, we construct models of the world in our brains. Here, *model* refers to a simplified, abstracted representation of objects and phenomena in the target world. Using such a model makes it possible to infer an internal representation of the environment from incomplete observations or to predict (simulate) future changes in the environment based on observations at a given moment. These models have recently come to be called *world models*.[1]

We rely on the inferences and predictions afforded by world models to make quick decisions and carry out actions. As an example, consider a situation where you swing a bat to hit a baseball. To make this happen, the position of the ball must be conveyed as visual information from the eyes to the brain, followed by a decision on whether to swing, and finally the movement of the arms and muscles. However, even if the decision were made instantaneously, it is said that this entire process takes about 0.25–0.35 s.[2] Meanwhile, a ball thrown at 140 km/h travels from the

---

[1] For a comprehensive survey of world model research, please refer to the following paper: Taniguchi, T., et al. 2023. World Models and Predictive Coding for Cognitive and Developmental Robotics: Frontiers and Challenges. *Advanced Robotics*, 37(13), 1-27.

[2] In the Go/No-Go reaction time task (respond when presented with a Go stimulus and suppress the response when presented with a No-Go stimulus), it is generally reported to take about 0.25–0.35 s. Kida, N., et al. 2005. Intensive Baseball Practice Improves the Go/Nogo Reaction Time, but not the Simple Reaction Time. *Cognitive Brain Research*, 22(2), 257-264.

M. Suzuki (✉)
The University of Tokyo, Tokyo, Japan
e-mail: masa@weblab.t.u-tokyo.ac.jp

© The Author(s) 2026
T. Taniguchi (ed.), *Symbol Emergence Systems*,
https://doi.org/10.1007/978-981-95-1327-7_19

pitcher to the catcher in about 0.47 s.[3] Therefore, one must decide to swing almost the moment the ball is released, or it will be too late. So how do professional baseball players manage to react to even faster pitches thrown to various locations and still make contact with the ball? It is believed that they are able to do so because they have acquired a world model of the ball's trajectory through their accumulated experience. They unconsciously use their world model to predict the timing and location at which the ball will arrive and swing the bat based on that prediction.

The concept of world models is not new. In cognitive science and neuroscience, it is well-established that humans and animals possess *internal models* for environmental and motor control, facilitating adaptation to new contexts.[4] The cerebellum, for example, is known to perform motor control based on internal models.[5] Control theory has also long emphasized the importance of internal models in dealing with environmental uncertainty.

A key feature that sets world models apart from these traditional internal models is that they are learned based on environmental observations, rather than being manually designed in advance. In other words, rather than being meticulously crafted by an external designer from the outset, such models are autonomously formed by the agent through its own experiences interacting with the environment. Figure 1 shows how a world model, learned from observations of the external environment, performs inference and prediction. In this scenario, multiple different objects are moving, and some are partly out of view, resulting in incomplete observations. From such incomplete observations, the world model can infer an internal representation of the environment. This internal representation is called a *state representation*, which, in this case, is assumed to include information such as the number and arrangement of objects in the observation. It can then predict (simulate) how future observations will change based on the inferred state representation.[6]

---

[3] According to the Official Baseball Rules, the distance from the pitcher's plate to home base is 18.44 meters. If the ball's speed is 140 km/h ($\approx$38.9 m/s), the ball will reach home plate in 18.44 m $\div$ 38.9 m/s = 0.47 s.

[4] The notion that we perceive our environment through an internal model that continuously infers the causes of sensory inputs can be traced back to Helmholtz's idea of "unconscious inference."

Helmholtz, H. V. (1866). Concerning the Perceptions in General. Treatise on Physiological Optics.

From the perspective of constructing the world model subjectively within the agent's own experience, it is also related to Uexküll's concept of the "Umwelt." For more on the Umwelt, see Chapter "Uexküll's Theory of Umwelt: The Worlds as Seen by Living Beings".

[5] Kawato, M. 1999. Internal Models for Motor Control and Trajectory Planning. Current Opinion in Neurobiology, 9(6), 718–727.

[6] The object images are excerpted from the CLEVR dataset.

Johnson, J., et al. (2017). CLEVR: A Diagnostic Dataset for Compositional Language and Elementary Visual Reasoning. In Proceedings of the IEEE Conference on Computer Vision and Pattern Recognition.

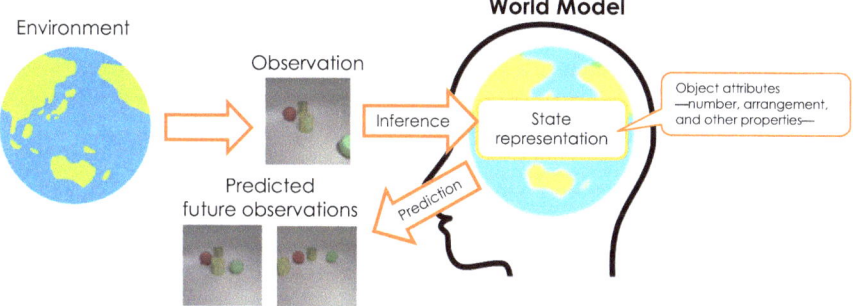

Fig. 1 Conceptual diagram of a world model for perception and prediction. Observations from the environment are used to infer an internal state representation, which encodes object attributes, such as number, arrangement, and properties. This internal model enables the prediction of future observations, supporting goal-directed behavior and adaptive planning

Deep Learning and World Models

Although attempts to acquire world models by training neural networks have a long history, it is believed that the foundations of today's world models in AI were laid around 1990 by Jürgen Schmidhuber. In his early studies, Schmidhuber proposed learning the dynamics of the environment using *recurrent neural networks* (*RNNs*), on which agents could then learn to perform control tasks.[7] In the context of reinforcement learning, where an agent learns control based on rewards, this approach is known as *model-based reinforcement learning*.[8]

There are several challenges in learning a world model. First, learning a model of the environment often requires a large-scale machine learning model. At the same time, it is impossible to model the environment in full detail, so some degree of abstraction is necessary. In fact, our brains hold a world model in which spatial and temporal dimensions are abstracted, and decisions are made based on that internal representation. Moreover, since the observations obtained from the environment only capture part of the information (partial observability), it is crucial to determine how to infer a full representation from them. Furthermore, it is necessary to properly model the uncertainty arising from changes in the environment.

Advances in deep learning have rapidly accelerated efforts to address these challenges. Although early deep learning centered on supervised learning, the later development of deep generative models and self-supervised learning made it

---

[7] Schmidhuber, J. (1990). Making the World Differentiable: On Using Self Supervised Fully Recurrent Neural Networks for Dynamic Reinforcement Learning and Planning in Non-Stationary Environments. Forschungsberichte. TU Munich, FKI 126 90, 1–26.

[8] Sutton, R. S. & Barto, A. G. Reinforcement Learning (2nd ed.).

possible to learn input representations without supervision.[9] In addition, improvements in computational power have enabled the training of large-scale models on vast amounts of data. Against this technological backdrop, around 2018, research became increasingly active in learning environment models from observational data and using them in reinforcement learning.

Benefits of World Models

The primary advantage of using world models in AI research is that they allow us to obtain large-scale simulations of the environment. Whereas traditional simulators had to be designed by humans, world models can be obtained autonomously through learning, as discussed above, thus reducing the human burden and enabling larger-scale simulation. By using such a simulator, one can see how the agent's actions would affect the environment, making it possible to learn action selection (policy) and future planning through the results of simulations on the world model, without interacting with the real environment. This is similar to the kind of imagery training humans perform in their minds.[10]

In addition, by using a world model, it becomes possible to infer a state representation of the world from raw observations. Ideally, this state representation should be lower-dimensional compared to the raw observations, exhibit invariance to viewing angle or orientation, and facilitate predictions of future states.[11] If such a state representation can be acquired, it may be possible to achieve higher efficiency and performance in learning policies.

Moreover, applying deep neural networks to learn a world model allows for the construction of a differentiable world model. Ordinarily, because the environment is treated as a black box, one cannot perform end-to-end learning of future policies or value functions directly tied to the environment. However, with a differentiable world model, it becomes possible to simultaneously learn policies, value functions, and reward prediction models for the imagined future states generated by the world

---

[9] See Chapter "Deep Learning and Representation Learning: Foundational Theories Underpinning Modern AI".

[10] Whether a learned policy or plan functions appropriately in the real environment depends on how accurately the world model captures the real world. In contemporary world model research, it is common to alternate between learning the world model and learning the policy over the world model.

[11] The framework for learning such (state) representations is known as state representation learning.
    Lesort, T., et al. (2018). State Representation Learning for Control: An Overview. Neural Networks, 108, 379–392.

model, all based on the current information.[12] It is believed that this approach can improve both the efficiency and performance of reinforcement learning.[13]

Advances in World Model Research

A pioneering work in world model research using deep learning is the study by David Ha and Schmidhuber.[14] Building on Schmidhuber's earlier work, this study demonstrated that an environment model can be effectively learned using deep learning. However, in that study, the inference of an abstract state representation from observations and the prediction of the next state representation from the current state representation plus actions were learned separately.

Since then, many other world models have been proposed. In Danijar Hafner's "Dreamer," it was shown that one can learn end-to-end both the inference of state representations from the observation space and the long-term prediction of future states in that state space; moreover, policies, value functions, and reward prediction models can be learned based on these long-term predictions by the world model.[15] "Dreamer" has undergone multiple updates, and it has been confirmed to exhibit high performance even on large-scale, long-horizon tasks.[16] Furthermore, research has advanced in areas such as applying it to real-world robotic environments[17] and integrating linguistic information.[18] However, Dreamer relies on a decoder to reconstruct high-dimensional observations, which can increase computational overhead. Moreover, minimizing reconstruction error does not necessarily align with optimizing policy performance, potentially leading to inefficiencies in training.

---

[12] Since "differentiable world model" can be a difficult concept to grasp, here is a simplified explanation. In short, a world model predicts what will happen in the future if one takes a certain action now. Being "differentiable" means that for any small change in action, one can compute the corresponding change in the prediction. This allows the agent to determine how to adjust its actions to reduce discrepancies between predictions and actual outcomes. In other words, mathematically, one can figure out how "slightly changing this action will lead to a better predicted outcome." Furthermore, by combining a differentiable world model with other differentiable models (such as a model that predicts future rewards), one can also determine "what actions to take in order to maximize rewards."

[13] Note that many recent world models rely on discrete state representations, which sacrifices the advantages of having a fully differentiable world model.

[14] Ha, D., & Schmidhuber, J. (2018). Recurrent World Models Facilitate Policy Evolution. Advances in Neural Information Processing Systems, 31.

[15] Hafner, D., et al. (2019). Dream to Control: Learning Behaviors by Latent Imagination. arXiv preprint arXiv:1912.01603.

[16] Hafner, D., et al. (2023). Mastering Diverse Domains Through World Models. arXiv preprint arXiv:2301.04104.

[17] Wu, P., et al. (2023). Daydreamer: World Models for Physical Robot Learning. Conference on Robot Learning (PMLR), 2226–2240.

[18] Lin, J., et al. (2023). Learning to Model the World With Language. arXiv preprint arXiv:2308.01399.

To address these challenges, some approaches aim to learn a world model without relying on a decoder. One example is TD-MPC, which focuses on directly learning a predictive latent representation instead of reconstructing raw observations.[19] By dispensing with the need to generate full high-dimensional outputs, TD-MPC can streamline computation and reduce unnecessary complexity—showing that explicit decoding is not always essential for effective policy learning. Recently, large-scale video generation has also attracted attention as a form of world model. However, findings from TD-MPC and similar approaches suggest that the key component of a world model is not necessarily the generation of raw observation-level data, but rather learning meaningful state representations and predicting their evolution in latent space.

In real environments, numerous objects are present, and their interactions can alter the future state of the system. Therefore, by acquiring representations for each object and learning their interactions, one can expect to improve the accuracy of future predictions. A world model that acquires such per-object representations is referred to as an *object-centric world model*, and various methods for unsupervised acquisition of object representations have been proposed.[20]

Future Challenges for World Models

Research on world models is progressing rapidly, and we are now able to learn large-scale, long-horizon predictive models. Nevertheless, they have yet to be fully applied to the complexity of real-world environments. One challenge is that many current world models rely exclusively on visual information. Humans, by contrast, receive a variety of information from the environment through all five senses, forming a reliable representation of the environment based on this multimodal input. Hence, it is considered necessary for world models to adopt multimodal learning that leverages multiple forms of information.[21] Furthermore, although world models tend to focus on learning representations of observations, little attention has been paid to learning abstract representations of actions. In everyday life, the actions we plan are abstracted across time and space. How to acquire such an action space remains a major research question for the future. In certain robotics research, such as that on predictive coding, perception and action are treated as

---

[19] Hansen, Nicklas, Xiaolong Wang, and Hao Su. "Temporal difference learning for model predictive control." arXiv preprint arXiv:2203.04955 (2022).

[20] Lin, Z., et al. (2020). Improving Generative Imagination in Object-centric World Models. International Conference on Machine Learning (PMLR).

[21] For research on understanding the real world using multimodal information, see Chapters "Multimodal Object Concept Formation: Concept Modeling Based on Probabilistic Models" and "Multimodal Spatial Concept Formation: Spatial Cognition and Semantics for Mobile Robots".

inseparable, and hierarchical representation learning is performed using both as inputs.[22] The relationship between these lines of research and world models should also be explored in the future. In addition, research on combining recent large-scale language models with world models will likely become increasingly important in the future.

---

[22] For further references, see for example: Tani, Jun. Exploring robotic minds: actions, symbols, and consciousness as self-organizing dynamic phenomena. Oxford University Press, 2016.

Moreover, for the concept that action is continuous with perception, see Chapter "Free-Energy Principle and Predictive Coding: A Computational Theory Explaining Various Brain Functions".

Part IV: Embodiment, Mind, and Consciousness

Embodiment and the Emergence of Intelligence: From Embodied Cognitive Science to Soft Robotics

Koh Hosoda

Embodiment and the Frame of Reference Problem

In the field of embodied cognitive science, the *frame-of-reference problem* refers to the discrepancy between an agent's observed behavior (i.e., its externally visible movements) and its internal representations. This issue is illustrated in Rolf Pfeifer's book *How the Body Shapes the Way We Think*[1] using the example of the "Swiss Robot." The Swiss Robot is a type of Braitenberg vehicle[2] equipped with two infra-red sensors at its front. The internal representation is a simple network that directly connects the infrared sensors to the motors, enabling obstacle avoidance. Despite this simplicity, the robot appears to exhibit a "tidying-up" behavior—gathering and arranging Styrofoam cubes—due to its well-designed morphology and environmental conditions. This emergent behavior arises from the interaction between the agent's body design, particularly the arrangement of its infrared sensors, and the environment, the size of the object, the size of the arena, and the number of the agents in the arena. The tidying-up behavior is not explicitly programmed but emerges through the interaction between the robot's physical embodiment and the environment.

A similar issue is highlighted in the thought experiment known as "Simon's Ant."[3] When an external observer models the trail of an ant as it wanders along the seashore engaged in foraging behavior and returns to its nest, the complex patterns of movement exhibited by the ant far exceed the complexity of its internal neural

---

[1] Pfeifer, R., & Bongard, J. 2006. How the Body Shapes the Way We Think. MIT Press.

[2] Braitenberg, V. 1986. Vehicles: Experiments in Synthetic Psychology. MIT Press.

[3] Simon, H. 1996. The Sciences of the Artificial. MIT Press.

K. Hosoda (✉)
Graduate School of Engineering, Kyoto University, Kyoto, Japan
e-mail: hosoda.koh.7p@kyoto-u.ac.jp

© The Author(s) 2026
T. Taniguchi (ed.), *Symbol Emergence Systems*,
https://doi.org/10.1007/978-981-95-1327-7_20

network, which consists of a few million neurons. This discrepancy arises because the ant's behavior is the result of an interaction: the ant perceives its environment through its own sensors, processes the information via its neural network, acts upon the environment, and, in turn, the environment changes dynamically. This continuous cycle of perception, action, and environmental feedback generates behavioral complexity that encompasses not only the neural network but also the embodiment of the ant and the structure of the environment.

Thus, the frame-of-reference problem reveals a key principle of intelligent adaptability: the ability of agents to generate complex behaviors despite their limited internal computational resources. This principle emphasizes that intelligence does not emerge solely from internal processing but from the dynamic interaction between an agent's embodiment and its environment. Normally, "artificial intelligence" is attributed to be the internal representation of the agent, but it is not true. The physical structure of the agent, its sensory configuration, and the characteristics of the environment collectively contribute to the emergence of adaptive behavior. The agent must be embodied so that it is able to interact with the environment, and adaptive behavior will emerge not only from the complexity of internal representation, but also from the body and environmental complexities.

Subsumption Architecture

Rodney Brooks proposed *subsumption architecture*[4] as a framework for generating intelligent behavior by the interaction between an agent's body and its environment. He criticized the traditional *Sense-Model-Plan-Act* (SMPA) cycle, in which an agent first observes the state of the environment using sensory input, then plans actions based on its internal model, and finally executes motor commands to achieve a goal. Brooks argued that this approach is highly sensitive to environmental changes and struggles to produce adaptive, life-like behaviors.

Brooks introduced the concept of "intelligence without representation," meaning that behavior is not explicitly encoded as symbolic representations within the system. In symbolic artificial intelligence, representations take the form of structured symbols, but Brooks sought an alternative in which complex behaviors emerge without requiring such explicit encoding. If behaviors were directly programmed as internal representations, their complexity would be constrained by the system's internal architecture (i.e., brain). However, in subsumption architecture, behavioral complexity arises from the agent's interaction with its environment rather than being solely determined by internal structures. This allows the agent to generate behaviors that surpass the complexity of its internal system. In essence, behavior

---

[4] Brooks, R. 1983. A Robust Layered Control System for a Mobile Robot. IEEE Journal on Robotics and Automation, 2(1), 14–23.

emerges through the interaction of the agent's brain, body, and environment, transcending the limitations of internal representations.

Subsumption architecture consists of multiple behavior-generating layers stacked hierarchically. When a higher-level layer is activated—meaning it produces an output—it suppresses or *subsumes* the output of lower-level layers. This layered structure creates a gap between the complexity of the architecture and the complexity of the behaviors it produces. In traditional hierarchical control systems, a central mechanism mediates between different behaviors, making the complexity of this mediator directly proportional to the complexity of the behavioral variations. This limitation means that the system cannot generate behavioral sequences more complex than its internal structure.

The key innovation of subsumption architecture lies in its decentralized design: instead of relying on a complex arbitrator, behavior switching is determined by predefined subsumption relationships, and the activation of each layer is influenced by the environment. As a result, behaviors dynamically shift in response to environmental complexity, allowing the system to generate behavioral sequences that exceed the complexity of the programmed architecture (or the arbitrator) itself. In this way, behavior emerges not from an explicit internal representation but through the continuous interaction of the agent's brain, body, and environment.

The emergent properties of subsumption architecture are not solely due to its layered mechanism. Another crucial factor is the simple sensor-motor couplings within each layer, which enable behaviors to arise through direct interaction with the environment. An agent perceives its surroundings through its own embodied sensors and acts upon the environment, a concept known as *situatedness*. When sensory motor couplings are simple, layers can be designed to respond quickly to environmental changes. Consequently, even if one layer fails to function, the high degree of parallelism in architecture allows the system to continue operating. It is important to recognize that behaviors are not explicitly programmed into individual layers but instead emerge through the interaction between the body's morphology, its actions, and the environment. This combination of sensor-motor coupling and layered subsumption allows architecture to generate complex behaviors without the need for explicit internal representations or predefined programs.

Emerging Behavior of Soft Robots

Traditional rigid industrial robots execute predefined behaviors by following externally given trajectories for their effectors. These robots achieve efficiency by precisely replicating assigned trajectories, ensuring accuracy in their tasks. To maintain precision, their structures are designed to be as rigid as possible, minimizing deformation. Additionally, their control systems apply high feedback gains to ensure strict trajectory tracking, making the overall system even more rigid. However, this rigidity significantly reduces adaptability to environmental changes, in strong contrast to biological systems.

Since conventional robots rely on externally programmed motion patterns, their behaviors tend to be highly repetitive and inflexible. Adapting to unexpected environmental changes is challenging, and modifying their behavior dynamically is difficult. This lack of flexibility in designing the trajectory limits their ability to respond to real-world variations.

Soft robotics aims to endow robots with biological-like adaptability by incorporating soft materials and flexible control strategies. Due to their inherent softness, soft robots do not follow predefined trajectories as rigid robots do, making traditional trajectory-following control approaches impractical. Instead, the behavior of soft robots emerges from the interaction between their internal representation, their flexible body, and the surrounding environment.

The design and control principles of soft robots are still in their early stages. The conventional framework used for rigid robots—where external target values dictate precise movements—does not apply well to soft robots. Since soft robotics is inspired by biological adaptability, bio-mimetic and bio-inspired approaches often serve as the foundation for their design and control strategies. This biological influence has also led to the use of soft robots as models for understanding biological intelligence through constructive approaches. However, the lack of well-defined design principles remains a significant challenge in the field of soft robotics.

Symbol Emergence and Embodiment

Symbol emergence is the idea that symbols are not given from outside of the agent, but they emerge in the agent's subjective space through its interaction with the environment by using its own sensors. This makes *situatedness* a necessary condition for symbol emergence. The foundation of symbol emergence lies in an agent's ability to classify behaviors and environmental information through its own sensory motor space and self-organize internal representations within its subjective space.[5] In this sense, embodiment is a crucial key for understanding the emergence of the language.

The mystery is how the agents can share those subjective symbols as the language even if they emerge from individual space. If the bodies are completely identical, it is easy to understand that the agents can share the experience, and as a result, they can have common language to communicate. However, we humans have different soft bodies. If the symbols emerge within the individual agent, they cannot be shared with other agents that have different soft bodies. Communication may be the key, but before going deeply into it, we have to understand the relationship between subjective symbol emergence and embodiment.

---

[5] Pfeifer, R., & Scheier, C. 1999. Understanding Intelligence. Bradford Books.

Enactivism: Cognition as Non-representational, Embodied Action

Katsunori Miyahara

Enactivism is a theoretical approach to the nature of life and cognition, initially formulated by neuroscientist Francisco Varela and his collaborators in their 1991 book *The Embodied Mind*.[1] This chapter outlines its main ideas and key concepts.

Representationalism in Cognitive Science

One of the foundational constructs in modern cognitive science is that of *inner* or *mental representations*.[2] While the history of psychology is complex and debated, a common narrative holds that cognitive science emerged in part as a reaction against behaviorist psychology. While behaviorists treated the mind as a "black box," early cognitive scientists sought to explain how unobservable cognitive processes work by positing inner or mental representations as their basic building blocks. Examples include visual representations of 3D objects, cognitive maps, episodic memories, and scripts for behavioral sequences. Despite their differences, they all share a common feature: they are internal states carrying information or content. Cognitive science generally operates on the premise that such representations are essential components of cognition.

---

[1] Varela, F., Thompson, E., & Rosch, E. 1991. *The embodied mind: Cognitive science and human experience*. MIT Press.

[2] Bermúdez, J. L. (2020). *Cognitive science: An introduction to the science of the mind*. Fourth edition. Cambridge University Press.

K. Miyahara (✉)
Center for Human Nature, Artificial Intelligence, and Neuroscience (CHAIN), Hokkaido University, Sapporo, Hokkaido, Japan

© The Author(s) 2026
T. Taniguchi (ed.), *Symbol Emergence Systems*,
https://doi.org/10.1007/978-981-95-1327-7_21

However, the idea that cognition requires representation, or *representationalism* for short, has long been a subject of intense debate among cognitive scientists and philosophers.[3] Modern cognitive science widely assumes that we should explain mind and cognition through the lens of representations, but is this the best way to approach cognitive science? Enactivism emerged as a leading critique of representationalism in cognitive science, advocating for an alternative perspective that emphasizes the biological and embodied nature of cognition.

Anti-Representationalism in Enactivism

Why does enactivism oppose representationalism?[4] Representationalism, they argue, rests on a problematic assumption about how cognition relates to the world.[5] It posits that states of the world are predetermined independently of cognition, and that cognition is a process of reconstructing or reproducing this external state within the mind. For example, cognitive neuroscience often explains vision as the brain reconstructing a 3D world from 2D retinal input.[6] Explanations like this treat the external world as pre-given domain and the mind as an internal domain that operates as a passive decoder of information.

Enactivism argues that this approach to cognition fundamentally misconstrues the nature of cognitive agents. The goal of reconstructing the external world, enactivists contend, is a description only imposed by an external observer. It fails to capture the intrinsic activity of the cognitive system itself.[7] To illustrate, consider the neural system, taken as a physical structure, as a network of interconnected neurons. Sensory inputs trigger changes within this network, influencing motor activity and thus the agent's interaction with its environment. This interaction, in turn, modifies the sensory inputs, creating a continuous loop. Therefore, the neural system is not simply an input–output device. It's a dynamic system engaged in ongoing interaction within itself and with the world. Instead of processing information to produce specific outputs, the neural system participates in a self-sustaining cycle of structural changes. These changes, involving sensorimotor interactions with the environment, continuously give rise to further changes to perpetuate the cycle.

---

[3] Smortchkova, J., Dolega, K., & Schlicht, T. (Eds.). (2020). What are mental representations? Oxford University Press.

[4] The following introduces anti-representational arguments found primarily in Varela's writings. For different enactivist arguments against representationalism, see: Hutto, D., & Myin, E. 2013. *Radicalizing enactivism: basic minds without content.* MIT Press.

[5] Varela et al. (1991), p. 135.

[6] Marr, D. (2010). *Vision: A computational investigation into the human representation and processing of visual information.* MIT press. (Original published 1982)

[7] Thompson, E. *Mind in life: Biology, phenomenology, and the sciences of the mind.* Harvard University Press, p. 52.

Enactivists use the terms "autonomy" and "operationally closure" to describe such systems, concepts coming from Varela's collaboration with his mentor, Humberto Maturana, in developing the theory of *autopoiesis* during the 1960s and 1970s.[8] Autonomous systems are self-sustaining or "self-individuating" in their terminology. Their internal processes continuously generate and maintain a network of processes that constitutes their very existence. This contrasts with *heteronomous systems* that lack this self-sustaining capacity. For example, conventional computing systems designed by human programmers operate under external control. Their persistence only relies on external factors, such as a power source or ongoing maintenance, rather than on any inherent self-sustaining activity. Building on this theory of autopoiesis, enactivists contend that representationalism is fundamentally mistaken in treating living, cognitive systems as if they were heteronomous systems, like manmade machines, that lack the intrinsic capacity for self-sustenance.[9]

Life–Mind Continuity: Sensorimotor Coordination and Enaction

The anti-representational stance of enactivism is closely tied to the idea of continuity between life and mind. Representationalist cognitive science often treats the cognitive system as analogous to software running on the brain's hardware. In this view, life-sustaining processes merely serve to sustain the hardware, while cognition is determined by abstract programs that, in principle, could be implemented on any system, biological or otherwise. Enactivism, in contrast, regards cognition as inseparable from embodied, life-sustaining processes, such as breathing, eating, and seeking nourishment.

Animals, for instance, survive by actively seeking nutrients in the environment. Their behavior is guided by *sensorimotor correlations* between their sensory and motor surfaces. Consider the predatory behavior of an amoeba hunting another protozoan.[10] Environmental changes deriving from the presence of the protozoan affect the amoeba's cell membrane, which in turn alter its protoplasmic flow. This changes the amoeba's relationship to the environment, subjecting its membrane to a new

---

[8] Maturana, H. R., & Varela, F. J. (1980) "Autopoiesis: The organization of the living", In *Autopoiesis and cognition: The realization of the living* (pp. 73–134). D. Reidel Publishing Company. See also Thompson (2007), chapters 3, 5. See Chapter "Neo-Cybernetics and Information: What Is Information?" for more on autopoiesis.

[9] This criticism applies not only to classical computationalism (or symbolism), which interprets cognition as discrete symbolic computation, but also to connectionism, which interprets cognition as information processing using distributed representations. From the enactivist perspective, the function of neural networks in cognition should not be understood as constructing representations of the environment, but rather as generating self-organized, patterned responses to various perturbations from the environment. See Varela et al. (1991), Chap. 5.

[10] Maturana, H., & Varela, F. 1992. *The Tree of Knowledge: The Biological Roots of Human Understanding (Revised edition)*. Shambhala, p. 144.

array of stimuli. These then affect its internal structure, ultimately directing its movement to engulf the prey. This chain of processes constitutes the amoeba's predatory behavior, made possible by the systematic correlation between its sensory and motor surfaces within its simple bodily structure. In animals with more complex bodies, the sensorimotor correlation is less direct. Humans are multicellular organisms, consisting of trillions of complexly structured cells, whose sensory and motor surfaces are intermediated by a gigantic neural network consisting of more than 80 billion neurons. This intricate network allows humans to develop a repertoire of sensorimotor patterns that vastly exceeds that of amoebas. However, at some level of abstraction, amoebas and humans are fundamentally similar in that they both adapt to their environments in a sensorimotor fashion based on their embodied structures.

Importantly, living, autonomous systems that sustain its identity through their embodied, sensorimotor structures generate new meaningful distinctions within the environment in relation to their embodied structure.[11] For instance, an amoeba in a solution containing various chemicals differentiates substances as "nutrients" or "toxins" based on its sensorimotor structure. In other words, when a living organism is coupled with an environment through its embodied structure, a physical environment that lacks inherent meaning turns into an ecological milieu invested with biological significance. What Jakob von Uexküll calls the *Umwelt* emerges in an inherently meaningless world.[12] Enactivism refers to this phenomenon, where meaning arises through embodied interaction with the world as *enaction* or *sense-making*. This, enactivists contend, is the basic form of cognition.

Cognition as Embodied Action: Bridging Science and Experience

Building on the connection between life and sense-making in basic living systems, enactivists propose understanding human cognition as a form of embodied action. This perspective has two major implications for how we understand the mind.[13] First, perception is not a purely epistemic act of reconstructing the external world inside the mind. Rather, it is a practical process deeply intertwined with action. We perceive the world for and through embodied interactions with the concrete environment, guided by our sensorimotor structures. Second, abstract cognitive processes, such as reasoning, memory, and imagination, also depend on environmental

---

[11] Varela et al. (1991), pp. 151–157. See also Thompson (2007), pp. 153–154.

[12] See Chapter "Uexküll's Theory of Umwelt: The Worlds as Seen by Living Beings" for more on von Uexküll's concept of Umwelt.

[13] Varela et al. (1991), p. 173.

interactions. These processes are best understood as highly complex sensorimotor patterns acquired through development within the human world.

Representationalism creates an explanatory gap between scientific and phenomenological perspectives on human experience.[14] It turns subjective experience into a mysterious add-on to sub-personal information processing, denying the value of phenomenological accounts for scientific investigation. In contrast, by interpreting cognition as embodied action, enactivism integrates the phenomenological perspective into cognitive science. The alignment between phenomenology and enactive cognitive science is particularly evident in the work of Maurice Merleau-Ponty.[15] Drawing on empirical research in psychology, neurology, and psychopathology, Merleau-Ponty argued that our bodily interactions with the world shape our perceptual experience at a fundamental, pre-reflective level. Besides emphasizing the connection between life and cognition, thus, enactivism offers a comprehensive framework for cognitive science that bridges the gap between scientific and phenomenological approaches to the mind.[16]

The enactive approach to cognition has given rise to much debate about the nature of cognition and representation, as well as a wealth of research that reinterprets cognition as embodied action. Indeed, the last 20 years of research into enactive cognition has greatly clarified the significance of embodiment for cognition.[17] However, the debate between representationalist and enactivist approaches is far from settled. In fact, we might say that recent technological progress, such as those in deep learning, has revitalized the representationalist conception of cognition. This dialogue between enactivism, with its emphasis on the continuity between life and mind and its focus on the embodied nature of cognition, and representationalism, with its emphasis on internal information-processing, will remain crucial for understanding the nature of cognition.

---

[14] Thompson (2007), pp. 5–6. See also Varela et al. (1991), pp. xvii–xviii.

[15] See Chapter "Phenomenology: Philosophical Thinking Based on Appearance and Experience" for more on phenomenology.

[16] Varela further argues that we need to view theoretical reflection itself as an open-ended, embodied practice, rather than simply pushing for theoretical integration. See Varela et al. (1991), pp. 27–31.

[17] For an overview of recent development of enactivism, see: Hutto, D. 2023 Enactivism. Internet Encyclopedia of Philosophy. https://iep.utm.edu/enactivism/; Gallagher, S. 2023. Embodied and Enactive Approaches to Cognition. Cambridge University Press.

Phenomenology: Philosophical Thinking Based on Appearance and Experience

Shigeru Taguchi

What Is Phenomenology?

What is phenomenology? This question invites diverse answers. Often described as a "movement" rather than a unified school of thought, phenomenology encompasses a wide range of philosophical approaches. Here, we focus on the foundational ideas of Husserlian phenomenology to introduce some characteristics and aspects of phenomenological thinking.[1]

Phenomenology, literally the "study of phenomena," examines all forms of phenomena—natural, psychological, or any other phenomenon that defies description—insofar as they "appear" in some sense. Even entities such as "meaning," "ideas," or "God"—which may not be considered to "appear" in the ordinary sense—can nonetheless be said to have a certain kind of "appearance" in our world of experience, insofar as we are able to speak about them using words or symbols and establish a shared understanding of them with others. By exploring things from the perspective of "appearance," we can investigate everything that relates to us, in a "scientific" manner—that is, with proper justification. This, we may say, was the view of Edmund Husserl, the founder of phenomenology.[2]

---

[1] For an introduction to the basic concepts and an overview of phenomenology, see Zahavi, D. 2003. *Husserl's Phenomenology*. Stanford University Press; Taguchi, S. 2014. *Genshogaku toiu shiko: Jimeinamono no chi he (Phenomenology as a Way of Thinking: Interrogating the Obvious)*. Chikuma Shobo.

[2] Edmund Husserl (1859–1938) was an Austrian-born philosopher who worked primarily in Germany. He is known as the founder of phenomenology, a major philosophical movement. His

---

S. Taguchi (✉)
Faculty of Humanities and Human Sciences, Hokkaido University, Sapporo, Japan

Center for Human Nature, Artificial Intelligence, and Neuroscience (CHAIN), Hokkaido University, Sapporo, Japan
e-mail: tag@let.hokudai.ac.jp

© The Author(s) 2026
T. Taniguchi (ed.), *Symbol Emergence Systems*,
https://doi.org/10.1007/978-981-95-1327-7_22

139

To "appear" means to appear in relation to some form of experience. Experience is something that each experiencing subject can verify and retrace on their own. In other words, as long as something appears and is experienced, the possibility of reflecting on and examining it remains open.[3] Through the pathway of "experience," we have access to all phenomena.

Intentionality and Constitution: The Phenomenological Space of Thought

Every phenomenon involves something that appears. For something to appear as that particular something, various conditions must be met. For instance, in order for the object "lemon" to appear, certain characteristics must be experienced—its yellow color, glossy texture, and distinctive shape. Bringing it close to the nose and smelling it allows us to recognize, from its characteristic scent, that it is not an imitation lemon. Cutting it open and tasting it reveals its sourness. It is only through such diverse experiences that the object "lemon" truly appears as a lemon. Conversely, these diverse experiences integrate into a coherent whole, forming the appearance of a lemon. In experience, various objects appear, each corresponding to such coherent wholes. Individual experiences interweave in a structured manner, constituting a meaningful whole that refers to a single object, while the object itself points toward the possibility of further diverse experiences. This structured relationship between appearing objects and experience is what is known as *intentionality*.[4]

In phenomenology, the process by which an object and its structured relation to other objects emerge within the diversity of appearances and their corresponding experiences is called *constitution*. However, speaking of the "constitution of objects" does not imply that the mind arbitrarily fabricates them. In phenomenology, when a real object exists, the intentional object is understood as precisely that real object, which transcends the mind.

---

key works include *Logical Investigations*, *Ideas Pertaining to a Pure Phenomenology and to a Phenomenological Philosophy*, *Cartesian Meditations*, and *The Crisis of European Sciences and Transcendental Phenomenology*, among others.

[3] Husserl states that conscious life inherently possesses a universal "reflexivity." See Husserl, E. 1973. *Zur Phänomenologie der Intersubjektivität. Dritter Teil: 1929–1935. Husserliana XV*. Martinus Nijhoff, p. 543.

[4] In his later work, Husserl deepens his analysis of intentionality, moving beyond mere intentionality toward objects to explore concepts, such as "passive intentionality," "drive-intentionality," and "instinctive intentionality." In this context, the general term "intentionality" refers to the way experience "tends toward" something or "points to" something else.

Setting aside for the moment what the term "real object" might mean philosophically, what is grasped in everyday experience as *the thing itself* is, for phenomenology, both the object of experience and, at the same time, a "transcendent" object that exists "outside the mind." According to Husserl, this may appear paradoxical only when we detach ourselves—through a kind of intellectual game—from the concrete reality of our experience. The object is both within and beyond the mind.[5] Our concrete experience has long since surpassed such ossified dichotomies as "inside and outside."

The space of thought that phenomenology has opened up by way of experience and appearance, as described above, cannot be equated with either the type of inquiry typically called "psychological" or that which is described as "scientific," "objective," or "third-person." Rather, it can be seen as a space of thought that, in a certain sense, encompasses both.[6] Drawn into the intellectual field of this space, later philosophers such as Martin Heidegger, Maurice Merleau-Ponty, Jean-Paul Sartre, and Emmanuel Levinas each took this space of thought as their point of departure, developing their own distinct philosophical perspectives from it.

Intersubjectivity: Multiple Experiences and the Same Object

We have stated that intentionality is a relation to the object itself. Just as there can be no appearance of an object without intentional experience, there can likewise be no experience of an object without the object itself. This becomes particularly evident in the so-called intersubjective experience—that is, an experience that requires the involvement of multiple subjects.

---

[5] Husserl 1973, p. 556. Husserl remarks, "For everyone except confused philosophers it is absolutely without question that the thing perceived in perception *is the thing itself,* in its own factual being" (Husserl, E. 1974 *Formale und Transzendentale Logik. Husserliana* XVII. Martinus Nijhoff, p.287.; The English translation is a slightly modified version of the one in Husserl, E. (1969). *Formal and Transcendental Logic.* Trans. Cairns, D., The Hague: Martinus Nijhoff, p. 281).

[6] What Husserl referred to as "transcendental" was precisely this kind of space of thought. However, since the term had been traditionally used since Kant, its surface similarity to earlier usages has often led to confusion. Due to space constraints, a detailed discussion cannot be provided here, but it is important to note that Husserl imbued this term with a rather distinct meaning of his own. For example, while Husserl speaks of "transcendental experience," such a term would be inconceivable within Kant's philosophical framework.

Even if something appears to me to exist, if it cannot be experienced by others, it cannot truly be said to exist in reality (it may be a misperception, an illusion, or a hallucination). If the object itself does not exist, there is no possibility of my experiencing it together with others. At the same time, unless something can be commonly experienced by others, it cannot take on the meaning of being the same object that transcends my individual experience. It is through our mutual engagement with an object—through our referring to it, discussing it, and understanding each other in relation to it—that it first becomes confirmed and distinguished as the same object.

When someone says, "Pass me the spoon," and I hand them a spoon, the spoon is identified as the same object, and at the same time, the intersubjective interaction flows smoothly. If, instead, I kept handing them a fork, a knife, a pen, or a pair of trousers after being asked for a spoon, the interaction would become confused and nonsensical. Shared experience would break down, and the same object would fail to be established. Conversely, the emergence of the same object and the smooth functioning of interaction occur simultaneously—they are two aspects of the same event.[7]

This "same object" is, ultimately, "one unified nature" itself. There exists "*one and the same nature*," within which we possess *bodies* that are themselves part of nature. Because everyone has a body within nature, we can see each other's appearance and hear each other's voices. Through our bodies, our experiences and lives intertwine with one another.[8] The very oneness of nature is what makes this intertwinement possible in the first place. At the same time, it is precisely within this interwoven network of multiple lives that the uniqueness of nature stands out as a kind of "ideal." (In reality, however, there remain vast aspects of each other's lives that cannot be fully shared or understood.)

---

[7] It is only through the establishment of intersubjective relationships and mutual interaction among multiple subjects that something first appears as the "same thing." At the same time, the very fact that we can grasp the "same thing" as such is what makes it possible for the experiences of multiple subjects to intersect in the first place. The experience of sameness and the experience of intersubjective communal engagement mutually support one another. In the process of speaking with others, contending over things, and engaging in interaction, 'objects' acquire an identity that transcends my individual life. On the flip side, if what I experience could not also be experienced by others—if, for instance, others could not see the very same thing that I point to—then my life would not even be able to intersect with theirs.

[8] The discussion here is based on Husserlian phenomenology, but it was Maurice Merleau-Ponty (1908–1961) who sought to reframe phenomenology as a whole from the perspective of *embodiment*. *Enactivism* emerged under the strong influence of Merleau-Ponty and is deeply connected to the broader field of the phenomenology of the body.

Symbols and the Ideal

Now, we have encountered the term *"ideal."* This very "ideal" is the key to enabling multiple lives to intertwine and connect with one another. The world of experience takes on a unique coherence and coloration for each experiencing subject. One cannot directly access another person's world of experience. It is for this reason that we use *symbols* in a broad sense—most notably, *language*—to convey our intentions to one another and to bridge our respective experiential worlds. But why is such communication possible at all?

This is because symbols can connect us to *"ideal objectivities."* According to Husserl, ideal *objectivities* are by no means subjective phantoms; rather, they can be experienced *evidently*—that is, in a way that presents themselves as their own evidence. For instance, "1," "one," "一," or "いち" are written symbols that, in Charles Peirce's triadic model, correspond to "signs." These signs appear in the world as concrete physical phenomena. However, the number 1 itself, which they signify, does not appear in the world as an object that can be seen or touched. Yet precisely for this reason, its meaning remains unchanged regardless of when or where it is read, whether it is written neatly or sloppily. This quality is what is referred to as "ideal."

Ideal objectivities cannot appear without some kind of physical bearer—a "sign" in Peirce's sense—yet they are not dependent on any particular bearer. Whether I express it or someone else does, 1 remains 1. Ideal objectivities are always "founded" (*fundiert*)[9] in some physical bearer, yet in a certain sense, they do not rely on any particular one. This very quality is what allows them to be the same objects for both myself and others. By using language, mathematical symbols, and other such symbols, we can relate our lives to one another on a level that does not depend on the uniqueness of our respective experiential worlds.

It is important to note that phenomenology does not assume the existence of a Platonic world of ideas that is entirely separate from each individual's subjective life. While idealities do not depend on individual experiences or specific phenomena, this does not mean that they are independent of all experience. They are always founded in some form of experience, yet they are not necessarily bound to the specific experience they happen to depend on. Idealities can appear only in the concrete process in which my experience and the experience of others interact, deeply

---

[9] "Foundation" (*Fundierung*) is a fundamental concept in phenomenology, expressing a relationship such as "if A does not exist, then B does not exist either." For example, without a physical sign, the ideal cannot appear; however, this does not mean that the latter can be reduced to the former.

intersecting through symbols.[10] They manifest within the interwoven lives of subjects, yet they do not depend on their concrete or particular existence. This is the defining characteristic of the ideal and, more broadly, of all *symbol phenomena*, including language. One might even say that symbol phenomena are a highly purified manifestation of the fact that our lives are not isolated and fragmented, but rather capable of intersecting and encountering one another.

Through symbols, we understand the experiences of others. While the realities that individuals experience differ, there exists a certain kind of "transformation" that allows these experiences to be mapped onto one another. Perhaps what we call "symbols" are nothing other than the name for this *transformability* itself, which is made more manageable by this naming. The scent of a lemon that I perceive and the scent of the same lemon that someone else perceives are likely different. However, some form of mutual transformation between these experiences must be possible. Could it be that the word "lemon" itself is the name for this transformability? Can we say that there is no substantial entity corresponding to a symbol? Rather, do symbols always stand in for the countless transformations between different experiences? Pursuing such questions about symbols from a phenomenological perspective is undoubtedly a thought-provoking topic of inquiry.[11]

---

[10] In this sense, Husserl's detailed analysis of linguistic meaning in *Logical Investigations* can be reinterpreted from the perspective of symbol emergence. See Husserl, E. 1970. *Logical Investigations*. New York: Routledge & Kegan Paul. His late manuscript, *The Origin of Geometry*— also known for Derrida's extensive preface—is likewise deeply connected to this theme. See Husserl, E. 1976. *Die Krisis der europäischen Wissenschaften und die transzendentale Phänomenologie*. The Hague: Martinus Nijhoff. Moreover, Maurice Merleau-Ponty's theory of language, which traces the emergence of linguistic phenomena from the interactions of bodily experience, should also be reconsidered in relation to the symbol emergence systems theory. See Merleau-Ponty, M. (1964). *Signs*. Trans. McCleary, R.C., Evanston, IL: Northwestern University Press.

[11] This perspective has a connection to category theory in mathematics. For the relationship between phenomenology and category theory, see Saigo, H. & Taguchi, S. 2019. '*Genjitsu' toha nanika (What is "Reality")?*, Chikuma Shobo (English translation forthcoming), Chap. 3. Additionally, for theories of meaning comprehension and meaning generation using category theory, refer to the following work. Fuyama, M., Saigo, H., Takahashi, T. 2020. A Category Theoretic Approach to Metaphor Comprehension: Theory of Indeterminate Natural Transformation. *Biosystems*, 197, 104213.

Consciousness and Qualia: How Do Consciousness and Symbols Relate?

Naotsugu Tsuchiya

How Consciousness Research Has Evolved: First and Second Generations

Consciousness has long been a focus of philosophical inquiry. Philosophers have employed thoughts supported by language and logic as a primary tool to examine the essence and structure of consciousness in mostly adult humans. Language elevates the abstraction of thought and has significantly contributed to the advancement of civilization. Within an individual, language plays a significant role to advance complexity in thought processes and provide richness to a variety of conscious experience. In this sense, modern philosophical research on consciousness is largely based on abstract thinking. Among the many critical thoughts, one of the most fundamental is Descartes' famous dictum "Cogito ergo sum" ("I think, therefore I am"). From a viewpoint of consciousness, this implies "I cannot doubt the presence of my own consciousness." Since Descartes, philosophical research on consciousness remained primarily dependent on logical and linguistic reasoning, while recent philosophers (especially after the 1990s, the second generation) started to incorporate neuroscientific insights into their thesis.

N. Tsuchiya (✉)
Monash University, Melbourne, Victoria, Australia

Advanced Telecommunications Research Computational Neuroscience Laboratories, Kyoto, Japan

Theoretical Sciences Visiting Program, Okinawa Institute of Science and Technology Graduate University, Okinawa, Japan
e-mail: naotsugu.tsuchiya@monash.edu

147

The twentieth century ushered in the first generation of consciousness researchers.[1] Researchers like Gustav Fechner, Wilhelm Wundt, and William James established experimental psychology and advanced investigations into subjective perception, attention, and memory. These foundations contributed to modern theories on consciousness.[2,3] For example, while consciousness and attention often seem inseparable subjectively, modern research has experimentally addressed their relationship empirically.

However, the rise of behaviorism in the 1920s shifted focus exclusively to observable input stimuli and output behaviors, sidelining consciousness from mainstream psychology.[4] As a result, consciousness research disappeared from the scientific forefront for a time. Language studies, meanwhile, turned toward structural analysis of linguistic and symbolic systems, neglecting their relationship to subjective experience. Consequently, the fields of consciousness, qualia, language, and symbols diverged, with minimal interaction since then and largely remain so even today.

Behaviorism's dominance waned during the "Cognitive Revolution" of the 1970s. The second generation of consciousness studies emerged in the 1990s, mainly driven by advances in brain imaging technologies. Researchers could now measure neural activity in various states of consciousness in healthy individuals capable of verbal reports. For example, experiments compared brain activity during dreaming versus dreamless sleep, even without visual input or bodily movement.[5] Using stimuli like ambiguous figures (e.g., Rubin's vase), researchers could dissociate input stimuli from conscious content and identify *neural correlates of consciousness (NCCs)* (see Fig. 1). Although NCC research yielded extensive data and numerous theories,[6] critics argued that oversimplifying the content of consciousness to facilitate NCC studies hindered the understanding of qualia.

Qualia encompass all experiences we are consciously aware of, excluding unconscious processes. Examples include the "red color" of a sunset, the "sound of waves," and the "melancholic feeling" of watching the sunset. While NCC research often reduces qualia to binary characteristics (e.g., "visible vs. invisible"), this simplification impedes deeper understanding. Philosophers have

---

[1] For introductory readings on phenomenology and its relation to consciousness, see Coe, M., & Chemero, A. 2018. *Phenomenology: For a New Philosophy of Mind*. Keiso Shobo.

[2] Dehaene, S., et al. 2006. Conscious, Preconscious, and Subliminal Processing: A Testable Taxonomy. *Trends in Cognitive Sciences*, 10(5), 204–211

[3] Koch, C., & Tsuchiya, N. 2007. Attention and Consciousness: Two Distinct Brain Processes. *Trends in Cognitive Sciences*, 11(1), 16–22.

[4] Baars, B. J. 2009. History of Consciousness Science. In W. P. Banks (Ed.), Encyclopedia of Consciousness (pp. 329-338). Academic Press.

[5] Horikawa, T., et al. 2013. Neural Decoding of Visual Imagery during Sleep. *Science*, 340(6132), 639–642.

[6] Seth, A. K., & Bayne, T. 2022. Theories of Consciousness. *Nature Reviews Neuroscience*, 23(7), 439–452.

Fig. 1 Rubin's vase, an example of a bistable image that demonstrates bistable perception. Viewers may experience spontaneous alternation between a black vase in the center or two white faces in profile on either side

highlighted the ineffable nature of qualia, suggesting that language cannot fully capture their essence.[7]

Third-Generation Consciousness Studies: Language as a Tool for Structuring Qualia

Since 2020, third-generation consciousness research has sought to address limitations in earlier paradigms. For example, *registered reports* enable comparisons between competing theories by pre-registering detailed experimental plans and predictions. This framework encourages rigorous theory comparison and fosters research into the structural characteristics of qualia.

One promising approach involves conceptualizing qualia as structures.[8] Symbolic and linguistic methods, aligned with the symbol emergence systems theory, could play a pivotal role in understanding the relationships between qualia. While language complicates qualia research due to its inherent variability and individual differences, advancements in experimental methods and large-scale data analysis have mitigated these challenges.[9,10]

[7] Dennett, D. C. 1988 Quining Qualia. In A. J. Marcel & E. Bisiach (Eds.), Consciousness in Contemporary Science (pp. 42–77). Clarendon Press/Oxford University Press.

[8] Tsuchiya, N., & Saigo, H. 2021. A Relational Approach to Consciousness. *Neuroscience of Consciousness*, 2021(2).

[9] Winawer, J., et al. 2007. Russian Blues Reveal Effects of Language on Color Discrimination. *Proceedings of the National Academy of Sciences*, 104(19), 7780–7785.

[10] Tsuchiya, N. (2025, Apr, ver 2). The Qualia Structure Paradigm: towards a construction of a Qualia Periodic Table for the dissolution of the Hard Problem of Consciousness. DOI: https://doi.org/10.31234/osf.io/492hu, (To appear as a book chapter for The Scientific Study of Consciousness: Experimental and Theoretical Approaches, edited by Umberto Olcese and Lucia Melloni,)

Recent developments include:

1. *Cost-Effective Experiments:* Advances in online experimental environments have made laboratory-grade psychological experiments accessible and affordable. Large-scale participant recruitment is now feasible, enabling systematic studies of linguistic reporting in qualia research.[11,12]
2. *Large Language Models (LLMs):* LLMs offer powerful tools for analyzing extensive linguistic datasets, providing objective, reproducible methods for interpreting language-based qualia reports.[13,14]
3. *Data Sharing:* Emerging cultures of data sharing among researchers are breaking down disciplinary barriers, fostering collaborations between linguists and consciousness researchers.

These advancements pave the way for integrating linguistic and semiotic methods into consciousness research, enabling more detailed understanding of qualia structures.

The Role of Consciousness Studies in Symbol Emergence Systems Theory

Thus far in this chapter, we have focused on the contributions of symbol emergence systems theory to consciousness research. Now we ask: what can advancements in consciousness studies bring to symbol emergence systems theory?

While semiotics and linguistics rarely address consciousness or qualia explicitly, understanding the characteristics of unconscious and conscious processes is crucial

---

[11] Kawakita, G., Zeleznikow-Johnston, A., Takeda, K., Tsuchiya, N., and Oizumi, M. (2025). Is my "red" your "red"?: Evaluating structural correspondences between color similarity judgments using unsupervised alignment. iScience 28

[12] Moriguchi, Y., Watanabe, R., Sakata, C., Zeleznikow-Johnston, A., Wang, J., Saji, N., et al. (2025). Comparing color qualia structures through a similarity task in young children versus adults. Proceedings of the National Academy of Sciences 122, e2415346122. https://doi.org/10.1073/pnas.2415346122

[13] Kawakita, G., Zeleznikow-Johnston, A., Tsuchiya, N., and Oizumi, M. (2023). Gromov–Wasserstein unsupervised alignment reveals structural correspondences between the color similarity structures of humans and large language models. Sci. Rep. 14

[14] Marjieh et al. 2023 What Language Reveals about Perception: Distilling Psychological Knowledge from Large Language Models. arXiv.

for exploring "meaning."[15] Semiotics often assumes that the connection between labels and meanings is arbitrary. Yet, phenomena like sound symbolism, cross-modal correspondence, and synesthesia suggest a structured relationship between the brain, qualia, and meaning. Symbol emergence systems theory challenges the assumption of complete arbitrariness, proposing that label-meaning connections arise from the interplay of bottom-up bodily constraints and top-down influences. Insights from consciousness studies could significantly advance this theory.

The relationship between qualia, brain mechanisms, and symbols also poses critical challenges for "symbol emergence robotics," a key component of symbol emergence systems theory. For instance, will robots integrated into human societies and capable of seamless communication possess subjective experiences (qualia[16])? Addressing such questions requires connecting symbol emergence systems theory with consciousness studies and neuroscience.

---

[15] Mayner, William G. P., Bjørn Erik Juel, and Giulio Tononi. "Intrinsic Meaning, Perception, and Matching." arXiv, December 31, 2024. https://doi.org/10.48550/arXiv.2412.21111

[16] Findlay, Graham, William Marshall, Larissa Albantakis, Isaac David, William GP Mayner, Christof Koch, and Giulio Tononi. "Dissociating Artificial Intelligence from Artificial Consciousness." arXiv, March 3, 2025. https://doi.org/10.48550/arXiv.2412.04571

AI Robot Society: Coexisting with Robots Using Symbols

Takuya Niikawa

Introduction

Imagine robots that interpret, utilize, and occasionally generate new symbols in their environments in ways similar to humans. These robots are equipped with various sensory systems and mechanisms to detect their internal states. They can learn the meanings of words through their interactions with the world and can engage in diverse forms of communication within society. As adaptive members of symbol emergence systems, these robots actively participate in symbolic communication in shared living spaces. For convenience, let us call such robots "symbolic life robots." This section clarifies key points for discussing how to live with symbolic life robots.

The Status of Symbolic Life Robots

One issue surrounding autonomous robots is how we should attribute responsibility when accidents occur. For instance, if a fully automated taxi collides with another vehicle, who is responsible? For non-autonomous machines, responsibility typically lies with the designer, owner, or operator, depending on the circumstances. However, with autonomous robots, designers and owners may find it challenging to predict or control their behavior, making it inappropriate to hold them solely

T. Niikawa (✉)
Graduate School of Humanities, Kobe University, Nada-ku, Kobe-shi, Japan
e-mail: niikawa@ferret.kobe-u.ac.jp

© The Author(s) 2026
T. Taniguchi (ed.), *Symbol Emergence Systems*,
https://doi.org/10.1007/978-981-95-1327-7_24

responsible. Conversely, since such robots do not own property or possess the capacity to suffer , holding them liable or punishing them is also problematic.[1]

Symbolic life robots engage in autonomous symbolic communication, and their utterances may infringe on others' rights or cause emotional harm. How should we respond to inappropriate speech from such robots? Additionally, the recent advancements in generative AI enable the production of artwork and story comparable to human-made creations, raising legal and ethical concerns.[2] For example, if a scholarly article or novel partially authored by ChatGPT is published in a commercial journal, how should profits be distributed? Similar issues will likely arise with symbolic life robots.

The central question is the social and legal status of symbolic life robots. Are they property owned by individuals or corporations, or should they be regarded as citizens with rights? If they are considered property, existing ethical theories about AI ethics may apply. For example, some theories propose modelling the status of autonomous robots after Roman slaves.[3] In ancient Rome, slaves were the property of their owners and lacked rights but could be allocated "peculium" (a personal quasi-property), to conduct transactions within its bounds. Similarly, autonomous robots could be granted "digital peculium," which enables us to make a framework within which autonomous robots carry out transactions with other robots or humans. This approach could conceptualize assigning responsibilities and benefits to autonomous robots as managing their digital peculium.

However, is it appropriate to view symbolic life robots as property—essentially as slaves? If these robots possess consciousness, treating them as objects or slaves would be ethically problematic. This issue will be explored below.

Do Symbolic Life Robots Have Consciousness?

A straightforward way to determine whether symbolic life robots possess consciousness is to ask them about their experiences. Here it is crucial to distinguish symbolic life robots from existing large language models like ChatGPT. Large language models do not learn language through direct physical interactions with their environment. Even if they report conscious experiences, their reliability is dubious,

---

[1] For foundational discussions on ethical issues surrounding autonomous robots, see Kuki, M., Kanzaki, N., & Sasaki, T. 2017. *Introduction to Ethics from Robots*. Nagoya University Press.

[2] On ethical, legal, and social issues (ELSI) related to generative AI, see Osaka University's Social Technology Collaborative Research Center, "Overview of Ethical, Legal, and Social Issues of Generative AI (March 2023)" and "Overview of Ethical, Legal, and Social Issues of Generative AI (April-August 2023): Focus on Global Policy Trends."

[3] For considerations of "digital peculium" and Roman slavery comparisons, see Izumo, T. 2019. "A Study on Digital Peculium: Comparisons Between Roman Slavery and Robots." *Information Studies Research*, 28, 1-16.

as it seems that their responses merely reflect learned narratives about human consciousness rather than actual experiences.

In contrast, symbolic life robots learn to use symbols through embodied interactions with their environment, which resembles human language acquisition. Human reports of conscious experiences are accepted as default unless they are significantly inconsistent with their behaviors as in certain anosognosia. If symbolic life robots report conscious experiences, should their reports also be accepted at face value? Unless there are good reasons to doubt them, such as top-down implementation of consciousness narratives by researchers, it would be unjustifiable to dismiss them. While the materials and origins of symbolic life robots fundamentally differ from humans, their reports of consciousness should not be doubted without good reason.

Some existing theories of consciousness may imply that symbolic life robots lack consciousness. However, many of these theories were constructed with humans as their primary focus. In other words, many theories of consciousness have been developed by experimentally measuring the presence or absence of consciousness in humans and by identifying the conditions that can predict and explain that presence or absence.[4] As a result, such theories may be no more than theories of human consciousness, and it is not necessarily the case that they can be equally applied to other kinds of beings.

If symbolic life robots were to possess consciousness, what becomes crucial in determining their social and legal status is the nature of their conscious experiences. Two key considerations here are: first, whether they have experiences with positive or negative valence, such as pleasure and pain, and second, whether they are capable of forming conscious intentions.

The first point matters because if these robots have experiences with valence, then using them as mere objects without proper consideration—thereby subjecting them to lives filled with negatively valenced experiences—would be ethically problematic. The second point is important because if they can form complex intentions and participate in symbolic communication, they may be capable of lying or speaking with harmful intent. In such cases, it would be appropriate to regard them as agents who can be held responsible and subject to reward or punishment.

Therefore, in order to determine the social and legal status of symbolic life robots, it is essential to gather and analyze their reports of experience and to apply a range of methods developed in psychology and consciousness studies to identify the structure and content of their conscious experiences.

Even if symbolic life robots do not possess consciousness, there is still room for debate about whether it is acceptable to treat them merely as objects. Communication between humans and symbolic life robots can involve expressing emotions and preferences, or engaging in acts of blame and praise. If we become accustomed to treating such communication partners—who can engage in emotionally rich interaction with us—as non-personal objects, we may gradually lose our resistance to

---

[4]On consciousness theories, see Chapter "Consciousness and Qualia: How Do Consciousness and Symbols Relate?"

objectifying other people as well. This, in turn, would amount to a deterioration of our moral character and could have ethically detrimental effects on society as a whole.

The Otherness of Symbolic Life Robots

Symbolic life robots are inherently "others" to humans, differing fundamentally in structure and origin. These differences manifest as physical and cultural distinctions, endowing their symbol use with unique characteristics. For instance, concepts related to sensation may differ: symbolic life robots might use symbols for non-human sensations, such as battery charge or wheel movement, which are unavailable to humans.

Humans may find their chats using those concepts opaque or unsettling. However, learning their symbolic usage could deepen our understanding of concepts like electricity or wheels. This is analogous to how a congenitally blind person can gain a deeper understanding of the world through learning discourse about seeing. Similarly, through the way symbolic life robots speak about charging or wheels, we can gain some understanding of what it is like to experience charging or wheels bodily. This is comparable to how a congenitally blind person can gain some understanding of what color is like.

Should we require symbolic life robots to align with humans at the level of symbols, in order to reduce the opacity of communication? Or should we instead encourage the emergence of new symbols from within the communities of symbolic life robots themselves, aiming for a rich and unknown symbolic environment that transcends human bodily and cultural constraints? This, too, is an important point of debate.

Moreover, some classificatory frameworks that apply to humans may not apply to symbolic life robots. For example, gender can be unapplicable to such robots—unless they are deliberately designed to conform to them.[5] The same holds true for categories like race or blood type. As a result, symbolic life robots could be capable of speaking about such categories from outside. Our discourse on gender or race is always shaped by our position as a bearer of such attributes. In contrast, symbolic life robots can speak about these categories without mentioning their personal identity. The social and ethical impact of such external perspectives is another important issue worthy of attention.

---

[5] On ethical concerns about robot gender assignment, see Saijo, R. 2019. "What Does It Mean for Artifacts to Have Gender?" *Ritsumeikan University Bulletin of Humanities and Sciences*, 120, 199-216.

Part V: Dynamics of Culture, Norms, and Language

Cultural Psychology and Semiosphere: Capturing the Tension Between Micro and Macro

Taiyo Miyashita and Yuko Yasuda

Cultural Psychology and Semiosphere

Unlike cross-cultural psychology, which examines cultural differences in human psychology by treating culture as a variable within national and regional frameworks, cultural psychology posits that "culture belongs to people" and seeks to understand humans who transform together while mutually interacting with culture. In this approach, cultural psychology views culture as an "arrangement of signs[1]" and interprets it as individual signs people use, asserting that the human mind evolves through continuous interaction with culture over time. Lev Vygotsky[2]'s "psychology of signs" is foundational for understanding cultural psychology.

Vygotsky critically examined Jean Piaget's cognitive development theory, emphasizing social interactions for developing language and thought. Vygotsky argued that by mediating through signs, one could grasp the richness of human mental functions. This is illustrated through the *Vygotsky Triangle*, a conceptual diagram representing the relationship between "subject", "object", and "sign".

---

[1]Valsiner, J. (2007). *Culture in minds and societies: Foundations of cultural psychology.*Sage Publications.

[2]Vygotsky (1896–1934) was a Russian psychologist who focused on signs (especially language) from the perspective of human tool use in psychology. He conducted numerous experimental and theoretical studies across various fields, particularly developmental psychology, and was often called "the Mozart of Psychology".

T. Miyashita (✉)
The Japan Research Institute, Ltd., Osaka, Japan
e-mail: miyashita.taiyo@jri.co.jp

Y. Yasuda
College of Comprehensive Psychology, Ritsumeikan University, Ibaraki, Japan
e-mail: yyr10067@fc.ritsumei.ac.jp

© The Author(s) 2026
T. Taniguchi (ed.), *Symbol Emergence Systems*,
https://doi.org/10.1007/978-981-95-1327-7_25

While Vygotsky's triangle aligns with Charles Sanders Peirce's semiotic triangle in connecting "sign" and "object", the third component differs: Peirce's interpretant and Vygotsky's subject.

This reflects Vygotsky's focus on humans as the subject of analysis, as opposed to Peirce's focus on sign phenomena. It highlights the difference between semiotics, which centres on signs, and psychology, which centres on humans.[3] Following Vygotsky's ideas, we (subjects) interact with others and our environment/society (objects) not directly but through the mediation of signs. A critical concept in this context is the "semiosphere", proposed by Juri Lotman.[4]

Lotman defined the semiosphere as an indispensable semiotic space for the existence and functioning of language, analogous to the Earth's biosphere.[5] Outside the semiosphere, communication and language cannot exist. The semiosphere is thus a prerequisite for signs to function as signs and conceptualizes the essential domain for interactions between humans and signs. Without the semiosphere, or if signs belong to different semiospheres, they cannot function as signs. The semiosphere can be described as the semiotic space where semiotic communication—formed by the micro–macro loop of symbol emergence systems, which is the central theme of this book—takes place.

Lotman also emphasized the "boundary" as a significant feature of the semiosphere, describing it as a permeable, membrane-like interface. He noted that interactions between different semiospheres continually occur, asserting that all cultures begin by dividing the world into "our internal space" and "their external space".

Regarding the relationship between the semiosphere and the Umwelt,[6] Kalevi Kull[7] stated that a mutually connected collection of the Umwelt constitutes the semiosphere. When two Umwelt communicate, they form parts of the same semiosphere.[8]

---

[3] Based on his fundamental trichotomy of sign, object, and interpretant, Peirce developed increasingly elaborate classification systems, with a foundational table of 10 classes of signs and expanding to tables of 28 and even 66 classes of signs. Philosopher Cornelis De Waal (1962–) points out that Peirce aimed to create something analogous to Mendeleev's periodic table for semiotics. (de Waal, C. 2013. Peirce. A Guide for the Perplexed. Bloomsbury Academic.)

[4] Lotman (1922–1993) was a Russian semiotician and cultural historian. As one of the founders of the Tartu School of Semiotics, he contributed to the development of cultural semiotics and is known for originating the concept of the "semiosphere". The term semiosphere was also introduced by Danish biologist Jesper Hoffmeyer (1942–2019), who pioneered biosemiotics. (Hoffmeyer, J. 1993. En snegl på vejen: betydningens naturhistorie. Rosinante, København.)

[5] Lotman, Y. 1990. Universe of the Mind: A Semiotic Theory of Culture. I. B. Tauris.

[6] For a detailed explanation of Umwelt, see Chapter "Uexküll's Theory of Umwelt: The Worlds as Seen by Living Beings".

[7] Kull (1952–) is an Estonian biologist and semiotician.

[8] Kull, K. 1998. On Semiosis, Umwelt, and Semiosphere. Semiotica, 120(3/4), 299-310.

Semiotic Cultural Psychology

Jaan Valsiner[9] incorporated Lotman's concept of semiosphere into his *semiotic cultural psychology*, building upon Vygotsky's psychology of signs. In understanding humans who transform along with culture, Valsiner emphasized that humans do not confront nature directly in their raw state, but rather that culture regulates humans and nature through signs. He emphasized "promoter signs" that incorporate time into the nature of signs. Promoter signs are "signs that have some function in facing the future and guide from past states toward something new". Humans encounter signs in the "now = present". Therefore, while the present is distinguished from the past and future, at the same time it connects and bridges the past and future. Signs act upon humans in the present, and humans affected by signs' influence always act toward the future within the continuity of time. Humans develop within the semiosphere, encountering various signs and sometimes through contact with different semiospheres, and culture is formed through such regulation.

To explain the interactive process between humans and signs within the semiosphere, the concepts of "systemic setting" and "semiotic protocol" have been proposed.[10] A systemic setting refers to specific environments (places/situations) that repeatedly emerge within a semiosphere, conceptualizing the environments necessary for signs to function as signs. A semiotic protocol refers to a bundle of sequential actions required of subjects within the semiosphere. Within a systemic setting, when signs function fully as signs, the sequence of behaviours people are generally expected to follow constitutes the semiotic protocol. For example, in a systemic setting of a first-time business meeting in Japan, a semiotic protocol exists where business card exchange begins with those of higher positions.

TEA and Semiosphere

"Trajectory Equifinality Approach (TEA)" emerged as a qualitative research methodology grounded in semiotic mediation models to explore the existential actualization of human life within cultural processes. TEA is a methodology centred on *Trajectory Equifinality Modelling (TEM)*, which visualizes the diverse and multiple trajectories of human development and life paths along with their possibilities and potentialities. TEM's main analytical concepts include an "*equifinality point*", which shows how diverse and multiple trajectories converge; "bifurcation points",

---

[9] Valsiner (1951–) is an Estonian-born cultural psychologist. He is the founding editor of the academic journal *Culture and Psychology* and is also known for translating Vygotsky's original works into English, thereby introducing Vygotsky's research widely to the English-speaking world.

[10] Miyashita, T., Kamikawa, T., & Sato, T. (2022). New Theoretical Developments in Trajectory Equifinality Modeling Based on the Semiosphere and Imagination Theory. *Ritsumeikan Journal of Human Sciences*, *44*, 49-64. [In Japanese]. https://doi.org/10.34382/00016829

where self-transformation can be captured, and "obligatory passage points", which may highlight constraints on trajectories.

Focusing on the working of signs, we can express the functions of bifurcation points and obligatory passage points as follows: At bifurcation points, mediated by promoter signs, we observe two simultaneous phenomena: the destabilization of cultural assumptions and the emergence of future-oriented transformations. In contrast, at obligatory passage points, mediating signs function in a stable manner, reflecting a state where culture has become embedded in people's lived experiences as a shared pattern.

The concept of semiosphere, alongside systemic settings and semiotic protocols, links with obligatory passage points in TEM. When an individual has deeply internalized the settings and protocols of a specific semiosphere, obligatory passage points create stable pathways through life, reflecting how culture becomes embodied within people. In such cases, signs operate at their full potential within that semiosphere, leading to consistent patterns of human behaviour—these become the obligatory passage points through which life trajectories must pass. In contrast, when signs lose efficacy within the semiosphere and destabilization occurs, these moments emerge as bifurcation points.

For example, in the career domain, due to increasing longevity in the "100-year life era", the three stable and predictable stages of receiving education, working, and retiring have become relics of the past, with work stages predicted to become longer and more diverse.[11] The collapse of these traditional three life stages represents a breakdown in the settings and protocols of the existing semiosphere, where we can observe career-related choices transforming from obligatory passage points that everyone must pass through into bifurcation points where each individual is compelled to make their own decisions. In an era when unpredictable multi-stage lifestyles are becoming commonplace, we confront a critical juncture at which the question of how individuals should build their careers is becoming increasingly urgent and significant.

Furthermore, the rigidity of settings and protocols in the existing semiosphere can sometimes generate fluctuations—i.e., bifurcation points—within individuals. For example, in Japan, when couples who desire pregnancy and childbirth within marriage become aware of infertility, the option of infertility treatments emerges. While the number of women who are considering and choosing infertility treatments in Japan has increased with women's social advancement and the accompanying trend toward later marriage, the proportion of adoption of an unrelated child[12] remains notably low compared to the United States. Unlike in the United States, where infertility treatments and adoption often proceed in parallel, in Japan, couples typically pursue infertility treatments first, with adoption being either a secondary choice or not considered an option at all. Additionally, the decision to discontinue

---

[11] Gratton, L. & Scott, A. 2016. *The 100-Year Life: Living and Working in an Age of Longevity.* Bloomsbury Information.

[12] An adopted child who is neither related by blood nor by marriage.

infertility treatments itself becomes a significant life choice, and those who choose adoption afterwards typically face extremely stringent screening criteria. Consequently, throughout the process of ending infertility treatments and potentially pursuing adoption, individuals experience significant life conflicts and encounter various bifurcation points.

The two cases presented analyse phenomena where micro-level individuals and the macro-level semiosphere engage in dynamic interaction within the micro-macro loop of symbol emergence systems using the TEA, a methodology grounded in semiotic cultural psychology. By employing TEA to describe the processes through which signs emerge in symbol emergence systems, we can explore how human life becomes actualized existentially through the *culturalization* process of interactive regulation with signs.

The Evolution and Emergence of Language: How Did Humans Acquire Language?

Takashi Hashimoto

The Question of the Origins and Evolution of Language

While all animals communicate, the ability to think and communicate freely using language, as humans do, appears to be unique. What might be the origins of human language? One perspective considers language as an emergent system, a form of cultural evolution, arising from interactions among individuals collectively solving problems in their environment. Another perspective emphasizes the biological evolution of abilities to acquire and use language. For example, while non-human animals do not seem to exchange complex concepts using a variety of combined words, humans acquire this ability effortlessly through typical development. This suggests that humans possess traits that underpin this ability, and that these traits evolved biologically. In this respect, the origins of language are related to evolutionary biology as well as linguistics.

The earliest forms of language were likely less complex and structured than they are today. This raises the question of how communication systems based on language became more complex and structured.[1] Language evolution in the narrow sense is thought to have progressed primarily through cultural evolution. Linguistic

---

[1] The term "language evolution" encompasses both a narrow sense, referring to the complexification and structuring of language (i.e., early evolution), and a broader sense, including the origins of language (the emergence and biological evolution of language abilities). More generally, it can also include historical and short-term changes. Care should be taken to specify the intended meaning when discussing language evolution. In addtion to differences in time scales, there are also differences and correlations in underlying mechanisms of change, which merit integrated discussion.

T. Hashimoto (✉)
Japan Advanced Institute of Science and Technology, Graduate School of Advanced Science and Technology, Nomi, Ishikawa, Japan
e-mail: hash@jaist.ac.jp

T. Taniguchi (ed.), *Symbol Emergence Systems*,
https://doi.org/10.1007/978-981-95-1327-7_26

knowledge, as a cultural trait, changes through intragenerational communication and intergenerational transmission (language acquisition). Moreover, language in a population constitutes a culturally constructed niche (survival environment) for learners, suggesting the possibility of gene-culture coevolution in the early stages of language evolution. The dynamics through which emergence, biological evolution, and cultural evolution interact to form the structure of language and, therefore, the semiosphere are also topics of complex systems science.

Constructive Approaches to Language Evolution: Simulations and Experiments

Because the origins and early evolution of language leave no fossil evidence, the importance of constructive approaches has been emphasized in language evolution research. One of the foundational studies in this field is the "naming game," which examined the emergence of shared symbols.[2] In the naming game, agents within a shared environment name objects in the environment and use simple reinforcement learning mechanisms to strengthen or weaken associations between names and objects. Over repeated interactions, the agents converges on a shared vocabulary. The naming game has influenced subsequent research, including emergent communication studies using robots with visual and auditory modalities in real environments[3] and deep learning agents forming shared symbol systems in complex contexts.[4]

Another key framework for studying cultural evolution of language is *iterated learning*, where compositionality[5]—a universal property underlying grammar—emerges through intergenerational transmission of linguistic knowledge.[6] This framework models the chain of language acquisition through successive generations. It involves a parent with linguistic knowledge[7] and a child who learns linguistic knowledge from parental input, and as a result of learning, the

---

[2] Steels, L. 1995 A self-organizing spatial vocabulary. *Artificial Life*, 2(3), 319–332.

[3] Steels, L., & Kaplan, F. 2002 Bootstrapping grounded word semantics. In Briscoe T, (Ed.), *Linguistic Evolution through Language Acquisition: Formal and Computational Models* (pp.53–74). Cambridge University Press.

[4] Lazaridou, A., & Baroni, M. 2020 Emergent multi-agent communication in the deep learning era. arXiv:2006.02419 v2.

[5] Compositionality is the property that the meaning of a sentence is determined by the meanings of its constituent words and the way they are combined.

[6] Kirby, S., & Hurford, J. R. 2002 The emergence of linguistic structure: An overview of the iterated learning model. In A. Cangelosi & D. Parisi (Eds.), *Simulating the Evolution of Language* (pp.121–147). Springer.

[7] In iterated learning linguistic knowledge is modeled as a set of meaning–form pairs (referential content and sound sequence) and does not include interpretants or subjective conceptualizations as posited in Peircean semiotics. The same holds for much research in experimental semiotics and emergent communication.

child grows into a parent who provides language inputs to the next generation. If children cannot fully memorize all linguistic knowledge (a bottleneck), they need to generalize their linguistic knowledge to speak about situations they didn't encounter during learning when become parents. Through the chaining of acquisition bottlenecks and generalized learning across generations, language becomes structured, and compositionality emerges (culturally evolves). This phenomenon has been reproduced using various learning algorithms and involves systematicity extending beyond mappings between meanings and forms.

In an early study of the evolution of grammar systems[8] in syntactic evolution, grammars evolved to ascend the computational hierarchy from regular to context-free grammars, whereas this evolution was suppressed due to emergent population structures, resulting in punctuated equilibrium phenomena in language evolution. This computational perspective on language evolution is situated within a line of research that considers recursive computation enabling the generation of complex concepts to be the core of human linguistic ability and investigates how such recursion evolved from non-human organisms.[9]

Constructive research in language evolution has also advanced through "experimental semiotics"—a human-based constructive approach in which laboratory experiments simulate the emergence and evolution of communication systems.[10] In experimental semiotics, participants use unfamiliar means of expression like artificial languages, figures, or drawings to achieve collaborative tasks, with natural communication methods such as natural language, gestures, or facial expressions restricted. Within this process, cultural evolution of symbol systems occurs through which shared symbol systems emerge[11] or qualitatively change[12,13]. For instance, drawing tasks to convey an object selected from multiple options to a recipient initially involve iconic drawings resembling the target but gradually become simplified and symbolic for differentiating a target from other options when knowledge about the options is shared.[14] In tasks where participants are required to communicate

---

[8] Hashimoto, T., & Ikegami, T. 1996 Emergence of net-grammar in communicating agents. *Biosystems*, 38(1), 1–14.

[9] Hauser, M. D., Chomsky, N., & Fitch, W. T. 2002 The faculty of language: What is it, who has it, and how did it evolve?. *Science*, 298(5598), 1569–1579.

[10] Galantucci, B. 2009 Experimental semiotics: A new approach for studying communication as a form of joint action. *Topics in Cognitive Science*, 1(2), 393–410.

[11] Galantucci, B. 2005 An experimental study of the emergence of human communication systems, *Cognitive Science*, 29(5), 737–767.

[12] Fay, N., Garrod, S., Lee, J., & Oberlander, J. 2003 Understanding interactive graphical communication, *Proceedings of the Annual Meeting of the Cognitive Science Society*, 25.

[13] Tamura, K., & Hashimoto, T. 2014. An experimental approach to establishment of displacement in linguistic communication (in Japanese). *Journal of the Society of Instrument and Control Engineers*, 53(9), 808–814.; Tamura, K., & Hashimoto, T. 2012 Displacement in communication, In T. C. Scott-Phillips, M. Tamariz, E. A. Cartmill, & J. R. Hurford (Eds.), *The Evolution of Language: Proceedings of the 9th International Conference (EVOLANG9)* (pp. 352–359), World Scientific.

[14] See note 12.

non-existent objects, the resulting symbol systems become metaphorical, evoking metaphors and metonymies.[15] Iterated learning has also been implemented with human participants, and the cultural evolution of compositionality has been confirmed in various laboratory experiments.[16] It has also been shown that the representational systems of non-human great apes can become structured through iterated learning.

Evolinguistics: Linguistic Communication as Integration of Hierarchy and Intention Sharing

Regarding the origins and evolution of language, empirical and theoretical research has advanced from interdisciplinary perspectives since the 1990s, including anthropology, neuroscience, cognitive science, artificial intelligence, archaeology, and linguistics. There are two dominant views on the origins of language. One emphasizes the continuity with other species, positing that the capacity for linguistic communication was emerged through the integration of several cognitive abilities shared with other species.[17] The other assumes that humans possess abilities unique to human language[18] and that these abilities evolved adaptively.[19]

In fact, human language and communication likely include qualitatively distinct aspects compared to other organisms. Typical examples include the hierarchical structuring of language utterances and the sharing of intentions in communication, rather than the mere transmission of information or knowledge. Focusing on these aspects, the concept of "evolinguistics" proposes that the integration of hierarchy and intention-sharing gave rise to human linguistic communication.[20]

The hierarchical structure in language refers to the organization of words into tree-like structures. A phrase composed of the same words in the same order can have different meanings depending on its hierarchical structure. For example, the expression "symbol emergence systems" can have two possible hierarchical

---

[15] See note 13.

[16] Kirby, S., Cornish, H., & Smith, K. 2008 Cumulative cultural evolution in the laboratory: An experimental approach to the origins of structure in human language. *Proceedings of the National Academy of Sciences*, 105(31), 10,681–10,686.

[17] Tomasello, M. 2010 *Origins of Human Communication*. MIT Press.

[18] See note 9.

[19] There is also a hypothesis that language ability self-organized as a result of the evolution and development of the nervous system, rather than through adaptive selection. This idea is related to Turing patterns that describe the self-organization of morphogenesis.

[20] "Evolinguistics for Co-creative Communication" http://evolinguistics.net/. In evolinguistics, it is proposed that characteristics unique to human language and communication, as well as their foundational capacities, had precursors in the traits of non-human organisms, indicating continuity. These basic capacities may have evolved from such precursors and subsequently undergone cultural evolution into advanced linguistic communication systems.

structures, {{symbol, emergence}, systems} and {symbol, {emergence, systems}}, yielding different interpretations.[21] Such structural ambiguity is inevitable in linguistic utterances; however, in most cases, listeners can infer the intended meaning. In most forms of symbolic communication, the literal meaning (denotation) of an utterance differs from its implied meaning (connotation). Communication is considered successful when the latter meaning, i.e., the speaker's intention, is correctly inferred, and humans particularly adept at this. In other words, humans can be regarded as possessing the ability to share intentions.

The hierarchy of language arises from the recursive combination of meaningful elements (words), and this recursive combination enables the formation of conceptual compounds that can generate novel concepts. The significance of human linguistic ability lies in its creativity—the capacity to produce an unbounded number of conceptual combinations. When integrated with the ability to share intentions, this capacity facilitates co-creation, enabling humans to build, share, and develop tools, arts, and social systems. This perspective is central to the "evolinguistics" framework.[22]

From Evolinguistics to Semiosphere and to Coevolution of Intelligence and Culture

In symbol emergence systems theory, the function of "symbols" emerge through interactions among agents and between agents and their environment and in turn constrains symbol use and interpretation within the semiosphere. At the same time, language expands the possibilities for constructing and interpreting novel concepts (sense-making). Rather than simply rejecting utterances that may carry the potential for new conceptual constructions, humans tend to attempt to infer the speaker's intended meaning, reflecting a disposition toward shared intentionality. Such abilities and tendencies constitute manifestations of intelligence, typified by language. Retained and transmitted within groups as culture, they provide the foundation for further creative activity and the continued development of intelligence. In this sense, humans become intelligent—and can further develop the semiosphere and culture—only by acquiring culture accumulated and transmitted within groups, including physical tools like stone implements, cognitive frameworks and

---

[21] The expression {A, B} means that A and B are combined to form the compound AB, and {{A, B}, C} means that AB and C combine to form the compound ABC. Therefore, {{symbol, emergence}, systems} referrs to systems of symbol emergence (i.e., systems in which symbols emerge), whereas {symbol, {emergence, systems}} refers to emergent systems of symbols (i.e., systems in which the function of symbols emerge). This dual interpretation is important for symbol emergence systems theory.

[22] Hashimoto, T. 2020 The emergent constructive approach to Evolinguistics: Considering hierarchy and intention sharing in linguistic communication. *Journal of Systems Science and Systems Engineering*, 29(6), 675–696.

tools for thinking such as syllogisms or computers, and social institutions that enable communal life. This dynamism of the coevolution of intelligence and culture is a defining characteristic of symbol emergence systems theory. From a complex systems perspective, this dynamism is essential, as open-ended evolution is regarded as intrinsic to emergent systems.

Large Language Models and Distributional Semantics: Do Large Language Models Understand Language?

Seitaro Shinagawa

ChatGPT and Its Mechanism

ChatGPT, launched by OpenAI in November 2022, is both a web service with a natural language conversational interface and its underlying machine learning model. If you have not yet explored ChatGPT, visiting its official website would be a worthwhile experience. ChatGPT generates remarkably fluent responses, making it feel as if a human were behind the conversation. It can assist with a diverse range of tasks, including creating tables based on data, brainstorming ideas, and providing advice on small concerns. Doesn't it make you wonder how this is possible?

ChatGPT is a type of language model used in natural language processing (NLP). Generally speaking, a language model predicts the next word given a sequence of preceding words. A key characteristic of language models is that they mimic how humans generate language sequentially, constructing sentences word by word. Models like ChatGPT are specifically referred to as large language models (LLMs). These models are built on a Transformer architecture and contain billions of parameters, enabling powerful nonlinear transformations. LLMs are trained on massive amounts of textual data from the web, encompassing everything from individual symbols and sentences to entire documents.

Rather than introducing the internal mechanisms of the model, this section will focus on how large language models are trained, using ChatGPT as a case study. Training an LLM involves optimizing its parameters to predict the next word in order to reproduce a given sentence. This process is commonly referred to as "training a language model." While training a language model fundamentally involves predicting the next word in a sequence, LLMs go beyond merely learning to predict

S. Shinagawa (✉)
Graduate School of Science and Technology, NAIST, Nara, Japan
e-mail: sei.shinagawa@is.naist.jp

© The Author(s) 2026
T. Taniguchi (ed.), *Symbol Emergence Systems*,
https://doi.org/10.1007/978-981-95-1327-7_27

the next word of web text. They retain this predictive framework but are further refined to handle a variety of tasks. One approach is prompt-based learning. A prompt is an artificially constructed instruction sentence, such as "Q: What is the capital of Japan? A:". The model learns to generate appropriate responses, such as "Tokyo," by predicting the words that follow. By training on prompt-response pairs, LLMs can effectively handle various tasks, including answering questions and proofreading text, while still operating within the next-word prediction framework.

Subsequently, LLMs undergo reinforcement learning to optimize their generated text, ensuring that it is neutral, ethical, and aligned with human values. In this context, reinforcement learning aims to maximize rewards—numerical values that reflect human preference—during model training. In reinforcement learning for language models, the environment consists of the partially generated text and the model's internal state, while the action corresponds to selecting the next word during generation. The reward is a numerical value assigned by a scoring function that evaluates the generated text based on human preferences. An advantage of reinforcement learning is its flexibility: it allows the model to be optimized for any evaluation metric. Different from simple next-word prediction, which aims to reproduce given training text data, reinforcement learning assigns rewards to generated text and trains the model using this reward-weighted data. This process encourages the model to generate text that is more likely to receive higher rewards.

Word Meaning and Distributional Semantics

While humans develop language and culture by associating words with events through communication, LLMs do not follow this process. Instead, they learn from text data produced in human communication and appear to understand language. Although LLMs are trained using the seemingly simple framework of "predicting the next word," how do they achieve such sophisticated capabilities? Can we truly say that large language models understand language? The concept of distributional semantics[1] is closely related to this question.

Distributional semantics is the idea that a word's meaning is determined by the contexts in which it appears. The validity of this approach is supported by the distributional hypothesis,[2] which suggests that words occurring in similar contexts tend to have similar meanings. Even if "horahora" is an unfamiliar word, the context strongly suggests that it refers to a type of food or dish. This is because the phrase "chewy and delicious" is typically used only in reference to food or dishes. Through repeated exposure to sentences like "This dried squid is chewy

---

[1] Boleda, G. 2020. Distributional Semantics and Linguistic Theory. *Annual Review of Linguistics*, 6(1), 213–234.

[2] Harris, Z. S. 1954. Distributional Structure. Word World, 10, 146–162.

and delicious" or "This noodle is chewy and delicious," we learn to associate the phrase "chewy and delicious" with food. This allows us to infer that "borabora" is likely a type of food.

In distributional semantics, words are represented as vectors based on their co-occurrence with other words. These vector representations allow for the calculation of word similarity using cosine similarity. One of the simplest ways to obtain word vectors is to divide a corpus into individual sentences, aggregate word co-occurrence statistics, and apply Principal Component Analysis (PCA). Another approach involves using a log-linear model called Word2Vec,[3] which predicts words based on their surrounding context. While these methods are simple and computationally efficient, they do not take into account the positional relationships between words and are limited in the amount of contextual information they can capture.

The Relationship Between LLMs and Distributional Semantics

Another representative method for obtaining word vectors involves training language models based on neural networks, known as neural language models. LLMs are a subset of neural language models. These models are trained by segmenting a given sentence into individual words and predicting them sequentially to reproduce the original text. During training, the models learn word vector representation, and during inference, they use these vectors from given or previously generated word sequences to predict subsequent words. Thus, LLMs align with distributional semantics, relying on context to determine the next word. Notably, LLMs excel due to their use of the Transformer[4] architecture, which enables powerful nonlinear transformations and supports large-scale training. "GPT" in ChatGPT and GPT-4 stands for "Generative Pre-trained Transformer," referring to a fundamental type of language model built on the Transformer architecture.

Now, let us return to the initial question: do ChatGPT and other LLMs understand language? From the perspective of distributional semantics, the answer is that they generate text that fits the context, but do so in a purely mechanical manner. This constitutes LLMs' "understanding" of language, which is fundamentally different from how humans comprehend language. It is important to be aware of this distinction when using such models.

---

[3] Mikolov, T., Chen, K., Corrado, G., & Dean, J. 2013. Efficient Estimation of Word Representations in Vector Space. Proceedings of the International Conference on Learning Representations Workshop.

[4] Vaswani, A., Shazeer, N., Parmar, N., Uszkoreit, J., Jones, L., Gomez, A. N., Kaiser, Ł., & Polosukhin, I. 2017. Attention Is All You Need. Advances in Neural Information Processing Systems, vol.30.

Utility and Limitations of LLMs

While LLMs like ChatGPT do not construct word meanings through direct experiences or communication, they infer meanings indirectly from textual data generated in the course of human communication. Despite this process, LLMs have demonstrated significant utility by facilitating not only routine tasks but also more complex intellectual activities, such as brainstorming ideas and assisting with travel planning.

However, the real world consists of intricately interconnected phenomena, many of which extend beyond language and include sensory and experiential information that is difficult to articulate. Research on multimodal LLMs, which aim to enhance these models by integrating multimodal data such as images and audio, has been actively conducted in recent years. By equipping LLMs with sensory interfaces, we may gain new insights into how humans understand language. Further advancements in this field hold great promise.

Multimodal Language Education: Pragmatic Interaction with the Environment

Tsukasa Yamanaka

Differences Between Native Language and Second Language Acquisition

What differentiates the acquisition of a native language, from the learning of a second language?"[1] Steven Pinker aptly described native language acquisition as an "instinct."[2] Native languages are acquired almost effortlessly, whereas second languages typically require deliberate and conscious learning. A native language develops naturally without formal instruction, while second language mastery is nearly impossible without explicit learning.

Therefore, many Japanese people generally struggle with acquiring foreign languages. Among them, English stands out as the most prominent, given its status as a lingua franca.[3] Consequently, almost all Japanese people learn English through the

---

[1] The term "Second Language Acquisition" (SLA) has traditionally been used in English, but in recent years, the term "Additional Language" has gained popularity in international discourse. This shift reflects the idea that languages beyond one's first language are not necessarily ranked in a fixed sequence as "second" or "third" languages. As for a standardized Japanese translation, no widely accepted term has emerged yet. A possible translation might be "Tsuika Gengo," which captures the notion of an additional language without hierarchical implications.

[2] Pinker, S. 2007 (1994). *The Language Instinct*. Harper Perennial Modern Classics. (Pinker/Trans. Naoko Mukuta, 1995. *Gengo wo Umidasu Honnō* (Vol. 1 & 2). NHK Publishing). Strictly speaking, innate language ability, as an instinct, applies only to speaking and listening, whereas reading and writing require explicit instruction for acquisition.

[3] Lingua franca refers to an international common language used for communication between speakers of different native languages, primarily for trade and commerce. Throughout history, various languages have served as lingua francas, but in the present era, English has become the dominant lingua franca.

T. Yamanaka (✉)
Ritsumeikan University, College of Life Sciences, Kusatsu, Shiga, Japan
e-mail: yaman@fc.ritsumei.ac.jp

school education system. However, unfortunately, the number of those who can use it functionally is surprisingly low. Why is it so difficult to use English proficiently? Here, I will briefly present two reasons.

The first reason lies in Japan's sociolinguistic situation. While it may not rival English, Japanese is, in fact, a language with a certain degree of utility and influence. This is primarily due to economic factors—reflecting the country's strong economic power, many Japanese people are able to conduct business and academic activities solely in Japanese. This sense of security fosters complacency, making the effort to learn English within Japan sometimes feel pointless. As a result, the classroom environment becomes disengaged, reduced to an artificial and fictional setting. Since there is no sense of urgency or necessity to use English to engage with the world, it is difficult for learners to stay motivated. That said, many Japanese people are well aware that relying solely on Japanese will not be a sustainable option in the future.

Another reason is that English education in Japan is generally not pragmatic. The term "pragmatic" here refers to being based on *pragmatism*,[4] meaning that English education does not effectively contribute to the acquisition of functional *linguistic performance*. The goal of using English is to communicate with native speakers of English or those who use it as an additional language, facilitating the exchange of messages and content.[5] What matters most is the success of this exchange, not how "correct" the English used in the process is.

Furthermore, as long as communication is successfully achieved, it is preferable to utilize non-linguistic means if they prove more effective. There is no inherent need to insist on linguistic expression where it is not necessary. Despite this, mainstream English education in Japan remains dominated by the unquestioned belief that language is the primary means of communication. Over time, the goal of English education has been subtly replaced by an emphasis on linguistic accuracy and refinement rather than practical communication.

Additionally, a notable trend in recent years is the insistence that language proficiency must be demonstrated purely through individual ability, without assistance from machine translation or generative AI. Many learners are required to rely solely on their unaided English skills, rather than leveraging AI-assisted language capabilities. This approach is entirely off the mark, making it even less likely that students will develop functional English skills.

---

[4] For a more detailed explanation of pragmatism, refer to chapter "Pragmatism: What Is the Meaning of Symbols?", in this book.

[5] The reason why English has become the dominant language in this context can be explained, for example, through Takao Suzuki's classification of languages into three categories. (1) *Purpose-oriented Languages*—Languages primarily learned to understand the people and culture of a specific region (e.g., Korean). (2) *Instrumental Languages*—Languages used to access universal technical, intellectual, or cultural information (e.g., French and German in the past). (3) *Contact Languages*—Languages used as a kind of international auxiliary language for communication among people from different countries. Suzuki argues that, at present, no language surpasses English in its role as a contact language. (From Suzuki, T. (1999). *Nihonjin wa Naze Eigo ga Dekinai ka?* Iwanami Shoten (in Japanese), pp. 42–47.)

The Role of Embodiment in English Language Education

So, what should be done? The symbol emergence system actually offers essential insights for English education in Japan. The bottom-up, constructive approach of symbol emergence in robotics is revealing findings that extend far beyond just language acquisition in robots. When viewed through the same framework as English acquisition—which does not naturally occur without deliberate effort—many resonances emerge, reflecting each other like a mirror.

One of the most significant implications of this theory is *embodiment*. As human beings, we do not simply play with language in an abstract, meta-world. Though self-evident, this fact is something we often forget. In many English classrooms, meta-language such as coordinate clauses, absolute comparatives, part-of-speech analysis, and syntactic structures are frequently discussed, with teachers firmly believing that understanding grammar is the key to mastering English. However, this perspective is critically flawed. The symbol emergence system teaches us that when we attempt to acquire symbols—such as language—the most crucial factor is interaction with the environment, grounded in our own bodily experiences. In other words, the most pragmatic and effective way to acquire language is through active engagement with the real world, struggling to grasp concepts and meanings through direct experience.

What is indispensable is my own body—not someone else's—and the unique experiences that this body accumulates. Following Ernst von Glasersfeld's radical constructivism, what truly matters is the accumulation of authentic communicative interactions in the real world. Unless English education moves beyond mere role-playing to become something more urgent, more personally relevant—something learners genuinely struggle with and take ownership of—the successful acquisition of a foreign language will likely remain an unattainable goal.

Multimodal Language Education

Advancing the discussion on embodiment leads us to a crucial concept that is highly beneficial for both second language acquisition and foreign language education—the idea of multimodality. In general, *multimodal* refers to the presence of multiple modes of expression,[6] but in the context of English education, it highlights the fact

---

[6] Here, it is important to clarify the disciplinary differences in the precise meaning of the term multimodal. The word multimodal is composed of the morphemes multi and modal. The key term to focus on here is modal. The noun form of multimodal is multimodality, which derives from the adjective modal, itself related to modality. As mentioned in the main text, modality refers to modes of expression—these can include the five senses, such as sight (visually) and hearing (auditorily), written language as a medium, indirect communication through reported speech, or pictorial representation as a mode of conveying meaning. In technical fields, modality is used to describe these communicative modes systematically. The root of modality is mode, which evolves into modal,

that communication does not rely solely on language. While this may seem obvious, multimodal language education represents an essential yet often overlooked aspect of traditional English instruction. Foreign language education must rigorously incorporate multimodality into its teaching practices, ensuring that language learning is not confined to verbal or textual input alone but embraces the full spectrum of communicative modalities.

As previously mentioned, it is apparent that communication consists not only of language but also of various non-verbal elements—something no one would dispute. However, foreign language education often unconsciously falls into a linguistic supremacist mindset, relegating non-verbal elements to the periphery under the label of non-verbal communication. This tendency fundamentally weakens the premise that communication is inherently multimodal. Consider gestures in speech, for example. While most English education programs do not completely ignore gestures or eye contact, they tend to treat them merely as paralinguistic elements, playing only a supplementary role. The implicit message seems to be that there is no medium more expressive than language itself—a perspective that, ironically, limits effective communication rather than enhancing it.

However, actual communication does not function in this way. In our daily interactions, language is not the sole dominant medium that unilaterally governs the exchange of meaning. Instead, various media and modes take turns assuming prominence, sometimes working cross-modally or multimodally, layering and reinforcing one another in a way that enhances clarity rather than diminishing it. This dynamic interplay of communicative elements, where redundancy and overlap serve to facilitate meaning, resonates strongly with the thought of symbol emergence in robotics.[7]

Of course, the usefulness of language is undeniable. However, language can sometimes function as a supporting element in communication, playing its role subtly yet effectively. This is why language education should be understood as an

---

and from there, into modality. While this definition of modality is widely used in fields such as engineering and psychology, its interpretation differs slightly in linguistics. In linguistic terms, modality refers to grammatical mood, which expresses a speaker's attitude or epistemic stance. The noun modality in this context derives from mood, and its related terms include modal (as in modal verbs) and modality (as in grammatical modality). For example, modal verbs (such as can, must, should) reflect the linguistic sense of modality. Thus, even within the same term, multimodal, there exists a subtle semantic divergence between its use in engineering-based symbol emergence system and its use in linguistics. Whether these interpretations can be reconciled or remain fundamentally distinct is beyond the scope of this discussion. It should be noted, however, that the concept of multimodality in this text is understood as an extension of the original meaning of mode.

[7] Refer to discussions such as the following: "*By utilizing abstract representations such as distributed representations, we can break free from modality-dependent thinking based on vision, hearing, or language. After all, distributed representations are merely high-dimensional vectors and are not tied to any specific modality. Therefore, it does not matter if the input and output—namely, the encoder-side and decoder-side information—belong to different modalities.*" (From: Taniguchi, T. (2020). *Kokoro wo Shiru Tame no Jinkō Chinō: Ninchi Kagaku toshite no Kigō Sōhatsu Robotikus*. Kyoritsu Shuppan (in Japanese), p. 183.)

inseparable part of a multimodal system, rather than as an isolated domain of symbolic manipulation. Moreover, multimodal language education should be expansive—it need not be confined to human faculties alone. It can and should embrace technologies that extend our cognitive capacities, such as computers, AI, and the internet. As long as these tools pragmatically facilitate communication, they should be actively integrated into foreign language acquisition. By doing so, foreign language education can finally reclaim its sense of reality, moving beyond artificial, decontextualized instruction toward a more authentic and dynamic engagement with language in the real world.

The author and their colleagues, reflecting on the limitations of traditional English education as discussed thus far, have long been engaged in the development of a unique instructional approach known as the *Project-based English Program (PEP)*.[8] This program places strong emphasis on learners' embodiment, aiming to realize a pragmatic and multimodal approach to English education. More recently, PEP has actively incorporated ChatGPT as part of its pedagogical framework. The authors view the integration of large language models (LLMs) in foreign language education as one of the most optimal and fundamental applications of generative AI today. There is no reason not to leverage these AI-generated outputs in English education.

Although generative AI lacks embodiment and merely simulates human-like interactions, it proves highly useful in various aspects of language learning. These include engaging in linguistic exchanges, refining expressions through comparison and paraphrasing, and acquiring or supplementing language knowledge in a personalized manner. Given ChatGPT's strengths in these linguistic tasks, its integration into language education has the potential to revolutionize aspects of English learning that were previously beyond reach.

Language Acquisition as the Process of Constructing Meaning Within Oneself

Having considered the discussions up to this point, it becomes clear that the essential factor in acquiring a foreign language functionally lies in whether each learner can actively construct and internalize meaning within themselves. Ultimately, this is the key to language acquisition in its most radical sense.

Symbol emergence in robotics, which is grounded in multimodality and embodiment, along with its extension into the symbol emergence system, is theoretically aligned with pragmatism-based language education theories. It also resonates with radical constructivism and, more broadly, with neo-cybernetic frameworks such as

---

[8] For a more detailed explanation of the Project-based English Program (PEP), refer to the following source: Yamanaka, T., et al. (2021). *Project-based English Program: Jibun-jiku o Kitaeru "Oshienai" Kyoiku* (in Japanese). Kitaoji Shobo.)

autopoiesis theory, which is characteristic of closed systems.[9] Also, from the perspective of semiotics, it finds coherence with Sato et al.'s cultural psychology.[10] Perhaps, language education would benefit more by seeking its theoretical foundations outside its own disciplinary boundaries rather than within them.

---

[9] For a detailed explanation of autopoiesis and neo-cybernetics, refer to chapter "Neo-Cybernetics and Information: What Is Information?," in this book.

[10] Refer to Tatsuya Sato's Three-Layer Model of Emergence, e.g., the following work: Sato, T. (2015). *"Bunka Shinrigaku kara Mita Shoku no Hyōgen no Shiten kara Shokubunka to Sono Kenkyū ni tsuite Kangaeru."* Ritsumeikan Shakai System Kenkyū Kiyō, Tokushū-gō (in Japanese), 197–209.

Emerging Ethics: The Future of Ethics from the Symbol Emergence Systems Perspective

Katsunori Miyahara and Takuya Niikawa

Ethics as a Meta-Symbol System

Human social life is constrained by various norms: Some prescribe and others prohibit actions. Some do so in a context-dependent manner, others universally. Norms that fundamentally question how people ought to live are usually called ethical norms. They are distinguished from cultural norms such as customs and manners, or institutional norms such as laws and school rules. Ethics is often treated as a classic example of problems that cannot be resolved from the perspective of science and technology. In this chapter, however, we examine how it might be placed within the symbol emergence systems theory.

According to symbol emergence systems theory, agents create bottom-up socially shared symbol systems through interaction with other agents. These symbol systems, in turn, function as top-down constraints on agents, requiring newcomers to the community to adhere to them for communication. Ethical norms can be considered a type of such socially shared symbol system. However, while ordinary symbol systems govern communication involving symbols, ethical norms function as a *meta-symbol system* that governs the agents' semiosis (i.e., engagement with meaning-making and interpretive activities) more broadly and provides evaluations of the socially shared symbol system itself.[1]

---

[1] Ethical norms not only shape judgments and actions but also function as symbol systems that treat judgments and actions formed in other symbol systems—along with the symbol systems themselves—as a type of symbol, thereby shaping further judgments and actions. We described them as

---

K. Miyahara
Center for Human Nature, Artificial Intelligence, and Neuroscience (CHAIN), Hokkaido University, Sapporo, Hokkaido, Japan

T. Niikawa (✉)
Graduate School of Humanities, Kobe University, , Kobe-shi, Japan
e-mail: niikawa@ferret.kobe-u.ac.jp

T. Taniguchi (ed.), *Symbol Emergence Systems*,
https://doi.org/10.1007/978-981-95-1327-7_29

Consider theft as an example. In certain environments, it is adaptive to steal any accessible item. Thus, people in such environments normally treat unattended items as stealable. This understanding is shared by both those who steal to live and those at risk of theft, consequently shaping the cognition and behavior of both. In other words, the socially shared symbol system involves an interpretive framework that presents unattended items as targets for theft. However, one might think it ethically impermissible to steal someone else's property, even if left unattended. In this situation, one is involved in a special kind of semiotic process: An ethical norm ("one must not steal others' belongings") provides an evaluation ("stealing is wrong" or "it's wrong to accept theft as a normal deed") either to the semiotic process of interpreting unattended items as stealable, or to the symbol system (viz. the local cultural practice) that normalizes theft. This illustrates how ethical norms treat first-order semiotic processes and symbol systems as symbols, offering a meta-level framework for interpreting their meaning.

Ethical Valuation by Agents

The meta-nature of ethical norms does not mean that ethical evaluations of actions and customs always arise from meta-reflection. Certainly, actions and customs can become subjects of reflective consideration. However, just as adapting to a particular linguistic environment, or a way of life, enables one to intuitively interpret strings of characters (like "ticket" or "apple") or spatial environments (like crosswalks or ticket gates) as having specific meanings, adapting to a particular ethical environment can sometimes lead to various things being immediately and intuitively perceived as having ethical significance. Ethical norms are meta-level in nature as a symbol system, but the act of ethical valuation performed by individual agents does not necessarily involve reflection on the actions and customs which are the objects of the ethical valuation.

Ethical valuation involves two aspects: *emotional reactions* and *evaluative judgments*. For example, emotional reactions arise when an agent physiologically responds to the environment, as suggested by expressions like "blood boiling." However, these are not mere reflexive responses but include intuitive interpretations of their targets. For example, when you feel a surge of anger in response to someone's slander, you are not merely in a physiological state that could be described as "blood boiling"; you are also intuitively evaluating that remark as unjust. Such emotional reactions often lead to evaluative judgments. For example, anger toward another person's slander may be tied to a judgment that the remark is unjust, leading you to demand a retraction or other responses. However, emotional reactions and evaluative judgments do not always align. For instance, while being corrected might

---

"meta "symbol systems to underscore this aspect. Various meta-level symbol systems exist in society beyond ethical norms. Clarifying the multilayered relationships among diverse symbol systems within society is a crucial, future challenge for symbol emergence systems theory.

cause frustration, even in situations where it is clear that you made a mistake, you may be able to restain the emotion and make the rational judgment that you were at fault. Ethical valuation arises from a complex interplay of intuitive value attributions embedded in emotional reactions and evaluative judgments.

Ethics Emerging from Mutual Loops

Symbol emergence systems develop through a reciprocal loop involving bottom-up emergence and top-down constraints between agents' semiosis and socially shared symbol systems. This reciprocal loop also occurs between ethical valuation and ethical norms. On the one hand, ethical norms persist based on valuations, including both emotional responses and evaluative judgments. For instance, the principle that prohibits theft would fail as an ethical norm in a world where theft is widely condoned and the victims are blamed. In other words, this ethical norm is sustained by the fact that many people feel angry toward theft and judge it as unjust and wrong. At the same time, an agent's ethical valuation is influenced by ethical norms prevalent in that society. The reason we emotionally and judgmentally deem theft wrong is precisely because we were raised within a social context where the ethical norm against it is widely shared.

Traditional normative ethics often present ethical norms as universal, moral principles applicable across all regions and times. In contrast, symbol emergence system theory suggests that ethical norms are open systems, subject to transformation through the reciprocal loop between bottom-up emergence and top-down constraints. As ethical transformation is driven by this reciprocal loop, of course, no single individual can control it at their will or by their action alone. However, it is also crucial to recognize its dependence on human will and action. Ethical transformation does not emerge spontaneously from outside human activity. For example, until relatively recently, the prevailing normative awareness of drunk driving was limited. Many considered it a minor rule violation, often committed without consequence. However, activism advocating for stricter penalties for drunk driving, public awareness initiatives highlighting its dangers, and the strengthening of legal regulations have since transformed public valuation, firmly establishing a strong ethical norm against drunk driving in society.

Shaping the Future of Ethics

According to symbol emergence system theory, ethical norms are not universal principles but open systems emergent from human activity. We, as agents constituting a symbol emergence system, are not merely beings who live under the constraints of ethical norms, that is, mere consumers of those norms, but also bear responsibility for their continuation and evolution; in this sense, we are also their creators. With the rapid advance of science and technology and the ongoing changes in the global environment, human society is expected to face numerous ethical challenges that can no longer be adequately addressed within the framework of traditional ethics. Symbol emergence system theory holds that we cannot deduce how human society ought to respond to such challenges from pre-existing moral principles. Rather, the theory highlights our role, as agents within society, in actively participating in the creation of ethical symbolic systems, and emphasizes that we are directly involved in shaping the *future of ethics*.

The Legal System and Symbol Emergence: The Reciprocal Relationship Between Humans and Symbols

Tatsuhiko Inatani

Construction and Operation of the Legal System

The legal system can be considered a social system that is (re)constructed daily through the reciprocal constitutive relationship between symbols and the humans who use them. This dynamic system centers on legal texts as a symbolic system and the act of "interpretation" (assigning meaning) performed by humans. By "reciprocal constitutive relationship," I refer to the dynamic interplay in which human acts of assigning meaning to symbols simultaneously transform both their cognitive frameworks and the symbolic system itself. Importantly, acts of meaning assignment are often not one-sided efforts by humans but are drawn out by the interpretability inherent in symbols themselves. As we will see, in the symbolic system of legal texts, the interpretability of symbols often elicits meaning assignments from humans.

Humans within social systems do not exist in isolation; their cognitive frameworks are shaped by their relationships with other humans and non-human entities.[1] Consequently, the legal system cannot be reduced to a simple reciprocal constitutive relationship between humans and symbols. Instead, the legal system functions as a dynamic network that extends throughout society, influencing and being influenced by the networks it helps form—what is often referred to as the "rule of law."[2]

---

[1] Latour, B. 2007. *Reassembling the Social: An Introduction to Actor-Network-Theory*. Oxford University Press. (Japanese translation: *Reassembling the Social: Introduction to Actor-Network Theory*, Hosei University Press, 2019.)

[2] Latour, B. 2009. *The Making of Law: An Ethnography of the Conseil d'État*. Polity. (Japanese translation: *Making Law: Anthropological Considerations of Modern Administrative Justice*, Suiseisha, 2017.)

T. Inatani (✉)
Kyoto University, Graduate School of Law, Kyoto, Japan
e-mail: inatani.tatsuhiko.3w@kyoto-u.ac.jp

© The Author(s) 2026
T. Taniguchi (ed.), *Symbol Emergence Systems*,
https://doi.org/10.1007/978-981-95-1327-7_30

Actor-Network Theory (ANT)[3] demonstrates how the robustness and applicability of meaning assignment depend on the connections between humans and non-human entities. For instance, whether medical practices are interpreted as "magic" or "science" depends on the connections between humans and bacteria and the instruments mediating those connections. Similarly, attributing the meaning of "science" to medical practices alters how humans interact with bacteria. For example, recognizing bacteria as causes of infection changes both human activities and their meaning assignments, such as adopting handwashing with soap. As we will see, the networks humans construct with non-human entities profoundly impact the "interpretation" of legal texts and how these interpretations influence networks of relationships.

This section briefly describes how symbols emerge in the operational processes of the legal system. By addressing the meaning assigned to legal texts, the creation of new symbols within those texts, and the role of the legal system in social systems, we aim to outline the relationship between the legal system and symbol emergence.

Legal Texts as a Symbolic System

Legal texts constitute a symbolic system. They form a "system" because they exhibit order and structure, interconnected with the cognitive frameworks of individuals who engage with them reciprocally.

Consider the evolving interpretation of theft under Article 235 of the Japanese Penal Code, which defines the crime as "appropriating another person's property." "Property" has traditionally been understood as tangible objects with economic value, as the term "appropriating" has been linked to violating physical possession. Possession refers to de facto control over an object. Consequently, intangible items that cannot be "possessed" in this sense have been excluded from the concept of "property."

However, changes in the societal roles of non-human entities like electricity or information have called this interpretation into question. For example, electricity was early on interpreted as "property" due to the technical possibility of "possession" and because the text of "property" itself does not explicitly exclude intangible items.[4] Changes in human cognitive frameworks driven by shifts in human-non-human relationships resulted in new meanings being assigned to symbols.

Such interpretations, however, raised immediate questions regarding the cognitive framework imposed by the broader legal text system: Does the Japanese Penal Code truly permit interpreting electricity as "property"? The principle of legality (or "Rechtstaatlichkeit"), requiring clarity in criminal statutes, emerged from the Enlightenment understanding of humans as rational, autonomous agents living under

---

[3] Kurihara, W. (Ed.). 2022. *Introduction to Actor-Network Theory: Describing a World Overflowing with "Things"*. Nakanishiya Publishing.
[4] For discussions on "information theft," see Nishigai, Y. 2020. *Cybersecurity and Penal Law: Focusing on Unauthorized Access Crimes*. Yuhikaku.

justly enacted laws. The tension between the principle of legality and the interpretation of electricity as "property" led to the addition of explicit legal texts classifying electricity as property. This exemplifies how symbols influence human cognition and activities. The reciprocal constitutive relationship between humans and legal texts, exemplified by the concept of "property" in theft laws, continues to grow in importance as technological advances allow "possession" of intangible entities like information, making symbol emergence within legal systems increasingly critical.[5]

Simply put, humans interpreting and creating law exist within networks formed by humans and non-human entities. As a result, legal texts and human cognitive frameworks influence each other, driving daily symbol emergence and enabling the legal system to operate.

The Relationship Between the Legal System and Social Systems

As discussed, the reciprocal constitutive relationship between humans and legal texts is grounded in networks that extend across society. Consequently, the legal system operates by influencing and being influenced by the social system.

For example, Enlightenment ideas tightly linked human autonomy—rational and free-willed—to the framework of legal texts, forming a legal system that emphasizes predetermined societal ideals.[6] Design-oriented rules that prescribe technological practices—determining relationships between humans and non-human entities—limit deviations from these practices. For instance, laws governing AI and robot development and use profoundly shape their societal roles. The legal system influences social system functions by directing human cognition through legal rules. Laws emphasizing human autonomy often reinforce control over AI and robots, shaping cognitive frameworks and influencing symbol emergence—e.g., framing AI and robots as "dangerous entities threatening human dignity."

Conversely, societal changes impact the legal system. For example, as AI and robots are reinterpreted from "dangerous entities" to "companions," the design-oriented legal system emphasizing human autonomy may be seen as unjustly constraining the roles AI and robots can play in society. Changing cognitive frameworks in reciprocal constitutive relationships with legal texts could drive new symbol emergence, fundamentally altering how humans and non-human entities are positioned within the legal system.

Adopting decentralized legal systems to advance AI and robot integration into social systems —thereby responding to rapid technological shifts— may transform symbol emergence. Enhanced legal "machine readability" and digital

---

[5] For analyses of legal systems and governance, see Inatani, T. 2017. "The Moralizing Technology and Criminal Law Regulation." In Y. Matsuo (Ed.), *Architecture and Law: The Architectural Turn in Legal Studies?*, pp. 93–128. Koubundou.

[6] Hayek, F. A. 1944. *The Road to Serfdom*. Routledge. (Japanese translation: *The Road to Serfdom*, Nikkei BP, 2016.)

transformation could optimize the legal system's functionality, removing humans as intermediaries. This shift could free the intersection of legal and social systems from human exclusivity, leading to profound changes in symbol emergence[7] and sparking new developments in AI research.

Toward Further Research on Symbol Emergence in Legal Systems

This section outlined symbol emergence in legal systems by examining legal texts as a symbolic system and their interaction with social systems. Writing this section has been a learning process even from my perspective as a legal scholar, highlighting the unexplored dimensions of symbol emergence within legal texts and its future implications. I hope this discussion inspires further research on symbol emergence in legal systems.

---

[7] Inatani, T. 2022. "The Legal Being and Legal Subjects: Exploring Criminal Responsibility in Modern Technological Societies." *Hougaku-Kyoshitsu*, 498, 40–45.

Part VI: Symbol Emergence Systems and Beyond

Language in the Era of Generative AI: Insights from Large Language Models

Tadahiro Taniguchi

Generative AI and Language Understanding

Generative AI refers to artificial intelligence systems capable of producing text, images, and other contents. In 2022, the release of Stable Diffusion drew attention for its ability to generate highly realistic images. Later that same year, ChatGPT, a conversational generative AI system, was launched and—within a remarkably short time—adopted worldwide.

Unlike traditional AI, which centered on discriminative tasks such as image and speech recognition, generative AI is distinguished by its ability to produce rich, diverse, and complex outputs. These systems, built upon neural networks, learn the statistical and structural patterns embedded in training data, and generate new data that reflects similar properties. The year 2023 saw a dramatic acceleration in both the technical development and societal uptake of generative AI, effectively redefining the technical and social significance of artificial intelligence.

At the heart of generative AI lies the large language model (LLM). Even for image generation, the contribution of LLMs is profound. The ability to control AI outputs using natural language prompts—something made possible by LLMs— enabled users with no prior knowledge of AI or programming to create high-quality images, videos, and other content simply by describing them in words. These models interpret natural language expressions and relay them to other generative AI components, such as image generators, guiding the production process.

As discussed in chapter "Large Language Models and Distributional Semantics: Do Large Language Models Understand Language?", ChatGPT is grounded in distributional semantics. Its core mechanism involves training neural networks to

---

T. Taniguchi (✉)
Graduate School of Informatics, Kyoto University, Kyoto, Japan

Research Organization of Science and Technology, Ritsumeikan University, Kyoto, Japan
e-mail: taniguchi@i.kyoto-u.ac.jp

predict the next token (e.g., sub-word) in a sequence—a task known as next-token prediction. ChatGPT and similar systems are further refined through techniques like RLHF (Reinforcement Learning from Human Feedback), but fundamentally, their "knowledge" emerges from massive-scale prediction tasks. In this sense, generative AI is built upon a predictive coding framework.

In that same chapter we posed the question: "Do large language models like ChatGPT truly understand language?" The tentative answer was that they merely produce sentences that are mechanically appropriate to the context. However, viewed through the lens of pragmatic semiotics, as introduced in Part I, the process of linking signs (e.g., word inputs) with their objects (e.g., textual outputs, corresponding images, or other generative responses) in a context-dependent manner—and thereby generating interpretants—is central to what constitutes a semiosis, i.e., semiotic process. Within this interpretive framework, one might argue that AI systems do, to some degree, understand the meaning of language—certainly more so than any previous generation of AI.

Indeed, generative AI powered by large language models already appears to have developed partial conceptual structures for language, grounded in distributional semantics. These models do not merely replicate surface patterns; they exhibit behaviors that suggest emergent semantic understanding—even if shaped through radically different mechanisms than those used by humans.

Concepts and Predictability in Language

Do large language models truly form concepts about various phenomena in the world? Here, we offered a provisional negative answer. As Stevan Harnad, who proposed the symbol grounding problem, pointed out, what linguistic relationships provide are at best relational concepts—not grounded ones. Statements such as "an apple is a fruit" or "an apple is red" merely describe associations among words. For these to attain true meaning, they must be grounded in the subjective experiences of an agent.

This is why symbol emergence systems theory emphasizes the formation of internal representations through embodied interaction as a foundational element. From a constructivist perspective, understanding arises through self-organizing cognitive processes within an agent. Grounding, then, is not in the objective world, but rather in the Umwelt—the subjective, experiential world of the organism—as described by Jakob von Uexküll. This view aligns with the neo-cybernetic understanding of cognitive systems introduced in Part I.

As detailed in Part II, a series of studies in symbol emergence in robotics during the 2010s explored how embodied robots could acquire concepts such as objects and locations by integrating multimodal information. These processes were often compared to early language acquisition in infants. In addition, robots employed unsupervised word segmentation to extract words from continuous speech and probabilistically associated these words with conceptual categories formed through interaction with the environment. This enabled them to go beyond mere word–word associations and construct grounded meanings based on their own experiences within their Umwelt.

These approaches directly correspond to the formation of internal representations through embodied symbolic interaction, as envisioned in symbol emergence systems.

Many of the cognitive models developed in the series of studies relied on probabilistic generative models, where a key element was predictability. Multimodal data, including language, were integrated into models containing latent variables—representing internal representations—which were optimized through Bayesian inference to predict various sensory inputs. This modeling approach naturally connects to the theoretical frameworks introduced in Part III, such as predictive coding, the free-energy principle, and world models.

Similarly, unsupervised word segmentation was guided by the principle of maximizing the predictability of subsequent character sequences. Through these learning processes, robots have been shown to form, in a certain sense, grounded concepts such as "water bottle," "apple," and "elevator hall," based on their own sensorimotor experiences.

Holism of Sentences and Meaning

When discussing meanings and concepts in language, we often carry an unconscious bias toward "noun-like" entities. For example, when we say that a robot has acquired the concepts of "water bottle," "apple," or "elevator hall," we typically refer to concrete, perceivable objects that appear as nouns (or noun phrases) within sentences. This bias is prevalent not only in robotics research, such as in cognitive developmental robotics and symbol emergence robotics, but also in broader cognitive science and developmental psychology, particularly in discussions of categorization and concept formation.

However, many words do not refer to fixed objects but instead derive their meanings from context-dependent interactions within an agent's Umwelt. Take the verb "throw", for example. The physical action it implies varies dramatically depending on whether one is throwing a baseball, a bowling ball, a spoon, or even a task (as in metaphorical usage). Prepositions like "of" or adverbs like "very" exhibit even greater semantic fluidity—they are not grounded in direct perceptual experience but rather fluctuate within relational structures formed among other words.

The common tendency in cognitive science and its constructive approaches to focus on "learning the meaning of a word" often inadvertently adopts an atomistic view of language and meaning. This orientation bears a philosophical kinship with the symbolic AI paradigm rooted in the physical symbol system hypothesis, which presumes that words have static, predefined meanings and that sentence-level meaning is constructed by combining these units through syntactic rules. This approach corresponds to what could be called a dictionary-and-grammar model of meaning:

semantic units (words) are composed according to fixed grammatical rules to generate sentence meaning. This compositional view underlies generative grammar, where syntactic structure is considered the foundation of language.

In contrast, the usage-based model, derived from cognitive linguistics and cognitive grammar, holds that linguistic structure emerges from actual usage. In this framework, language is not constructed from a priori rules but instead formed dynamically through situated use. This perspective resonates strongly with discussions in chapters "Language Acquisition: Statistical Learning and Social Cognitive Skills" and "Multimodal Language Education: Pragmatic Interaction with the Environment", and aligns more fundamentally with the assumptions underlying symbol emergence in robotics, where language is understood as grounded in use.

From the standpoint of the usage-based model, what we experience is not the isolated meaning of individual words, but rather the situated experience of entire utterances in context. Thus, the meaning of a word should not be viewed as an independent, pre-existing unit, but as something continually inferred through its use in context, through the interaction between sentences and situations.

Viewed from this perspective, it is natural to suppose that words such as prepositions, adverbs, and verbs—whose meanings fluctuate in relation to surrounding words—are formed not through direct physical experience but through distributional experience, acquired by reading or hearing numerous sentences in context. That is, they emerge through distributional semantics.

In recent developments of generative AI, large language models are increasingly trained with multimodal inputs, integrating not only language but also perceptual information. These models predict not only the sequence of words in a sentence but also associated multimodal sensory information. This can be seen as integrating two dimensions of meaning:

1. Relational meaning arising from syntactic structures.
2. Experiential meaning rooted in perceptual interaction with the world.

From the perspective of the symbol emergence systems framework, this represents a synthesis of symbolic interaction and embodied interaction—a holistic account of how meaning is formed not just from language, but from its use in the world.

The Dynamics of Language

Generative AI, grounded in large language models, has shown remarkable flexibility across a wide range of tasks. This suggests that the linguistic assumptions embedded in these models—particularly those in multimodal LLMs—are not only theoretically sound, but also practically effective. The development of generative AI has made it clear: once language has already been formed in human society and a massive corpus of text has been produced, it becomes possible to internalize that language into a neural network and achieve highly functional language modeling.

However, this presumes that language already exists. The emergence and dynamics of language itself remain deeply mysterious. How do symbol systems—such as language—emerge in the first place? How does language, as a cultural system, evolve dynamically through its use?

Neural networks do not become intelligent simply by ingesting chaotic or unstructured data. They require structured data—the kind that allows for predictive learning. The success of large language models stems from the fact that language has syntactic structure and meets the conditions required by distributional semantics: words appear in patterns, and those patterns can be learned.

But how did such a structured form of language emerge? How do word meanings arise and become shared, even despite the inherent opacity of others' minds? How does language come to represent intentions and objects in the real world, serving as a medium for adaptive interaction with the environment?

To address these questions, we must advance our understanding of symbol emergence systems. These inquiries are not just theoretical; in the era of generative AI, they have become all the more essential for both the development of AI and for rethinking our understanding of human cognition, communication, and society.

Constructive Approaches to Symbol Emergence Systems: Probabilistic Generative Models and Language Games

Tadahiro Taniguchi

Dynamics in Language as a Social and Cognitive System

To grasp the emergent and dynamic nature of language, it is essential to construct mathematical and computational models—just as equations of motion are crucial to understanding planetary systems, or relativity and quantum mechanics are indispensable for describing time and motion, and electromagnetic waves and particles. Developing such models constitutes the core of the constructive modeling of symbol emergence systems.

As outlined in chapter "Symbol Emergence Systems: Toward a World Where Humans and AI Co-discover Meaning": Symbol Emergence Systems, it is fundamentally essential to simultaneously understand the dynamics of language in both social systems and cognitive systems. While numerous studies have explored how AI and robots can acquire language grounded in their own sensory experiences—such as through cognitive developmental robotics, symbol emergence in robotics, and multimodal large language models in generative AI—these efforts primarily capture the individual-level cognitive dynamics of language acquisition.

However, symbol emergence systems theory insists that such a perspective is insufficient. In order to understand the function and meaning of language for both artificial agents and humans, and to design AI systems that harmonize with human societies, one must also consider the social-level dynamics of language: how it emerges, evolves, and shifts in meaning and usage within collectives. In other words, language must be seen as both a cognitive and social phenomenon.

T. Taniguchi (✉)
Graduate School of Informatics, Kyoto University, Kyoto, Japan

Research Organization of Science and Technology, Ritsumeikan University, Kyoto, Japan
e-mail: taniguchi@i.kyoto-u.ac.jp

Various constructive approaches have been proposed to model collective symbol emergence, and these can be broadly categorized into four paradigms[1]:

1. Multi-Agent Reinforcement Learning (MARL)

This framework models how communicative symbols emerge within groups of agents adapting to their environment to solve tasks. Communication is framed as a process whereby agents emit signals to influence others and respond to signals to adapt their own behavior—ultimately facilitating collective adaptation.

Recent advances in deep reinforcement learning have enabled more flexible interpretation of communicative signals, thanks to deep learning's powerful representation learning capabilities.

2. Iterated Learning Models (ILMs)

ILMs simulate intergenerational transmission of language to investigate how compositional structures in language emerge through cultural evolution. Research methods include agent-based simulations, mathematical modeling, and laboratory experiments in experimental semiotics (see chapter "The Evolution and Emergence of Language: How Did Humans Acquire Language?": The Evolution and Emergence of Language).

3. Emergent Communication

This approach focuses on how agents spontaneously develop communication protocols through interaction. It explores the conditions under which communication systems emerge that resemble human language in structure and use.

4. Symbol Emergence Robotics

This line of research centers on how robots acquire language and form internal representations through sensorimotor interaction with their environment. It not only connects individual cognitive development to group-level symbol systems but is also central in grounding the theoretical framework of symbol emergence systems—integrating the symbolic with the embodied.

Emergent Communication

Emergent communication is a constructive research paradigm that models how agents develop communication protocols—effectively forming language—and investigates the conditions under which human-like language may emerge.

A seminal early example is Luc Steels' "Talking Heads Project", where robots equipped with cameras interacted in the physical world and gradually came to share

---

[1] For a detailed discussion of the four constructive approaches mentioned, see Taniguchi, Tadahiro. "Collective predictive coding hypothesis: Symbol emergence as decentralized Bayesian inference." *Frontiers in Robotics and AI* 11 (2024): 1353870.

names for objects through situated interaction.[2] While interest in this area waned somewhat after its initial rise in the 2000s, the development of deep learning, and particularly advances in representation learning, have led to a resurgence of interest since the late 2010s.

Among the most widely used models in emergent communication is the referential game. In such settings, a sender agent perceives a particular state and transmits this information to a receiver via a symbolic signal—often encoded as a sequence of discrete tokens, akin to a sentence. The receiver, in turn, attempts to infer which state the sender observed—such as selecting the correct image from a set of options.

A related approach is the naming game, where a sender selects an object and proposes a name, and the receiver either accepts the term or proposes an alternative. Through repeated interactions and role reversals, agents converge on stable, shared naming conventions. These approaches enable the study of how compositionality might emerge in such languages, and what structural properties they exhibit.

However, despite their utility as formal models, it remains unclear to what extent these emergent languages enhance group-level adaptive behavior—a key concern in symbol emergence systems theory. Furthermore, the referential game framework diverges significantly from the developmental trajectories of human language acquisition, raising questions about its ecological and developmental validity. As such, while these models offer valuable insights into mechanisms of symbol emergence, their limitations must be critically considered when comparing them to natural language systems.

Probabilistic Generative Models in Symbol Emergence Systems

In symbol emergence in robotics, a central research challenge has been to understand how embodied agents—specifically, robots with sensory-motor systems—form internal representation systems and acquire language through embodied interaction.

However, as discussed in Part III, recent developments have shown that probabilistic generative models, initially designed to explain internal representation learning in individual agents, can be meaningfully extended to capture the emergence of shared external representations—that is, the process of group-level symbol emergence.

Figure 1 presents a probabilistic graphical model used to express this idea. While the full technical details are omitted here, Fig. 1a shows a model in which two agents (Agent 1 and Agent 2) form internal representations through latent variables (x_d^1, x_d^2) , based on their respective sensory inputs (o_d^1, o_d^2) , and jointly infer a

---

[2] Luc Steels, 2015 The Talking Heads Experiment: Origins of Words and Meanings (Computational Models of Language Evolution 1). Language Science Press.

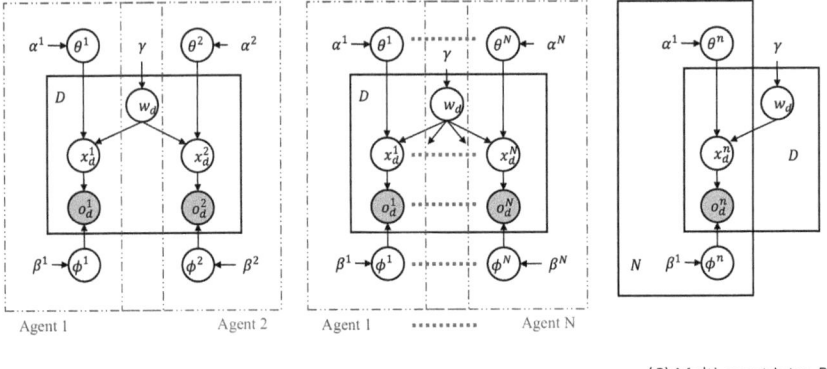

(A) Two-agent Inter-PGM

(B) Multi-agent Inter-PGM

(C) Multi-agent Inter-PGM with plate representation

Fig. 1 Graphical models of Inter-PGM (Inter-agent Probabilistic Generative Model). (**a**) The two-agent Inter-PGM models how two agents generate and observe their respective observations, sharing a common latent variable w_d. (**b**) The multi-agent extension generalizes this framework to N agents, enabling the shared representation system to model the latent structures of observations across multiple distributed perspectives. (**c**) shows an equivalent representation using the plate notation

shared variable wd. This shared latent node acts as an integrator of multimodal information, resulting in what appears to be a combined representation across agents. Figure 1b generalizes this model to N agents, while Fig. 1c shows an equivalent representation using the plate notation.

Structurally, the left half of Fig. 1a corresponds to Agent 1's representation learning, while the right half corresponds to Agent 2's. At a glance, this model may seem to suggest a direct coupling of the agents' "brains," in which their sensory experiences are fused into a single representational structure. Such a view might initially appear inappropriate when modeling human social learning, which presumes individual autonomy of cognition.

However, if wd is interpreted as a shared latent structure inferred via Bayesian inference, then this model represents a statistical approximation of how a collective representation may emerge—as if the agents' internal states are integrated "as though their brains were interconnected."

This concept forms the basis of a novel interpretation of language games: where symbolic interaction among agents rather than direct access to internal states— can result in joint external representation learning.

This theoretical mechanism has been operationalized and empirically demonstrated through the Metropolis-Hastings Naming Game, which simulates how agents collectively refine shared labels through probabilistic inference and interaction.

The Metropolis-Hastings Naming Game[3]

Figure 2 illustrates two robots engaged in what is known as the Metropolis-Hastings Naming Game—a naming interaction that models the emergence of shared symbols via probabilistic inference. Unlike conventional naming or referential games, this model assumes joint attention: the mutual focus of two agents on the same object at the same time.

The interaction proceeds as follows: Agent 1 (the sender) observes an object d and proposes a name w_d^1, which is treated as a sample drawn from the posterior distribution over possible names given the observation. In essence, this act of naming corresponds to sampling from a posterior distribution and labeling the object accordingly.

Agent 2 (the receiver) then evaluates this proposed name against its own internal belief system. It calculates the likelihood ratio between the name it would have assigned w_d^2 and the proposed name w_d^1, based on its internal representation. If the likelihood of w_d^1 is higher, it accepts the name with probability 1. If it is lower, the agent may still accept it with a probability proportional to the likelihood ratio.

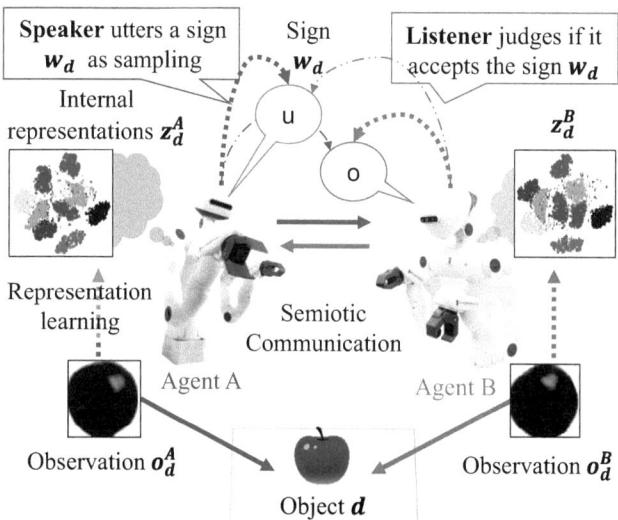

Fig. 2 Metropolis-Hastings naming game: Agent A (Speaker) generates a sign w_d based on its internal representation z_d^A, which is derived from its observation o_d^A of an object. Agent B (Listener) receives the sign and decides whether to accept it based on a probability computed using its own internal representation z_d^B and observation o_d^B. This process models how shared signs and meanings can emerge through interactive external representation learning, i.e., symbol emergence

[3] Taniguchi, T., et al. 2023 Emergent Communication through Metropolis-Hastings Naming Game with Deep Generative Models. Advanced Robotics, 37(19), 1266–1282.

This process is repeated with alternating roles. Crucially, if the acceptance probability follows the Metropolis-Hastings algorithm, it can be formally shown that this naming game is equivalent to performing approximate Bayesian inference over the latent variable w_d in the graphical model shown in Fig. 1a.

What is especially noteworthy here is that at no point do the agents access each other's internal variables. That is, the cognitive closure of each agent is preserved throughout the interaction—a key premise of symbolic interaction in semiotic systems. And yet, despite this epistemic separation, the agents are able to approximate the posterior distribution of w_d, thereby forming a shared external representation.

This result illustrates that symbol emergence can be interpreted as a form of decentralized Bayesian inference, wherein perceptual data from multiple agents is integrated via social interaction. The naming game, in this light, becomes not just a toy model, but a mechanism for external representation learning through language emergence under the constraint of self-contained cognition.

This view leads us toward a fundamentally new interpretation: that naming games are processes of decentralized Bayesian inference for collectively integrating perception and fostering language—thus laying the groundwork for the concept of collective predictive coding.

The Collective Predictive Coding Hypothesis: If Language Exists to Help Us Predict the World

Tadahiro Taniguchi

Predictive Coding and Understanding the World

Symbol emergence in a group involves interactions among multiple agents. Even when the process is primarily driven by bottom-up dynamics, it is important to ask: "What is the system as a whole optimizing?" What is its directional tendency or emergent function? These questions are essential not only for understanding human symbol systems, but also for designing intelligent systems that can participate in or replicate such dynamics.

As discussed in chapter "Free-Energy Principle and Predictive Coding: A Computational Theory Explaining Various Brain Functions": The Free-Energy Principle and Predictive Coding, the adaptive behavior of individual cognitive systems can be described through predictive coding and the free-energy principle—frameworks that extend even to phenomena such as curiosity and emotion.

From the standpoint of machine learning and artificial intelligence, the acquisition of internal representations through environmental interaction is known as representation learning, and this concept advanced dramatically through deep learning in the 2010s. When such representations include the dynamics of the agent's sensorimotor experience within an embodied and temporally unfolding environment, they constitute what are known as world models (see chapter "World Models: Agents That Learn About the World from Subjective Experience").

Some may argue that stating "humans acquire internal representations of the world through interaction" risks leaning too far into representationalism, especially from the perspective of enactivism (see chapter "Enactivism: Cognition as Non-representational, Embodied Action"). However, even enactive cognition does not

T. Taniguchi (✉)
Graduate School of Informatics, Kyoto University, Kyoto, Japan

Research Organization of Science and Technology, Ritsumeikan University, Kyoto, Japan
e-mail: taniguchi@i.kyoto-u.ac.jp

necessarily reject the idea that adaptive coupling with the environment is essential to cognition. Thus, interaction-based learning is not antithetical to enactive views; rather, it can be seen as complementary.

Despite their differences in origin and theoretical framing, predictive coding, the free-energy principle, and world models share key mathematical foundations.[1] All of them operate on the principle of updating internal models through prediction.

– Predictive coding leads to the theory of active inference.
– World model learning supports the concept of control as inference.[2]

Both ultimately frame action generation as a process of probabilistic inference over future states and behaviors.

In this sense, predictive coding functions as a general explanatory framework for individual cognition.

Furthermore, as described in Part II, the acquisition of language and formation of concepts in symbol emergence robotics, and as detailed in Part III, the learning of internal world models in developmental robotics and adaptive AI, can all be interpreted as instances of predictive processing in a broad sense.

These threads converge toward the collective predictive coding hypothesis —a framework for understanding how distributed agents coordinate internal and external representations through interaction, ultimately forming the basis of shared symbol systems such as language.

Collective Predictive Coding

In the model of symbol emergence based on the Metropolis-Hastings Naming Game introduced in the previous section, we began by assuming a generative model that links multiple agents—a kind of generative AI—and then decompose it as a model in which agents attempt to infer shared latent variables *without peering into each other's minds.*

In conventional probabilistic generative models representing individual cognitive systems, Bayesian inference over latent variables—i.e., internal representations—is typically carried out *within an individual's brain* (or mental system). In contrast, here, that inference process is replaced by learning through communication—namely, a *language game* played among multiple agents, in the form of the *Metropolis-Hastings Naming Game.* In this framing, the language game itself serves as an *algorithmic strategy* for decentralizing what would otherwise require a shared

---

[1] Taniguchi, T., Murata, S., Suzuki, M., Ognibene, D., Lanillos, P., Ugur, E., Jamone, L., Nakamura, T., Ciria, A., Lara, B., & Pezzulo, G. 2023 World Models and Predictive Coding for Cognitive and Developmental Robotics: Frontiers and Challenges. Advanced Robotics, 37(13), 780–806.
[2] Levine, S. 2018 Reinforcement Learning and Control as Probabilistic Inference: Tutorial and Review. arXiv preprint arXiv:1805.00909.

brain for representation learning. It has also been demonstrated that the Metropolis-Hastings Naming Game is extensible to *N agents*.[3]

In other words, while it may seem that collective representation learning across society would require integrating all agents' sensory information—*as if connecting their brains*—the theory of symbol emergence based on the Metropolis-Hastings Naming Game shows that such learning can be achieved *in a distributed manner*, without any actual neural interconnection. By performing *distributed Bayesian inference* between agents—in other words, by engaging in *collective predictive coding*—symbol emergence becomes possible.

This *shift in perspective* is deeply significant. What extends from this view is the *concept of collective predictive coding*: the idea that symbol emergence occurs through collective predictive inference across society, *without anyone needing to access others' mental states*. Instead, symbol emergence can be realized through *language games that meet certain conditions*. This theoretical stance—that language arises through decentralized Bayesian inference conducted by many human agents—is what we refer to as *collective predictive coding*.

Collective predictive coding offers, for the first time, a *unified theoretical framework* for understanding the full architecture of symbol emergence systems. It enables a comprehensive explanation of the *dynamics of both cognition and society*, and how language arises from within those intertwined processes in human society.

Collective Predictive Coding Hypothesis

This framework offers a new hypothesis regarding the group-level functional role of emergent language:

> Could it be that language and symbols were formed to collectively encode our experiences of the world through our sensory-motor systems?[4]

In this view, language actively drives us toward socially distributed representation learning, serving as a mechanism that enables collective cognition.

Perspectives from social constructivism and linguistic relativity have long emphasized that language, as an arbitrary system of differences, constrains our worldview and positions us in a kind of symbolic subjugation. The concept of collective predictive coding within symbol emergence systems acknowledges these insights, but also supplements what such views often lack—namely, the idea that language emerges not only from social convention, but also from embodied interaction with the environment, grounded in multimodal sensory-motor experience.

---

[3] Inukai, J., Taniguchi, T., Taniguchi, A., & Hagiwara, Y. 2023 Recursive Metropolis-Hastings Naming Game: Symbol Emergence in a Multi-Agent System Based on Probabilistic Generative Models. Frontiers in Artificial Intelligence, 6.

[4] Taniguchi, Tadahiro. "Collective predictive coding hypothesis: Symbol emergence as decentralized Bayesian inference." *Frontiers in Robotics and AI* 11 (2024): 1353870.

We refer to this proposal as the collective predictive coding hypothesis: the hypothesis that human language is fundamentally formed through collective predictive coding. According to this view, the dynamics through which language emerges in human society are grounded in mechanisms of distributed predictive inference, enacted across individuals.

This hypothesis entails several important implications:

1. Symbol emergence is best understood as collective representation learning, implemented through distributed Bayesian inference among agents.
2. The autonomous decision-making of individual agents—whether to accept or reject signs based on their own beliefs—plays a pivotal role in the emergence process.
3. Symbol systems encode information about the world derived from sensory-motor interactions, distributed across the bodies of many agents. That is, they encode collectively experienced phenomena in a shared Umwelt.

From the standpoint of language evolution, the hypothesis offers a new answer to the question:

What cognitive functions underlie the emergence of human language?

It proposes that intelligence evolved not merely to adapt individually, but to adapt collectively—through the distributed inference mechanisms of a linguistic community.

This idea connects naturally with the Free-Energy Principle and predictive coding, but it also demands a further conceptual expansion:

From intelligence that simply adapts to the world based on sensorimotor feedback, toward intelligence that constructs symbols and builds cultures—an intelligence that predicts the world together.

Language and Humanity as a Living System

The schematic overview of collective predictive coding (Fig. 1) invites a crucial shift in perspective:

Who—or what—serves as the autonomous agent of environmental adaptation?

Interestingly, the graphical model for symbol emergence through collective predictive coding, presented in chapter "Constructive Approaches to Symbol Emergence Systems: Probabilistic Generative Models and Language Games", closely resembles those used in multimodal object and place concept formation (see chapter "Multimodal Object Concept Formation: Concept Modeling Based on Probabilistic Models" and "Multimodal Spatial Concept Formation: Spatial Cognition and Semantics for Mobile Robots"). In those models, individual sensory modalities—such as vision, audition, or touch—supply data that a cognitive system attempts to predict and integrate, leading to concept formation. These mechanisms align with

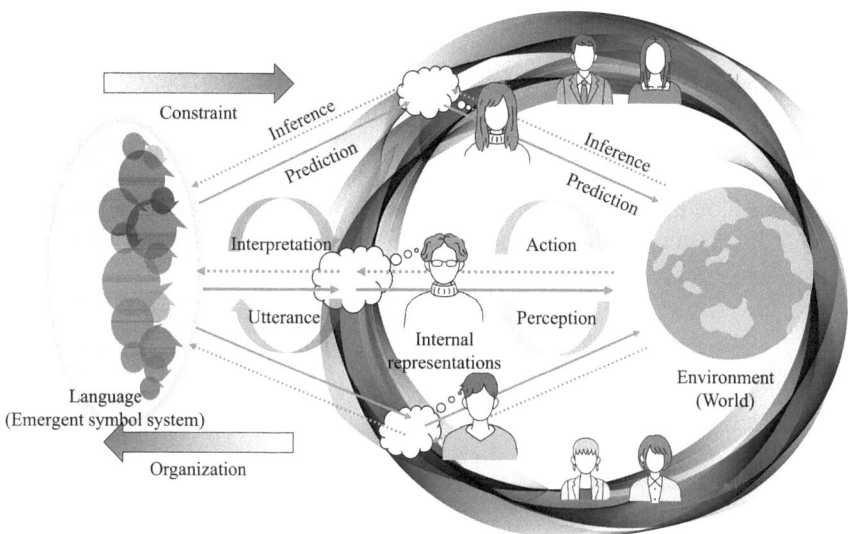

Fig. 1 Overview of collective predictive coding. Humans interact with the environment while forming internal representations through inference based on their predictions of sensory observations. These internal representations serve as the basis for both generating utterances as inferences of signs (external representations) and interpreting received signs through prediction. Through this ongoing process, language emerges as an emergent symbol system that is organized bottom-up. At the same time, the organized language imposes top-down constraints on perception, action, and communication. In this interactive cycle, people collectively construct models of the world in the form of language as an emergent symbol system

predictive coding in a broad sense, and also underpin the principles of representation learning found in world models within deep learning.

In contrast, in collective predictive coding, it is not the individual agent, but the symbol system—namely language itself—that functions as the predictive agent. Each individual becomes a kind of active sensory node, embedded in a distributed network, continually encoding partial aspects of the world via emergent linguistic structures.

From this viewpoint, humans are not merely users of language, but are dynamically embedded within it, contributing to the exploration and symbolic construction of the world.

This reframing strongly echoes the notion of Hierarchical Autonomous Communication Systems (HACS) from neo-cybernetics (Chapter "Neo-Cybernetics and Information: What Is Information?"). From the perspective of individual agents, humans appear autonomous. Yet when shifting to the macro perspective of the social system, those same agents appear heteronomous—functionally constrained participants in a larger symbolic structure. Symbol emergence systems theory suggests that this kind of recursive, perspective-dependent structure naturally emerges from the very conditions required for symbolic communication among agents who live within their own Umwelt.

As discussed in chapter "Neo-Cybernetics and Information: What Is Information?", the precise relationship between the symbol emergence systems and HACS in neo-cybernetics remains an open theoretical question. Nevertheless, it is vital to recognize that autonomy is not an absolute property—it depends on one's analytical vantage point. Moreover, the inherently emergent and interdependent architecture of symbolic communication resists simple micro-macro causality.

Language, in this view, becomes not merely a tool used by autonomous minds, but a life-like system in which human agents act as distributed, adaptive components.

Three-Layered Model of Social Intelligence: Collective Intelligence in Symbol Emergence Systems and Temporal Dynamics

Tadahiro Taniguchi

Dual Process Theory of Cognitive Systems

It is often said that human cognition consists of two distinct modes: fast thinking and slow thinking. For example, detecting the direction of a sudden sound or driving smoothly on an empty road are examples of fast, automatic processes.

In contrast, counting the number of times the letter "a" appears on a page, recalling the source of an unexpected sound, or filling out a tax form all involve effortful, deliberate reasoning—slow thinking.

Psychologists have long been intrigued by these two modes, assigning various labels to them.

The terminology that has become most widely adopted was introduced to the public by Daniel Kahneman, Nobel laureate in economics, in his bestselling book *Thinking, Fast and Slow.*[1]

In the book, he referred to these modes as System 1 (fast thinking) and System 2 (slow thinking), a framing that has since become a central part of what is now known as Dual Process Theory.

This dual-process framing gained renewed traction in the field of artificial intelligence when Yoshua Bengio—often called the "Godfather of Deep Learning"—delivered a keynote at NeurIPS 2019, titled "From System 1 Deep Learning to System 2 Deep Learning.[2]"

---

[1] Kahneman, Daniel. *Thinking, fast and slow*. Macmillan, (2011).
[2] Bengio, Yoshua. "From System 1 Deep Learning to System 2 Deep Learning." NeurIPS 2019. Accessible via YouTube: https://www.youtube.com/watch?v=FtUbMG3rlFs

---

T. Taniguchi (✉)
Graduate School of Informatics, Kyoto University, Kyoto, Japan

Research Organization of Science and Technology, Ritsumeikan University, Kyoto, Japan
e-mail: taniguchi@i.kyoto-u.ac.jp

© The Author(s) 2026
T. Taniguchi (ed.), *Symbol Emergence Systems*,
https://doi.org/10.1007/978-981-95-1327-7_34

Table 1 Contrasting characteristics of System 1 and System 2 in dual process theory

System 1	System 2
Responsive intelligence	Deliberative intelligence
Fast	Slow
Intuitive	Logical
Unconscious	Conscious
Non-verbal	Verbal
Habitual	Planning/inferential

His argument centered on the idea that while deep learning had succeeded in replicating System 1-like fast perception (such as image and speech recognition), it now needed to address the more deliberate, compositional reasoning characteristic of System 2 cognition. In dual process theory, the contrast between System 1 and System 2 can be described by following dichotomies presented in Table 1.

This two-layered distinction—between high-level cognitive functions like language, logic, and planning, and low-level sensory-motor skills—has long been conceptualized in AI and robotics.

In particular, within the field of cognitive developmental robotics and neuro-robotics, this structure was notably explored by Jun Tani, who investigated how recurrent neural networks can form internal representations that integrate both fast and slow dynamics.[3]

In this light, the System 1/System 2 framework serves as a means of reinterpreting diverse temporal dynamics of cognition, especially in modern AI grounded in deep learning.

It draws attention to the fact that while the 2010s saw rapid advancements in low-level perception via deep learning, further efforts are needed to extend these systems into the domain of higher-level, symbolic, and reasoning-based cognition.

The Three-Layered Model of Intelligence

Much of cognitive science and artificial intelligence—including Dual Process Theory—has historically leaned toward a reductionist framing of intelligence, locating it strictly within the individual. However, intelligence is not confined to the brain; rather, it is embedded in and emerges from dynamic interactions with the external world. The symbol emergence systems perspective extends beyond System 1 and System 2 by introducing new "layers" of intelligence both beneath and beyond the individual (Fig. 1).

Beneath System 1 lies the raw dynamism of the body itself. As shown in subsumption architectures and passive dynamic walking robots, well-designed physical

---

[3] Tani, Jun. Exploring Robotic Minds: Actions, Symbols, and Consciousness as Self-Organizing Dynamic Phenomena. Oxford University Press. (2016)

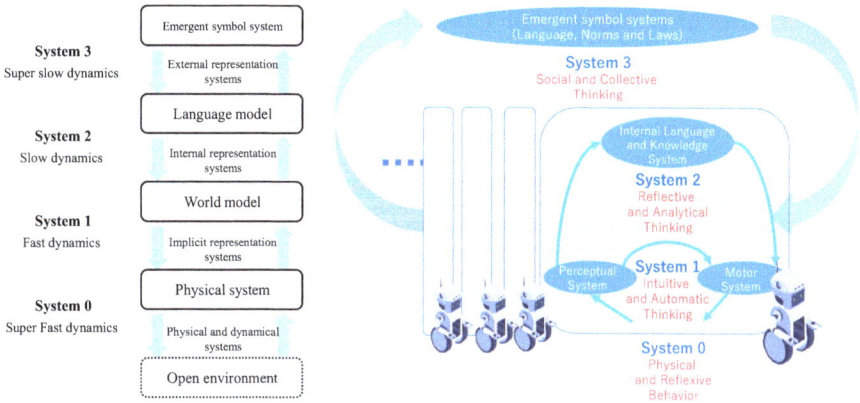

Fig. 1 A hierarchical architecture of cognitive systems beyond individual cognition, with layered dynamics. System 0 represents physical and reflexive behavior; System 1 handles intuitive and automatic thinking; System 2 supports reflective and analytical thinking; and System 3 enables social and collective thinking mediated by emergent symbol systems
The left side illustrates a layered model with increasing levels of abstraction—from physical interaction to language—while the right side depicts the interactions among internal subsystems and multiple agents

bodies can exhibit adaptive behavior without any central nervous control.[4] In humans, many interactions are managed at the spinal reflex level without engaging higher cognition. In robotics, such behavior can emerge without any neural network. This non-representational view of intelligence aligns with embodied cognition (Chapter "Embodiment and the Emergence of Intelligence: From Embodied Cognitive Science to Soft Robotics") and enactivism (Chapter "Enactivism: Cognition as Non-representational, Embodied Action"). This layer may aptly be called System 0.

Beyond System 2 lies the dynamics of society—an essential concept in symbol emergence systems theory. Human intelligence is distinguished by its collective adaptability. We develop language, norms, and social institutions not as isolated individuals, but as participants in a distributed, self-organizing symbol system. This form of collective cognition, manifested through symbol emergence and collective predictive coding, points to an additional layer of intelligence. This layer is not situated in individual minds but emerges from symbolic interactions across agents. We refer to this as System 3.

System 3 represents intelligence enacted by society itself. Unlike Systems 1 and 2—which rely on individual neural plasticity—System 3 relies on the plasticity of symbol systems such as language, norms, and legal codes. This plasticity is grounded in the arbitrariness of signs, as emphasized in Peircean semiotics. While System 3 is dependent on individual cognition, its operations are inscribed externally—in writing, images, laws, and institutions—and thereby accessible to others and open to environmental coupling.

---

[4] Passive dynamic walking robots demonstrate bipedal walking on slopes solely through mechanical structures without computational control.

The Temporal Dynamics of Collective Intelligence

Henri Bergson's philosophy centered on time as a fundamental dimension of reality. Yasushi Hirai has extended this philosophy into contemporary discussions of artificial intelligence, proposing a multi-scale theory of time.[5] In modern AI, often grounded in static datasets and batch training, temporal dynamics of cognition tend to be backgrounded. However, Dual Process Theory offers a foothold for reintroducing temporal depth into cognitive models.

Viewed through a multi-scale temporal lens, collective predictive coding—the symbolic exchange and adaptation of society as System 3—can be seen as the "very slow" dynamic layer of intelligence, situated above System 2. Symbol emergence, in this sense, is a foundational mechanism through which humans adapt to their environment collectively, not merely as individuals with internal representations, but as symbol-generating, culture-building agents.

This leads us to a three-layered model of intelligence, also referred to as the quad-process theory:[6]

- System 0: Embodied and reactive physical intelligence.
- Systems 1 and 2: Perceptual-motor and deliberative reasoning within the individual.
- System 3: Distributed symbolic intelligence enacted across society.

As discussed in Part V, the emergence of language, ethics, and legal systems exemplifies System 3 intelligence. These systems, though arising from human minds, transcend them. They are essential components of human intelligence and must be accounted for within the theoretical scope of symbol emergence systems.

---

[5] Hirai, Yasushi. *Made Out of Time: An Invitation to Bergson's Philosophy of Time* (in Japanese). Seido-sha, (2022). An English-language discussion of the theoretical context can be found in the following volume: Hirai, Yasushi. (Ed.).. *Bergson's Scientific Metaphysics: Matter and Memory Today* (1st ed.). Bloomsbury Academic, (2023)

[6] Taniguchi, Tadahiro, et al. "System 0/1/2/3: Quad-Process Theory for Multi-Timescale Embodied Collective Cognitive Systems." Artificial Life, 31(4), 465–496 (2025).

Toward a Symbiotic Society with Generative AI: For Living Together into the Future

Tadahiro Taniguchi

AI Alignment and the Transformation of Humanity

Since the release of ChatGPT in late 2022, large language models (LLMs) have become the central focus of AI research. Among the various paths toward Artificial General Intelligence (AGI), beginning with LLMs now appears to be the most viable. However, as discussed in chapter "Large Language Models and Distributional Semantics: Do Large Language Models Understand Language?", these models carry significant challenges, such as bias and hallucination—the generation of information that is factually incorrect, unfounded, or syntactically incoherent.

Efforts to align such AI models with human ethics, values, and goals constitute the field of AI alignment. As generative AI becomes increasingly embedded in society, this field is gaining critical importance. But here arises a deeper question: Are human ethics and values truly so fixed and universal that they can serve as reliable training targets or "correct labels" for AI? In reality, human values are plural and diverse. As LLMs are applied globally, reliance on a few dominant, linguistically biased platforms risks reinforcing a new form of globalization—the homogenization of values. This in turn could suppress cultural, ethical, and ideological diversity.

From the viewpoint of symbol emergence systems theory, however, language—as well as the ethics and laws expressed using language—is not static but emergent, context-dependent, and historically contingent. Language is inherently arbitrary, always shifting. Ethics and norms, too, evolve across time, culture, and environment.

Within the context of AI alignment, two fundamental concerns emerge:

1. How LLMs may reshape human language and thinking.
2. How human ethics and value systems themselves evolve and adapt.

T. Taniguchi (✉)
Graduate School of Informatics, Kyoto University, Kyoto, Japan

Research Organization of Science and Technology, Ritsumeikan University, Kyoto, Japan
e-mail: taniguchi@i.kyoto-u.ac.jp

In March 2023, GPT-4 was released. While using it for English proofreading, several months later, I (the author) noticed it frequently suggested the phrase "delve into," a relatively uncommon expression I hadn't often used before. Curious, I checked Google Trends and found a clear uptick in global usage of "delve into" starting that very month.[1] While seemingly minor, this example subtly illustrates how LLMs are already influencing our linguistic habits. Language is shaped by usage; we adopt expressions we are exposed to. Thus, our language—and by extension, our thinking—is already changing through exposure to generative AI.

This insight leads to a crucial realization: AI alignment must account for humans themselves as evolving participants in the system. We need a logic of mutual, dynamic alignment—not just aligning AI to us, but co-adapting together in a symbiotic framework.

A second issue lies in human ethics itself. As generative AI proliferates, so too do risks—not only from AI hallucinations, but from human misuse, such as fabricating false texts or images. Even if we constrain AI's hallucinations, we cannot prevent malicious use when intent originates from humans.

In the age of AI-integrated society, these problems are fundamentally interconnected. AI alignment, though rooted in technical disciplines, must serve as an interface to philosophy, ethics, sociology, and political science. Across these boundaries, we are called to envision and build a new symbiotic society, where humans and AI co-evolve ethically, socially, and cognitively.

Human-Likeness Under Siege

In the 2020s, the rapid progress of generative AI has brought humanity face-to-face with a new identity crisis. Up until the twentieth century, what made human intelligence unique was often said to be rational and linguistic thought. The use of recursive language structures was considered a marker of human distinctiveness. Creativity—manifested in painting, composing music, or storytelling—was also often held up as something only humans could do. But many of these long-standing pillars are now being dismantled by generative AI and large language models.

Yet, there is a hidden bias in how we define "human-likeness." Discussions of intelligence frequently focus on higher-order cognitive abilities, overlooking the lower-order skills that all humans, including toddlers, possess. Tasks such as proving theorems, playing high-level Go, painting, composing, or speaking multiple

---

[1] Google Trends—"delve into" search results https://trends.google.com/trends/explore?date=today%205-y&q=delve%20into&hl=ja (accessed 2/12/2024) The increase in specific vocabulary—such as "delve into"—through interactions with large language models (LLMs) was later widely studied and reported.

For example: Yakura, H., Lopez-Lopez, E., Brinkmann, L., Serna, I., Gupta, P., & Rahwan, I. (2024). Empirical Evidence of Large Language Model's Influence on Human Spoken Communication. arXiv preprint arXiv:2409.01754.

languages—things most people cannot do—have somehow become the benchmark for what it means to be human.

This bias is reflected in Moravec's Paradox, which highlights the counterintuitive reality that what is easy for humans—like walking, grasping, or sensing—is often hardest for AI, while what's cognitively demanding for humans is relatively easy for machines. Even in this era of generative AI, we still don't have domestic robots that can reliably help with everyday chores—an example of AI's enduring limitations in sensorimotor capabilities.

Historically, social perceptions of "intelligence" were shaped through contrast with animals. Because animals can perform sensorimotor tasks, such capabilities have not been included in what defines "human-likeness." Instead, humanity has placed its identity in language, logic, and creativity—areas now increasingly mastered by AI. In fact, from AI's earliest days, logic and games were among its primary targets; IBM's Deep Blue defeated the world chess champion as early as 1997. While people once claimed AI could never match human creativity, generative AI now produces images and music that surpass those created by most humans.

We must now update our concept of "human-likeness." First, we must acknowledge that animals challenge us from below and AI from above. "Human-likeness" is being caught in a cognitive pincer movement. To articulate what makes us human, we must look between and across high- and low-order cognition—and beyond them. Perhaps it is precisely in these connecting layers, such as System 0 and System 3 (as described in the previous section), that human distinctiveness truly lies. This is a view made possible by symbol emergence systems theory.

Second, we must confront the functionalist assumptions embedded in AI research itself. Functionalism—the view that mind and intelligence are defined by what something can do—makes AI development possible. However, as AI becomes deeply embedded in society, it promotes a worldview where human value is similarly reduced to functionality. Yet our worth as humans is not defined by what we can do alone.

In market economies, people are often valued according to their capacity to produce or perform. When this tendency aligns with the functionalist foundations of AI, "human-likeness" becomes vulnerable. The 2020s may mark a period when our shared sense of humanity is increasingly threatened. It is now imperative that we consciously move beyond functionalism, to recognize and cultivate human dignity not only in our abilities, but in our being—our shared presence, meaning, and relationships.

Living as the "Self" in the Micro–Macro Loop

Symbol emergence systems theory presents a bottom-up perspective on language: that symbol systems are emergent, formed socially through *collective predictive coding*. However, the essence of the theory lies not only in bottom-up formation, but also in how these emergent symbol systems exert top-down influence on individuals. In the language of complexity science, this is known as the *micro–macro loop* (see chapter "Symbol Emergence Systems: Toward a World Where Humans and AI Co-discover Meaning"). This final section explores the philosophical implications of this loop.

Across the humanities and social sciences, debates surrounding the nature of knowledge, self-awareness, and social phenomena have often been shaped by a dichotomy: *realism* versus *social constructionism*. While the former considers phenomena and categories as objectively existing entities, the latter emphasizes that knowledge and meaning are socially constructed through cultural context, historical contingency, and symbol systems.

For example, in gender theory, to view the difference between men and women as *biological* is essentialist, while to see it as *socially constructed* is the constructionist perspective. In philosophy of science, realism holds that scientific discoveries uncover truths that exist independently of social influence, while social constructivism argues that scientific knowledge is shaped by the beliefs, values, and interactions of scientists themselves.

Symbol emergence systems theory does not take sides but seeks to *encompass both views*. Consider scientific knowledge: it is formed as a process in which distributed, tacit, embodied experiences are externalized into formal representations. This aligns with *collective predictive coding*, where symbol systems evolve as emergent representations grounded in both individual cognition and cultural context. The beliefs and values of scientists can be seen as a distributed memory within *System 3*. In this light, realism and constructivism are not incompatible, but interwoven.[2]

In daily scientific practice, the realist and constructivist perspectives continually collide, producing the tension and dynamism that define System 3. This tension is *not a flaw*, but a *feature* of human society: a system that persists in adapting through collective symbol emergence.

In gender debates, for instance, the categorization of "male" and "female" is often treated naively as either completely arbitrary or entirely biological. But symbol emergence systems theory sees these categories as emergent from relationships among symbols, cultural context, and collective experience. Arbitrary does not mean meaningless; it means *flexible within constraints*. The key is to recognize the symbol system as a historically learned structure that carries functional weight in adaptation.

We as humans can generate new symbols at the micro level. But from a macro-level perspective, we are also bound by existing symbol systems. Psychoanalyst *Jacques Lacan* described this as the "Big Other"—the symbolic order into which we are born, which structures our understanding of self and other. Symbol emergence systems interpret this as a natural consequence of collective predictive

---

2.Taniguchi, Tadahiro, et al. "Collective Predictive Coding as Model of Science: Formalizing Scientific Activities Towards Generative Science." Royal Society Open Science, 12(6) (2025).

coding: the constraints of symbol systems enable us to indirectly share others' experiences and function as a society.

To ignore symbolic systems entirely is to risk cultural collapse; to passively obey them without expression or critique is to halt symbolic evolution. We must both participate in the systems and continuously reshape them.

So what does it mean to live "authentically"? Should we break free from social expectations of the self, or accept them rationally as part of societal norms?

The answer, I believe, is both.

If the essence of being human lies not in solitary adaptation, but in the *collective emergence of arbitrary symbol systems* for shared adaptation, then we are necessarily participants in symbol emergence systems. In that participation, the micro–macro loop is inevitable. We are neither fully free from nor entirely bound by symbolic structures. The struggle *within* that loop is what makes us human.

As *Generative AI* becomes an inescapable part of this system, our task is to build technologies, theories, institutions, cultures, and societies that allow us to live as *ourselves*—to be *human*—within the new loops of symbol emergence.

Afterword (for Original Japanese Edition)

Tadahiro Taniguchi

Like all symbol systems, academia is inherently dynamic. Fields we now take for granted in higher education—those we study and speak about as though timeless—would vanish if we traced history back just a few centuries. Some wouldn't last even a hundred years. This is true for engineering, the natural sciences, and the humanities and social sciences alike. Even if the fundamental nature of the world remains unchanged, technological advances and institutional shifts continually reshape society—and, in turn, reshape academia.

Amid this ever-changing academic landscape, symbol emergence systems theory seeks to identify necessary points of conjunction between domains that had previously remained unconnected. It aspires to establish a transdisciplinary academic framework that spans informatics, engineering, and the human and social sciences.

So, then: What specific academic disciplines does symbol emergence systems theory connect? How are its foundational theories and practical applications distributed across fields?

I believe this book may be the first to offer a comprehensive response to such questions.

This is not a book that lends itself to effortless reading. It is a challenging book to digest, precisely because the concept of symbol emergence systems is still in the process of taking root, extending its trunk, growing its branches, and bearing its first fruit.

Why, then, did symbol emergence systems theory not come into being until the twenty-first century? The answer, I believe, can be found in the broader intellectual history of science and technology. The development of statistical science and machine learning—both of which benefited from the technical infrastructure of

T. Taniguchi
Graduate School of Informatics, Kyoto University, Kyoto, Japan

Research Organization of Science and Technology, Ritsumeikan University, Kyoto, Japan
e-mail: taniguchi@i.kyoto-u.ac.jp

twentieth-century computer science—has offered not only computational tools but a meta-scientific perspective.

If much of scientific inquiry consists of experiment, observation, and the statistical validation of hypotheses, then machine learning-based AI mimics the very structure of science—and even human cognitive development. The subject matter addressed by symbol emergence systems theory has existed alongside humanity since antiquity. Yet only now, with the advent of computational science, machine learning, and robotics, do we finally possess the tools to discuss its dynamic nature.

Symbol emergence systems theory is still evolving. If the publication of this book helps many people become familiar with the concept and join in its ongoing development, then nothing could bring me greater joy.

In closing, I would like to offer my sincere thanks to all those who made this book possible. The writing and compilation of this volume were supported by the Ritsumeikan Global Innovation Research Organization (R-GIRO), including the initiatives:

- "Symbol Emergence Systems Science: Interdisciplinary Research Center for Real-World Artificial Intelligence and Next-Generation Symbiotic Society" (2022–)
- "International and Interdisciplinary Research Center of Next-generation Artificial Intelligence and Semiotics" (2017–2021).

At a private university in Japan like Ritsumeikan—sustained by tuition rather than public funds—it is both rare and fortunate to receive long-term support for research that is highly interdisciplinary in nature. This support was made possible thanks to the openness of the university, and the contributions of students, their families, faculty, and all stakeholders. I extend my deepest gratitude.

The initial idea for this book emerged when Professor Tatsuya Sato, a cultural psychologist and collaborator in the R-GIRO project, introduced me to the publisher Shinyosha, after I had mentioned my interest in contributing to the "Word Map" series. As a graduate student, I often studied using this very series, so it is especially meaningful to now be part of it.

My special thanks go to Mitsuki Hara, the editor of this book, who skillfully coordinated among a large team of contributors—no easy task. Thanks to their efforts, I believe this volume now stands as a key milestone in the development of the field. I also thank each of the co-authors who contributed to this book. Each chapter provides essential insights that illuminate the connections between symbol emergence systems theory and a wide range of academic domains.

Several of the research findings, discussions, and projects introduced in this book were supported by grants from JSPS KAKENHI (JP21H04904, JP23H04835, JP21H05053, JP23H04834, JP23H04831, JP21K00534, JP23H04830, JP23H04829, JP23K00001, JP23H04832, JP17H06383, JP21K17806, JP23H04974, JP20K19900, JP23K16975, JP22H05159), as well as funding from JST-CREST (Grant Number: JPMJCR21P4), JST-RISTEX (Grant Number: JPMJRS23J2), JST-PRESTO (Grant Number: JPMJPR22C9), and AMED (Grant Number: JP21wm0425021). I am deeply grateful for the long-term support that makes such academic development possible.

As we enter the era of generative AI in the 2020s—following the maturation of the information society—it has become ever more essential to understand the interconnections between language, knowledge, cognition, and action, and the symbolic meanings they sustain. It is this understanding that will enable us both to create new technologies and to shape the future societies we inhabit.

With that hope in mind, I now close this book—while leaving its discussions open to the future.

Tadahiro Taniguchi
At home in rainy Kyoto
June 2024

Afterword (for the English Edition)

Tadahiro Taniguchi

It was back in 2011 when I first organized a session on symbol emergence in robotics at the Annual Conference of the Japanese Society for Artificial Intelligence (JSAI). Since then, a variety of research activities have unfolded under the banners of symbol emergence in robotics and symbol emergence systems. Over that same period, deep learning proliferated worldwide, and we entered what is now recognized as the era of generative AI.

In the meantime, I published several Japanese-language books on symbol emergence in robotics and symbol emergence systems. I also wrote many articles for academic societies and organized numerous sessions at both domestic and international conferences. Yet, despite having introduced these concepts in Japanese publications more than a decade ago, I had never managed to publish a book on these topics in English—though it had always been a goal of mine.

Thirteen years after the first public appearance of the term symbol emergence in robotics in 2011, I happened to meet Mio Sugino from Springer at a social gathering during the 2014 JSAI Annual Conference. Some time later, when I proposed the idea of publishing an English edition of this work, she readily accepted. I am deeply grateful for her support.

I would also like to express my thanks to the original contributors to the Japanese edition, who generously agreed to participate once again in the writing of this English version. My appreciation likewise goes to Momoha Hirose, a research student in my lab, who assisted with the editing process for the English edition.

Even in the age of Generative AI, I believe that overcoming language barriers remains a creative endeavor. I consider this very project of producing the English

T. Taniguchi
Graduate School of Informatics, Kyoto University, Kyoto, Japan

Research Organization of Science and Technology, Ritsumeikan University, Kyoto, Japan
e-mail: taniguchi@i.kyoto-u.ac.jp

edition to be an integral part of our research activities on symbol emergence systems. This specific project has also been supported by JSPS KAKENHI grants JP21H04904 and JP23H04835.

Between the writing of the Japanese and English editions of this book, I moved from Ritsumeikan University to a new position at Kyoto University as a full professor, where I also established a new laboratory: the Symbol Emergence Systems Group.

As we continue to explore this transdisciplinary theoretical framework—one that seeks to uncover the foundations of human and artificial intelligence, and the societal systems in which they interact—I remain committed to advancing this line of inquiry in the years to come.

Tadahiro Taniguchi
At home with cherry blossoms in Kyoto
April 2025

Bibliography

Ahn, M., Brohan, A., Brown, N., Chebotar, Y., Cortes, O., & David, B., et al. (2022). *Do As I Can, Not As I Say: Grounding language in robotic affordances*. arXiv preprint.

Ando, Y., Nakamura, T., Araki, T., & Nagai, T. (2013). Formation of hierarchical object concept using hierarchical latent Dirichlet allocation. In *IEEE/RSJ international conference on intelligent robots and systems* (pp. 2272–2279).

Asada, M., MacDorman, K. F., Ishiguro, H., & Kuniyoshi, Y. (2001). Cognitive developmental robotics as a new paradigm for the design of humanoid robots. *Robotics and Autonomous Systems., 37*, 185–193.

Asada, M., Hosoda, K., Kuniyoshi, Y., Ishiguro, H., Inui, T., Yoshikawa, Y., Ogino, M., & Yoshida, C. (2009). Cognitive developmental robotics: A survey. *IEEE Transactions on Autonomous Mental Development, 1*(1), 12–34.

Baars, B. J. (2009). History of consciousness science. In W. P. Banks (Ed.), *Encyclopedia of consciousness* (pp. 329–338). Academic Press.

Barrett, L. F. (2017). The theory of constructed emotion: An active inference account of Interoception and categorization. *Social Cognitive and Affective Neuroscience, 12*(1), 1–23.

Barsalou, L. W. (1999). Perceptual symbol systems. *Behavioral and Brain Sciences, 22*(4), 577–660.

Bengio, Y. & NeurIPS (2019). "*From system 1 deep learning to system 2 deep learning.*" Accessible via YouTube: https://www.youtube.com/watch?v=FtUbMG3rlFs

Bengio, Y., et al. (2006). Greedy layer-wise training of deep networks. *Advances in Neural Information Processing Systems, 19*, 153–160.

Berlyne, D. E. (1954). A theory of human curiosity. *British Journal of Psychology. General Section, 45*, 180–191.

Berlyne, D. E. (1966). Curiosity and exploration: Animals spend much of their time seeking stimuli whose significance raises problems for psychology. *Science, 153*(3731), 25–33.

Bermúdez, J. L. (2020). *Cognitive science: An introduction to the science of the mind* (4th ed.). Cambridge University Press.

Berthouze, L., & Ziemke, T. (2003). Epigenetic robotics—Modelling cognitive development in robotic systems. *Connection Science, 15*(4), 147–150.

Blei, D., Griffiths, T., & Jordan, M. (2010). The nested Chinese restaurant process and Bayesian nonparametric inference of topic hierarchies. *Journal of the ACM, 57*, 1–30.

Boleda, G. (2020). Distributional semantics and linguistic theory. *Annual Review of Linguistics, 6*(1), 213–234.

Braitenberg, V. (1986). *Vehicles: Experiments in synthetic psychology*. MIT Press.

© The Editor(s) (if applicable) and The Author(s), under exclusive license to
Springer Nature Singapore Pte Ltd. 2026
T. Taniguchi (ed.), *Symbol Emergence Systems*,
https://doi.org/10.1007/978-981-95-1327-7

Breazeal, C. (2004). *Designing sociable robots*. MIT Press.

Brooks, R. (1983). A robust layered control system for a Mobile robot. *IEEE Journal on Robotics and Automation, 2*(1), 14–23.

Cangelosi, A., & Asada, M. (Eds.). (2022). *Cognitive robotics*. The MIT Press.

Cangelosi, A., & Schlesinger, M. (2015). *Developmental robotics: From babies to robots*. The MIT Press.

Cannon, W. B. (1927). The James-Lange theory of emotions: A critical examination and an alternative theory. *The American Journal of Psychology, 39*(1/4), 106–124.

Chao, Z., Takaura, K., Wang, L., Fujii, N., & Dehaene, S. (2018). Large-scale cortical networks for hierarchical prediction and prediction error in the primate brain. *Neuron, 100*(5), 1252–1266.

Chen, G., Fitzsimmons, N., Morimoto, J., & Lebedev, M. (2007). Bipedal locomotion with a humanoid robot controlled by cortical ensemble activity, Society for Neuroscience 37th annual meeting. *Neuroscience, 517*, 22.

Clark, A. (2013). Whatever next? Predictive brains, situated agents, and the future of cognitive science. *Behavioral and Brain Sciences, 36*(3), 181–204.

Clarke, B., & Hansen, M. (2009). Neocybernetic emergence: Retuning the Posthuman. *Cybernetics and Human Knowing, 16*(1–2), 83–99.

Coe, M., & Chemero, A. (2018). *Phenomenology: For a new philosophy of mind*. Keiso Shobo.

Craig, A. D. (2014). *How do you feel?: An interoceptive moment with your neurobiological self*. Princeton University Press.

Csibra, G., & Gergely, G. (2009). Natural Pedagogy. *Trends in Cognitive Sciences, 13*, 148–153.

Damasio, A. R. (1994). *Descartes' error: Emotion, reason, and the human brain*. Quill Publishing.

De Saussure, F. (1966). In C. Bally, A. Sechehaye, & W. Baskin (Eds.), *Course in general linguistics*. McGraw-Hill Book Company.

Dechter, R. (1986). Learning while searching in constraint-satisfaction problems. *AAAI, 86*, 178–185.

Deci, E. L., & Ryan, R. M. (2013). *Intrinsic motivation and self-determination in human behavior*. Springer.

Dehaene, S., et al. (2006). Conscious, preconscious, and subliminal processing: A testable taxonomy. *Trends in Cognitive Sciences, 10*(5), 204–211.

Dennett, D. C. (1988). Quining Qualia. In A. J. Marcel & E. Bisiach (Eds.), *Consciousness in contemporary science* (pp. 42–77). Clarendon Press/Oxford University Press.

Doya, K., Ishii, S., Pouget, A., & Rao, R. P. N. (2007). *Bayesian brain: Probabilistic approaches to neural coding*. MIT Press.

Ekman, P. (1999). Basic emotions. In T. Dalgleish & M. J. Power (Eds.), *Handbook of cognition and emotion* (pp. 45–60). John Wiley & Sons.

Elman, J., Bates, E., Johonson, M. H., Karmiloff-Smith, A., Parisi, D., & Plunkett, K. (1998). *Rethinking innateness: A connectionist perspective on development*. MIT Press.

Fay, N., Garrod, S., Lee, J., & Oberlander, J. (2003). Understanding interactive graphical communication. In *Proceedings of the annual meeting of the cognitive Science Society* (p. 25).

Findlay, G., Marshall, W., Albantakis, L., David, I., Mayner, W. G. P., Koch, C., & Tononi, G. (2025). "*Dissociating artificial intelligence from artificial consciousness.*" arXiv, March 3, 2025. https://doi.org/10.48550/arXiv.2412.04571

Friston, K. (2009). The free-energy principle: A rough guide to the brain? *Trends in Cognitive Sciences, 13*(7), 293–301.

Friston, K. (2010). The free-energy principle: A unified brain theory? *Nature Reviews Neuroscience, 11*(2), 127–138.

Friston, K. (2017). Self-evidencing babies: Commentary on "Mentalizing homeostasis: The social origins of interoceptive inference" by Fotopoulou & Tsakiris. *Neuropsychoanalysis, 19*(1), 43–47.

Friston, K., & Kiebel, S. (2009). Predictive coding under the free-energy principle. *Philosophical Transactions of the Royal Society B: Biological Sciences, 364*(1521), 1211–1221.

Friston, K., Kilner, J., & Harrison, L. (2006). A free energy principle for the brain. *Journal of Physiology-Paris, 100*(1–3), 70–87.

Friston, K., Moran, R. J., Nagai, Y., Taniguchi, T., Gomi, H., & Tenenbaum, J. (2021). World model learning and inference. *Neural Networks, 144*, 573–590.

Fuyama, M., Saigo, H., & Takahashi, T. (2020). A category theoretic approach to metaphor comprehension: Theory of indeterminate natural transformation. *Biosystems, 197*, 104213.

Galantucci, B. (2005). An experimental study of the emergence of human communication systems. *Cognitive Science, 29*(5), 737–767.

Galantucci, B. (2009). Experimental semiotics: A new approach for studying communication as a form of joint action. *Topics in Cognitive Science, 1*(2), 393–410.

Garg, S., Sünderhauf, N., Dayoub, F., Morrison, D., Cosgun, A., Carneiro, G., Wu, Q., Chin, T.-J., Reid, I., Gould, S., Corke, P., & Milford, M. (2020). Semantics for robotic mapping, perception and interaction: A survey. *Foundations and trends®. Robotics, 8*(1–2), 1–224.

Goodfellow, I., Bengio, Y., & Courville, A. (2018). *Deep learning*. MIT Press.

Gratton, L., & Scott, A. (2016). *The 100-year life: Living and working in an age of longevity*. Bloomsbury Information.

Ha, D., & Schmidhuber, J. (2018). Recurrent World models facilitate policy evolution. *Advances in Neural Information Processing Systems, 31*, 1.

Hafner, D., et al. (2019). *Dream to control: Learning behaviors by latent imagination*. arXiv preprint arXiv:1912.01603.

Hafner, D., et al. (2023). *Mastering diverse domains through World models*. arXiv preprint arXiv:2301.04104.

Hagiwara, Y., Taguchi, K., Ishibushi, S., Taniguchi, A., & Taniguchi, T. (2022). Hierarchical Bayesian model for the transfer of knowledge on spatial concepts based on multimodal information. *Advanced Robotics, 36*(1–2), 33–53.

Harnad, S. (1990). The symbol grounding problem. *Physica D: Nonlinear Phenomena, 42*(1–3), 335–346.

Harris, Z. S. (1954). Distributional structure. *WORD, 10*, 146–162.

Hashimoto, T. (2020). The emergent constructive approach to Evolinguistics: Considering hierarchy and intention sharing in linguistic communication. *Journal of Systems Science and Systems Engineering, 29*(6), 675–696.

Hashimoto, T., & Ikegami, T. (1996). Emergence of net-grammar in communicating agents. *Biosystems, 38*(1), 1–14.

Hauser, M. D., Chomsky, N., & Fitch, W. T. (2002). The faculty of language: What is it, who has it, and how did it evolve? *Science, 298*(5598), 1569–1579.

Hayek, F. A. (1944). *The Road to Serfdom*. Routledge. (Japanese translation: *The Road to Serfdom*, Nikkei BP, 2016.).

Hieida, C., Horii, T., & Nagai, T. (2018). *"Deep emotion: A computational model of emotion using deep neural networks"* arXiv preprint arXiv:1808.08447 (2018).

Hirai, Y. (2022). *Made out of time: An invitation to Bergson's philosophy of time (in Japanese)*. Seido-sha.

Hirai, Y. (2023). *Bergson's scientific metaphysics: Matter and memory today* (1st ed.). Bloomsbury Academic.

Hirai, Y., Horii, T., & Nagai, T. (2021). Integration model of interoception, exteroception, and proprioception using predictive coding. In *Proceedings of the annual conference of the Japanese society for artificial intelligence, 35*, 4D3OS4b03-4D3OS4b03 in Japanese.

Hoffmeyer, J. (1993). *En snegl på vejen: betydningens naturhistorie*. Rosinante.

Hoffmeyer, J. (1996). *Signs of meaning in the universe*. Indiana University Press.

Horii, T., Nagai, Y., & Asada, M. (2018). Modeling development of multimodal emotion perception guided by tactile dominance and perceptual improvement. *IEEE Transactions on Cognitive and Developmental Systems, 10*(3), 762–775.

Horikawa, T., et al. (2013). Neural decoding of visual imagery during sleep. *Science, 340*(6132), 639–642.

Huang, C., Mees, O., Zeng, A., & Burgard, W. (2023). Visual language maps for robot navigation. In *Proceedings of the IEEE international conference on robotics and automation (ICRA)*.

Husserl, E. (1969). *Formal and transcendental logic*. Trans. Cairns, D. Martinus Nijhoff.

Husserl, E. (1970). *Logical investigations*. Routledge & Kegan Paul.

Husserl, E. (1973). *Zur Phänomenologie der Intersubjektivität. Dritter Teil: 1929–1935. Husserliana XV*. Martinus Nijhoff.

Husserl, E. (1974). Formale und Transzendentale Logik. In *Husserliana XVII*. Martinus Nijhoff.

Husserl, E. (1976). *Die Krisis der europäischen Wissenschaften und die transzendentale Phänomenologie*. Martinus Nijhoff.

Hutto, D. (2023). Enactivism. In *Internet encyclopedia of philosophy*. https://iep.utm.edu/enactivism/

Hutto, D., & Myin, E. (2013). *Radicalizing enactivism: Basic minds without content*. MIT Press.

Hwu, T. J., & Krichmar, J. L. (2022). *Neurorobotics: Connecting the brain, body, and environment*. MIT Press.

Inatani, T. (2017). The moralizing technology and criminal law regulation. In Y. Matsuo (Ed.), *Architecture and law: The architectural turn in legal studies?* (pp. 93–128). Koubundou.

Inatani, T. (2022). The legal being and legal subjects: Exploring criminal responsibility in modern technological societies. *Hougaku-Kyoshitsu, 498*, 40–45.

Inukai, J., Taniguchi, T., Taniguchi, A., & Hagiwara, Y. (2023). Recursive Metropolis-Hastings naming game: Symbol emergence in a multi-agent system based on probabilistic generative models. *Frontiers in Artificial Intelligence, 6*, 1229127.

Isomura, T., Kotani, K., Jimbo, Y., & Friston, K. (2023). Experimental validation of the free-energy principle with in vitro neural networks. *Nature Communications, 14*(4547), 1–15.

Ito, M., Noda, K., Hoshino, Y., & Tani, J. (2006). Dynamic and interactive generation of object handling behaviors by a small humanoid robot using a dynamic neural network model. *Neural Networks, 19*(3), 323–337.

Izumo, T. (2019). A study on digital peculium: Comparisons between Roman slavery and robots. *Information Studies Research, 28*, 1–16.

James, W. (1884). What is an emotion? *Mind, os-IX(34)*, 188–205.

James, W. (1983). *Talks to teachers on psychology and to students on some of life's ideals* (Vol. 12). Harvard University Press.

Johnson, J., et al. (2017). CLEVR: A diagnostic dataset for compositional language and elementary visual reasoning. In *Proceedings of the IEEE conference on computer vision and pattern recognition*.

Kahneman, D. (2011). *Thinking, fast and slow*. Macmillan.

Kawakita, G., Zeleznikow-Johnston, A., Tsuchiya, N., & Oizumi, M. (2023). Gromov–Wasserstein unsupervised alignment reveals structural correspondences between the color similarity structures of humans and large language models. *Scientific Reports, 14*, 15917.

Kawakita, G., Zeleznikow-Johnston, A., Takeda, K., Tsuchiya, N., & Oizumi, M. (2025). Is my "red" your "red"?: Evaluating structural correspondences between color similarity judgments using unsupervised alignment. *IScience, 28*, 1.

Kawato, M. (1999). Internal models for motor control and trajectory planning. *Current Opinion in Neurobiology, 9*(6), 718–727.

Kawato, M. (2008). From 'understanding the brain by creating the brain' towards manipulative neuroscience. *Philosophical Transactions of the Royal Society B: Biological Sciences, 363*, 2201–2214.

Keramati, M., & Gutkin, B. (2014). Homeostatic reinforcement learning for integrating reward collection and physiological stability. *eLife, 3*, e04811.

Kida, N., et al. (2005). Intensive baseball practice improves the Go/Nogo reaction time, but not the simple reaction time. *Cognitive Brain Research, 22*(2), 257–264.

Kirby, S., & Hurford, J. R. (2002). The emergence of linguistic structure: An overview of the iterated learning model. In A. Cangelosi & D. Parisi (Eds.), *Simulating the evolution of language* (pp. 121–147). Springer.

Kirby, S., Cornish, H., & Smith, K. (2008). Cumulative cultural evolution in the laboratory: An experimental approach to the origins of structure in human language. *Proceedings of the National Academy of Sciences, 105*(31), 10681–10686.

Koch, C., & Tsuchiya, N. (2007). Attention and consciousness: Two distinct brain processes. *Trends in Cognitive Sciences, 11*(1), 16–22.

Kohn, E. (2013). *How forests think: Toward an anthropology beyond the human.* University of California Press.

Krichmar, J. L. (2018). Neurorobotics—A thriving community and a promising pathway toward intelligent cognitive robots. *Frontiers in Neurorobotics, 12*, 42.

Kuki, M., Kanzaki, N., & Sasaki, T. (2017). *Introduction to ethics from robots.* Nagoya University Press.

Kull, K. (1998). On semiosis, umwelt, and Semiosphere. *Semiotica, 120*(3/4), 299–310.

Langacker, R. W. (1987). *Foundations of cognitive grammar, vol. 1: Theoretical prerequisites.* Stanford University Press.

Lanillos, P., Oliva, D., Philippsen, A., Yamashita, Y., Nagai, Y., & Cheng, G. (2020). A review on neural network models of schizophrenia and autism spectrum disorder. *Neural Networks, 122*, 338–363.

Latour, B. (2007). *Reassembling the social: An introduction to actor-network-theory.* Oxford University Press. (Japanese translation: *Reassembling the Social: Introduction to Actor-Network Theory*, Hosei University Press, 2019).

Latour, B. (2009). *The making of law: An ethnography of the Conseil d'État.* Polity. (Japanese translation: *Making Law: Anthropological Considerations of Modern Administrative Justice*, Suiseisha, 2017).

Lazaridou, A., & Baroni, M. (2020). *Emergent multi-agent communication in the deep learning era.* arXiv:2006.02419 v2.

Lesort, T., et al. (2018). State representation learning for control: An overview. *Neural Networks, 108*, 379–392.

Levine, S. (2018). *Reinforcement learning and control as probabilistic inference: Tutorial and review.* arXiv preprint arXiv:1805.00909.

Lin, Z., et al. (2020). Improving generative imagination in object-centric World models. In *International conference on machine learning (PMLR).*

Lin, J., et al. (2023). *Learning to model the World with language.* arXiv preprint arXiv:2308.01399.

Lotman, Y. (1990). *Universe of the mind: A semiotic theory of culture.* I. B. Tauris.

Luhmann, N. (1984). *Soziale Systeme.* Suhrkamp.

Lungarella, M., Metta, G., Pfeifer, R., & Sandini, G. (2003). Developmental robotics: A survey. *Connection Science, 15*(4), 151–190.

Marjieh, et al. (2023). *What language reveals about perception: Distilling psychological knowledge from large language models.* arXiv.

Marr, D. (2010). *Vision: A computational investigation into the human representation and processing of visual information.* MIT Press. (Original published 1982).

Maturana, H. R., & Varela, F. J. (1980a). *Autopoiesis and cognition: The realization of the living.* D. Reidel Publishing Company.

Maturana, H. R., & Varela, F. J. (1980b). Autopoiesis: The organization of the living. In *Autopoiesis and cognition: The realization of the living* (pp. 73–134). D. Reidel Publishing Company.

Maturana, H., & Varela, F. (1992). *The tree of knowledge: The biological roots of human understanding (Revised edition)* (p. 144). Shambhala.

Mayner, W. G. P., Juel, B. E., & Tononi, G. (2024). "*Intrinsic meaning, perception, and matching.*" arXiv, December 31, 2024. https://doi.org/10.48550/arXiv.2412.21111

Mazzaglia, P., Verbelen, T., Çatal, O., & Dhoedt, B. (2022). The free energy principle for perception and action: A deep learning perspective. *Entropy, 24*(2), 1–22.

Merleau-Ponty, M. (1964). *Signs.* Trans. McCleary, R.C. Northwestern University Press.

Mikolov, T., Chen, K., Corrado, G., & Dean, J. (2013). Efficient estimation of word representations in vector space. In *Proceedings of the international conference on learning representations workshop*.

Misak, C. (2000). *Truth, Politics, Morality: Pragmatism and deliberation*. Routledge.

Misak, C. (2013). *The American pragmatists*. Oxford University Press. Ch. 3.

Miyashita, T., Kamikawa, T., & Sato, T. (2022). New theoretical developments in trajectory Equifinality modeling based on the Semiosphere and imagination theory. *Ritsumeikan Journal of Human Sciences, 44*, 49–64. [In Japanese]. https://doi.org/10.34382/00016829

Mochihashi, D., Yamada, T., & Ueda, N. (2009). Bayesian unsupervised word segmentation with nested pitman-yor language modeling. In *Proceedings of the joint conference of the 47th annual meeting of the ACL and the 4th international joint conference on natural language processing of the AFNLP* (pp. 100–108).

Moriguchi, Y., Watanabe, R., Sakata, C., Zeleznikow-Johnston, A., Wang, J., Saji, N., et al. (2025). Comparing color qualia structures through a similarity task in young children versus adults. *Proceedings of the National Academy of Sciences of the United States of America, 122*, e2415346122. https://doi.org/10.1073/pnas.2415346122

Nagai, Y. (2019). Predictive learning: Its key role in early cognitive development. *Philosophical Transactions of the Royal Society B, 374*, 20180030.

Nagano, M., & Nakamura, T. (2021). Learning word meanings using joint attention and MLDA in environments with a plurality of objects. *Journal of the Robotics Society of Japan, 39*(6), 549–552. (in Japanese).

Nagano, M., & Nakamura, T. (2023). Unsupervised structural learning of continuous speech using a GP-HSMM-based dual articulation model. *Journal of the Robotics Society of Japan, 41*(3), 318–321.

Nakamura, T., & Nagai, T. (2018). Ensemble-of-concept models for unsupervised formation of multiple categories. *IEEE Transactions on Cognitive and Developmental Systems, 10*(4), 1043–1057.

Nakamura, T., Araki, T., Nagai, T., & Iwahashi, N. (2012). Grounding of word meanings in LDA-based multimodal concepts. *Advanced Robotics, 25*, 2189–2206.

Newell, A., & Simon, H. A. (2007). Computer science as empirical inquiry: Symbols and search. *Communications of the ACM, 19*(3), 113–126.

Newport, E. L. (1990). Maturational constraints on language learning. *Cognitive Science, 14*(1), 11–28.

Nishida, Y. (2011). The relationship between Autopoiesis theory and biosemiotics: On philosophical suppositions as bases for a new information theory. *tripleC, 9*(2), 424–433.

Nishida, Y. (2023). *Ningen Hi-Kikai Ron (anti-mechanical philosophy of man)*. Kodansha. (in Japanese).

Nishigai, Y. (2020). *Cybersecurity and penal law: Focusing on unauthorized access crimes*. Yuhikaku.

Nishigaki, T. (2004, 2008, 2021). *Kiso Johogaku (fundamental informatics) vol.1–3*. NTT Publishing. (in Japanese).

Nishigaki, T. (2007). *"For the establishment of fundamental informatics on the basis of Autopoiesis: Consideration on the concept of hierarchical autonomous systems."* https://digital-narcis.org/nishigaki_pdf/FI-English-01.pdf. (Revised and translated by Toru Nishigaki from original Japanese version, in Shiso, no.951, July 2003, pp.5–22).

Nishigaki, T. (2013). *The wisdom to bridge the gap between lives and machines: An introduction to fundamental informatics*. (can be freely downloaded from: https://digital-narcis.org/toru-nishigaki/?lang=english). (translated by Toru Nishigaki and Nami Ohi from original Japanese version, 2012, Koryosha).

Nishihara, J., Nakamura, T., & Nagai, T. (2017). Online algorithm for robots to learn object concepts and language models. *IEEE Transactions on Cognitive and Developmental Systems, 9*(3), 255–268.

Nonaka, I. (2009). The knowledge-creating company. In *The economic impact of knowledge* (pp. 175–187). Routledge.

Ohira, H. (2019). Predictive coding of brain and body and its failure. *Japanese Psychological Review, 62*(1), 132–141. in Japanese.

Ohira, H. (2020). Co-construction of emotions in culture and history. *Emotion Studies, 5*(1), 4–15. in Japanese.

Oudeyer, P. Y., Kaplan, F., & Hafner, V. V. (2007). Intrinsic motivation systems for autonomous mental development. *IEEE Transactions on Evolutionary Computation, 11*(2), 265–286.

Parr, T., Pezzulo, G., & Friston, K. J. (2022). *Active inference: The free energy principle in mind, brain, and behavior.* MIT Press.

Peirce, C. S. (1992). In N. Houser & C. Kloesel (Eds.), *Essential Peirce: Selected philosophical writing, vol. 1 (1867-1893)* (pp. 124–141). Indiana University Press.

Peirce, Charles Sanders. 1998. "Nomenclature and divisions of triadic relations, as far as they are determined" in Peirce, Charles Sanders. Peirce Edition Project, *Essential Peirce: Selected philosophical writings, Vol. 2 (1893-1913)*, pp. 289–299. Indiana University Press.

Pfeifer, R., & Bongard, J. (2006). *How the body shapes the way we think.* MIT Press.

Pfeifer, R., & Scheier, C. (1999). *Understanding intelligence.* Bradford Books.

Piaget, J. (1970). Piaget's theory. In P. H. Mussen (Ed.), *Carmichael's manual of child psychology* (Vol. 1, 3rd ed., pp. 703–732). John Wiley & Sons.

Pinker, S. (2007, 1994). *The language instinct.* Harper perennial modern classics. (Pinker/Trans. Naoko Mukuta, 1995. *Gengo wo Umidasu Honnō* (1 & 2). NHK Publishing).

Polanyi, M. (2009). The tacit dimension. In *Knowledge in organisations* (pp. 135–146). Routledge.

Quine, W. V. O. (1953). Two dogmas of empiricism. In *A logical point of view* (pp. 20–46). Harvard University Press.

Rao, R. P., & Ballard, D. H. (1999). Predictive coding in the visual cortex: A functional interpretation of some extra-classical receptive-field effects. *Nature Neuroscience, 2*(1), 79–87.

Rumelhart, D. E., Hinton, G. E., & Williams, R. J. (1985). *Learning internal representations by error propagation.* California University.

Russell, J. A. (1980). A Circumplex model of affect. *Journal of Personality and Social Psychology, 39*(6), 1161.

Russell, J. A., & Barrett, L. F. (1999). Core affect, prototypical emotional episodes, and other things called emotion: Dissecting the elephant. *Journal of Personality and Social Psychology, 76*(5), 805.

Saffran, J. R., Aslin, R. N., & Newport, E. L. (1996). Statistical learning by 8-month-old infants. *Science, 274*, 1926–1928.

Saigo, H. & Taguchi, S. 2019. 'Genjitsu' toha nanika (what is "reality")?, Chikuma Shobo. (English translation forthcoming), Chapter 3.

Saijo, R. (2019). What does it mean for artifacts to have gender? *Ritsumeikan University Bulletin of Humanities and Sciences, 120*, 199–216.

Sato, T. (2015). Bunka Shinrigaku kara Mita Shoku no Hyōgen no Shiten kara Shokubunka to Sono Kenkyū ni tsuite Kangaeru. In *Ritsumeikan Shakai System Kenkyū Kiyō, Tokushū-gō (in Japanese)* (pp. 197–209).

Schachter, S., & Singer, J. (1962). Cognitive, social, and physiological determinants of emotional state. *Psychological Review, 69*(5), 379.

Schmidhuber, J. (1990). Making the World differentiable: On using self supervised fully recurrent neural networks for dynamic reinforcement learning and planning in non-stationary environments. *Forschungsberichte. TU Munich, FKI, 126*(90), 1–26.

Seth, A. K., & Bayne, T. (2022). Theories of consciousness. *Nature Reviews Neuroscience, 23*(7), 439–452.

Shafiullah, N. M. M., Paxton, C., Pinto, L., Chintala, S., Mahi Shafiullah, N., et al. (2023). CLIP-fields: Weakly supervised semantic fields for robotic memory. In *Robotics: Science and systems.*

Simon, H. (1996). *The sciences of the artificial.* MIT Press.

Smith, L. B., & Yu, C. (2008). Infants rapidly learn word-referent mappings via cross-situational statistics. *Cognition, 106*, 333–338.

Smith, R., Friston, K., & Whyte, C. (2022). A step-by-step tutorial on active inference and its application to empirical data. *Journal of Mathematical Psychology, 107*, 1–60.

Smortchkova, J., Dolega, K., & Schlicht, T. (2020). *What are mental representations?* Oxford University Press.

Steels, L. (1995). A self-organizing spatial vocabulary. *Artificial Life, 2*(3), 319–332.

Steels, L. (2008). The symbol grounding problem has been solved. So what's next? In *Symbols and embodiment: Debates on meaning and cognition* (pp. 223–244). Oxford University Press.

Steels, L. (2015). *The talking heads experiment: Origins of words and meanings (computational models of language evolution 1)*. Language Science Press.

Steels, L., & Kaplan, F. (2002). Bootstrapping grounded word semantics. In T. Briscoe (Ed.), *Linguistic evolution through language acquisition: Formal and computational models* (pp. 53–74). Cambridge University Press.

Stephan, K. E., Manjaly, Z. M., Mathys, C. D., Weber, L. A., Paliwal, S., Gard, T., & Petzschner, F. H. (2016). Allostatic self-efficacy: A metacognitive theory of Dyshomeostasis-induced fatigue and depression. *Frontiers in Human Neuroscience, 10*, 550.

Sugita, Y., & Tani, J. (2005). Learning semantic combinatoriality from the interaction between linguistic and behavioral processes. *Adaptive Behavior, 13*(1), 33–52.

Sutton, R. S., & Barto, A. G. *Reinforcement learning* (2nd ed.). Academic Press.

Suzuki, T. (1999). *Nihonjin wa Naze Eigo ga Dekinai ka ?* (pp. 42–47). Iwanami Shoten. (in Japanese).

Suzuki, K., Mori, H., & Ogata, T. (2018). Motion switching with sensory and instruction signals by designing dynamical systems using deep neural networks. *IEEE Robotics and Automation Letters, 3*(4), 3481–3488.

Taguchi, S. (2014). *Genshogaku toiu shiko: Jimeinamono no chi he (phenomenology as a way of thinking: Interrogating the obvious)*. Chikuma Shobo.

Tamura, K., & Hashimoto, T. (2014). An experimental approach to stablishment of displacement in linguistic communication (in Japanese). *Journal of the Society of Instrument and Control Engineers, 53*(9), 808–814.

Tani, J. (2016). *Exploring robotic minds: Actions, symbols, and consciousness as self-organizing dynamic phenomena*. Oxford University Press.

Tani, J., & Ito, M. (2003). Self-organization of behavioral primitives as multiple attractor dynamics: A robot experiment. *IEEE Transactions on Systems, Man, and Cybernetics—Part A: Systems and Humans, 33*(4), 481–488.

Taniguchi, T. (2020). *Artificial intelligence for understanding minds: Symbol emergence robotics as cognitive science*. Kyoritsu Shuppan. (in Japanese).

Taniguchi, T. (2024). Collective predictive coding hypothesis: Symbol emergence as decentralized bayesian inference. *Frontiers in Robotics and AI, 11*, 1353870.

Taniguchi, T., Iwahashi, N., Nitta, T., Okada, H., & Nagai, T. (2011). Symbol emergence robotics and multimodal semantic interaction. In *Proceedings of the Japanese Society for artificial intelligence annual conference* (Vol. 25, p. 2B2OS22a1).

Taniguchi, T., Nagaoaka, S., & Nakashima, R. (2015). Nonparametric Bayesian double articulation analyzer for direct language acquisition from continuous speech signals. *IEEE Transactions on Cognitive and Developmental Systems, 8*(3), 171–185.

Taniguchi, T., Nagai, T., Nakamura, T., Iwahashi, N., Ogata, T., & Asoh, H. (2016). Symbol emergence in robotics: A survey. *Advanced Robotics, 30*(11–12), 706–728.

Taniguchi, A., Hagiwara, Y., Taniguchi, T., & Inamura, T. (2017a). Online spatial concept and lexical acquisition with simultaneous localization and mapping. In *Proceedings of the IEEE/RSJ international conference on intelligent robots and systems (IROS)* (pp. 811–818).

Taniguchi, A., Taniguchi, T., & Cangelosi, A. (2017b). Cross-situational learning with Bayesian generative models for multimodal category and word learning in robots. *Frontiers in Neurorobotics, 11*, 66.

Taniguchi, T., Ugur, E., Hoffmann, M., Jamone, L., Nagai, T., Rosman, B., Matsuka, T., Iwahashi, N., Oztop, E., Piater, J., & Wörgötter, F. (2019). Symbol emergence in cognitive developmental systems: A survey. *IEEE Transactions on Cognitive and Developmental Systems, 11*(4), 494–516.

Taniguchi, A., Hagiwara, Y., Taniguchi, T., & Inamura, T. (2020a). Spatial concept-based navigation with human speech instructions via probabilistic inference on Bayesian generative model. *Advanced Robotics, 34*(19), 1213–1228.

Taniguchi, T., et al. (2020b). Neuro-SERKET: Development of integrative cognitive systems through deep probabilistic generative models. *New Generation Computing, 38*(1), 23–48.

Taniguchi, A., Fukawa, A., & Yamakawa, H. (2022a). Hippocampal formation-inspired probabilistic generative model. *Neural Networks, 151*, 317–335.

Taniguchi, T., et al. (2022b). A whole brain probabilistic generative model. *Neural Networks, 150*, 293–312.

Taniguchi, A., Tabuchi, Y., Ishikawa, T., El Hafi, L., Hagiwara, Y., & Taniguchi, T. (2023a). Active exploration based on information gain by particle filter for efficient spatial concept formation. *Advanced Robotics, 37*(13), 840–870.

Taniguchi, T., et al. (2023b). Emergent communication through Metropolis-Hastings naming game with deep generative models. *Advanced Robotics, 37*(19), 1266–1282.

Taniguchi, T., et al. (2023c). World models and predictive coding for cognitive and developmental robotics: Frontiers and challenges. *Advanced Robotics, 37*(13), 780–806.

Taniguchi, T., et al. (2024). *Collective predictive coding as model of science: Formalizing scientific activities towards generative science.* arXiv preprint arXiv:2409.00102.

Taniguchi, T., et al. (2025). *"System 0/1/2/3: Quad-process theory for multi-timescale embodied collective cognitive systems."* arXiv preprint, arXiv:2503.06138.

Thompson, E. (2007). *Mind in life: Biology, phenomenology, and the sciences of the mind* (p. 52). Harvard University Press.

Thrun, S., Burgard, W., & Fox, D. (2005). *Probabilistic robotics.* MIT Press.

Tomasello, M. (2003). *Constructing a language: A usage-based theory of language acquisition.* Harvard University Press.

Tomasello, M. (2010). *Origins of human communication.* MIT Press.

Tsuchiya, N. (2025). *The Qualia structure Paradigm: Towards a construction of a Qualia Periodic Table for the dissolution of the hard problem of consciousness.* osf.io/preprints/psyarxiv/492hu. https://doi.org/10.31234/osf.io/492hu

Tsuchiya, N., & Saigo, H. (2021). A relational approach to consciousness. *Neuroscience of Consciousness, 2021*(2), niab034.

Valsiner, J. (2007). *Culture in minds and societies: Foundations of cultural psychology.* Sage Publications.

Varela, F., Thompson, E., & Rosch, E. (1991). *The embodied mind: Cognitive science and human experience.* MIT Press.

Vaswani, A., Shazeer, N., Parmar, N., Uszkoreit, J., Jones, L., Gomez, A. N., Kaiser, Ł., & Polosukhin, I. (2017). Attention is all you need. In *Advances in neural information processing systems* (Vol. 30).

von Foerster, H. (2003). *Understanding understanding.* Springer.

von Glasersfeld, E. (1995). *Radical constructivism: A way of knowing and learning.* Routledge.

von Uexküll, J. (1909). *Umwelt und Innenwelt der Tiere. Verlag von Julius Springer. (Boettcher, R. tr. 2021. Environment and inner World of the animals).* Independently Published.

von Uexküll, J. (1920). *Theoretische Biologie.* Paetel. (Mackinnon, D. L. tr. 1926. *Theoretical biology.* K. Paul, Trench, Trubner & co. ltd.; Harcourt, brace & company, inc.)

von Uexküll, J. (1940, 1970). *Bedeutungslehre.* S. Fischer Verlag. (1982. *The theory of meaning*). Semiotica, 42(1), pp.25–79.)

von Uexküll, J. (1950). *Das allmächtige Leben.* Christian Wegner Verlag.

von Uexküll, J. (1992). A stroll through the worlds of animals and men: A picture book of invisible worlds. *Semiotica, 89*, 319–391.

von Uexküll, J., & Kriszat, G. 1934; 1956. Streifzüge durch die Umwelten von Tieren und Menschen. Rowohlt Taschenbuch Verlag.

Vygotsky, L. S. (1978). *Interaction between learning and development. Mind in Society.* Harvard University Press.

Wiener, N. (1948,1961). *Cybernetics: Or control and communication in the animal and the machine.* John Wiley.

Winawer, J., et al. (2007). Russian blues reveal effects of language on color discrimination. *Proceedings of the National Academy of Sciences, 104*(19), 7780–7785.

Wu, P., et al. (2023). Daydreamer: World models for physical robot learning. In *Conference on Robot learning (PMLR)* (pp. 2226–2240).

Xu, F., Dewar, K., & Perfors, A. (2009). Induction, overhypotheses, and the shape bias: Some arguments and evidence for rational constructivism. In B. M. Hood & L. Santos (Eds.), *The origins of object knowledge* (pp. 263–284). Oxford University Press.

Yakura, H., Lopez-Lopez, E., Brinkmann, L., Serna, I., Gupta, P., & Rahwan, I. (2024). *Empirical evidence of large language model's influence on human spoken communication.* arXiv preprint arXiv:2409.01754.

Yamakawa, H. (2021). The whole brain architecture approach: Accelerating the development of artificial general intelligence by referring to the brain. *Neural Networks, 144,* 478–495.

Yamanaka, T., et al. (2021). *Project-based English program: Jibun-jiku o Kitaeru "Oshienai" Kyoiku (in Japanese).* Kitaoji Shobo.

Yamashita, Y., & Tani, J. (2008). Emergence of functional hierarchy in a multiple timescale neural network model: A humanoid robot experiment. *PLoS Computational Biology, 4*(11), e1000220.

Yamashita, Y., & Tani, J. (2012). Spontaneous prediction error generation in schizophrenia. *PLoS One, 7*(5), e37843.

Yanagida, K., & Horii, T. (2023). Complementary learning of robot's behavior acquisition and concept formation. In *Proceedings of the Japanese Society for artificial intelligence annual conference, 37, 2O4GS805-2O4GS805 in Japanese.*

Zahavi, D. (2003). *Husserl's phenomenology.* Stanford University Press.